ABOUT THIS PUBLICATION

FOR SERVICE ASSISTANCE

Customer Service
1.704.898.0770

North Carolina General Statues is published by The Muliti-Media Group of Greater Charlotte in Charlotte, North Carolina. Copyright 2015 by the Multi-Media Group of Greater Charlotte. This book or parts thereof may not be reproduced in any form, stored in a retrieval system, or transmitted in any form by any means—electronic, mechanical, photocopy, recording or otherwise—without prior written permission of the publisher, except as provided by United States of America copyright law.

The records required by U.S. Code 2257(a) through (c) and the pertinent regulations 28 C.F.R. Cli. 1, Part 75 with respect to this publication and all materials associated with such records are maintained by The Multi-Media Group of Greater Charlotte, Publisher and available for review by Attorney General.

www.visionbooks.org

Copyright © 2015 by MMGGC
All rights reserved!

TID: 5107821
ISBN (10) digit: 1503243753
ISBN (13) digit: 978-1503243750

123-4-56789-01239-Paperback
123-4-56789-01239-Hardback

First Edition

090520140547

Printed in the United States of America

2015 EDITION

North Carolina Criminal Law And Procedure-Pamphlet # 78

Printed In conjunction with the Administration of the Courts

North Carolina Criminal Law and Procedure
Pamphlet Reference Guide

Chapters	Pamphlet
Chapter 1 Civil Procedure	1
Chapter 1 Civil Procedure (Continue)	2
Chapter 1A Rules of Civil Procedure	2
Chapter 1B Contribution.	2
Chapter 1C Enforcement of Judgments.	2
Chapter 1D Punitive Damages.	2
Chapter 1E Eastern Band of Cherokee Indians.	2
Chapter 1F North Carolina Uniform Interstate Depositions and Discovery Act.	2
Chapter 2 - Clerk of Superior Court [Repealed and Transferred.]	3
Chapter 3 - Commissioners of Affidavits and Deeds [Repealed.]	3
Chapter 4 - Common Law	3
Chapter 5 - Contempt [Repealed.]	3
Chapter 5A - Contempt	3
Chapter 6 - Liability for Court Costs	3
Chapter 7 - Courts [Repealed and Transferred.]	3
Chapter 7A – Judicial Department	3
Chapter 7A – Continuation (Judicial Department)	4
Chapter 7A – Continuation (Judicial Department)	5
Chapter 7B - Juvenile Code	5
Chapter 8 - Evidence	6
Chapter 8A - Interpreters for Deaf Persons [Recodified.]	6
Chapter 8B - Interpreters for Deaf Persons	6
Chapter 8C - Evidence Code	6
Chapter 9 - Jurors	6
Chapter 10 - Notaries [Repealed.]	6
Chapter 10A - Notaries [Recodified.]	6
Chapter 10B - Notaries	6
Chapter 11 - Oaths	6
Chapter 12 - Statutory Construction	6
Chapter 13 - Citizenship Restored	6
Chapter 14 - Criminal Law	7
Chapter 14 –Criminal Law (Continuation)	8
Chapter 15 - Criminal Procedure	9
Chapter 15A - Criminal Procedure Act (Continuation)	10
Chapter 15A - Criminal Procedure Act (Continuation)	11
Chapter 15B - Victims Compensation	11
Chapter 15C - Address Confidentiality Program	11
Chapter 16 - Gaming Contracts and Futures	11
Chapter 17 - Habeas Corpus	11

Chapter 17A - Law-Enforcement Officers [Recodified.]	11
Chapter 17B - North Carolina Criminal Justice Education and Training System [Recodified.] Chapter 17C - North Carolina Criminal Justice Education and Training Standards Commission	11
	11
Chapter 17D - North Carolina Justice Academy	11
Chapter 17E - North Carolina Sheriffs' Education and Training Standards Commission	11
Chapter 18 - Regulation of Intoxicating Liquors [Repealed.]	12
Chapter 18A - Regulation of Intoxicating Liquors [Repealed.]	12
Chapter 18B - Regulation of Alcoholic Beverages	12
Chapter 18C - North Carolina State Lottery	12
Chapter 19 - Offenses against Public Morals	12
Chapter 19A - Protection of Animals	12
Chapter 20 - Motor Vehicles	13
Chapter 20 - Motor Vehicles (Continuation)	14
Chapter 20 - Motor Vehicles (Continuation)	15
Chapter 20 - Motor Vehicles (Continuation)	16
Chapter 21 - Bills of Lading	17
Chapter 22 - Contracts Requiring Writing	17
Chapter 22A - Signatures	17
Chapter 22B - Contracts Against Public Policy	17
Chapter 22C - Payments to Subcontractors	17
Chapter 23 - Debtor and Creditor	17
Chapter 24 – Interest	17
Chapter 25 – Uniform Commercial Code	18
Chapter 25 – Uniform Commercial Code (Continuation)	19
Chapter 25A – Retail Installment Sales Act	20
Chapter 25B - Credit	20
Chapter 25C - Sales of Artwork	20
Chapter 26 - Suretyship	20
Chapter 27 - Warehouse Receipts [Repealed.]	20
Chapter 28 - Administration [Repealed.]	20
Chapter 28A - Administration of Decedents' Estates	20
Chapter 28B - Estates of Absentees in Military Service	20
Chapter 28C - Estates of Missing Persons	20
Chapter 29 - Intestate Succession	21
Chapter 30 - Surviving Spouses	21
Chapter 31 - Wills	21
Chapter 31A - Acts Barring Property Rights	21
Chapter 31B - Renunciation of Property and Renunciation of Fiduciary Powers Act	21
Chapter 31C - Uniform Disposition of Community Property Rights at Death Act	21
Chapter 32 - Fiduciaries	21
Chapter 32A - Powers of Attorney	21
Chapter 33 - Guardian and Ward [Repealed and Recodified.]	21

Chapter 33A - North Carolina Uniform Transfers to Minors Act	21
Chapter 33B - North Carolina Uniform Custodial Trust Act	21
Chapter 34 - Veterans' Guardianship Act	22
Chapter 35 - Sterilization Procedures	22
Chapter 35A - Incompetency and Guardianship	22
Chapter 36 - Trusts and Trustees [Repealed.]	22
Chapter 36A - Trusts and Trustees	22
Chapter 36B - Uniform Management of Institutional Funds Act [Repealed.]	22
Chapter 36C - North Carolina Uniform Trust Code	22
Chapter 36D - North Carolina Community Third Party Trusts, Pooled Trusts	23
Chapter 36E - Uniform Prudent Management of Institutional Funds Act	23
Chapter 37 - Allocation of Principal and Income [Repealed.]	23
Chapter 37A - Uniform Principal and Income Act	23
Chapter 38 - Boundaries	23
Chapter 38A - Landowner Liability	23
Chapter 39 - Conveyances	23
Chapter 39A - Transfer Fee Covenants Prohibited	23
Chapter 40 - Eminent Domain [Repealed.]	23
Chapter 40A - Eminent Domain	23
Chapter 41 - Estates	23
Chapter 41A - State Fair Housing Act	23
Chapter 42 - Landlord and Tenant	23
Chapter 42A - Vacation Rental Act	23
Chapter 43 - Land Registration	23
Chapter 44 - Liens	24
Chapter 44A - Statutory Liens and Charges	24
Chapter 45 - Mortgages and Deeds of Trust	24
Chapter 45A - Good Funds Settlement Act	24
Chapter 46 - Partition	24
Chapter 47 - Probate and Registration	25
Chapter 47A - Unit Ownership	25
Chapter 47B - Real Property Marketable Title Act	25
Chapter 47C - North Carolina Condominium Act	25
Chapter 47D - Notice of Settlement Act [Expired.]	25
Chapter 47E - Residential Property Disclosure Act	25
Chapter 47F - North Carolina Planned Community Act	25
Chapter 47G - Option to Purchase Contracts	25
Chapter 47H - Contracts for Deed	25
Chapter 48 - Adoptions	26
Chapter 48A - Minors	26
Chapter 49 - Bastardy	26
Chapter 49A - Rights of Children	26
Chapter 50 - Divorce and Alimony	26
Chapter 50A - Uniform Child-Custody Jurisdiction and	

Enforcement Act	26
Chapter 50B - Domestic Violence	26
Chapter 50C - Civil No-Contact Orders	26
Chapter 51 - Marriage	26
Chapter 52 - Powers and Liabilities of Married Persons	27
Chapter 52A - Uniform Reciprocal Enforcement of Support Act [Repealed.]	27
Chapter 52B - Uniform Premarital Agreement Act	27
Chapter 52C - Uniform Interstate Family Support Act	27
Chapter 53 - Banks	27
Chapter 53A - Business Development Corporations and North Carolina Capital Resource Corporations	28
Chapter 53B - Financial Privacy Act	28
Chapter 54 - Cooperative Organizations	28
Chapter 54A - Capital Stock Savings and Loan Associations [Repealed.]	28
Chapter 54B - Savings and Loan Associations	29
Chapter 54C - Savings Banks	29
Chapter 55 - North Carolina Business Corporation Act	30
Chapter 55A - North Carolina Nonprofit Corporation Act	31
Chapter 55B - Professional Corporation Act	31
Chapter 55C - Foreign Trade Zones	31
Chapter 55D - Filings, Names, and Registered Agents for Corporations, Nonprofit Corporations, and Partnerships	31
Chapter 56 - Electric, Telegraph and Power Companies [Repealed.]	31
Chapter 57 - Hospital, Medical and Dental Service Corporations [Recodified.]	31
Chapter 57A - Health Maintenance Organization Act [Recodified.]	31
Chapter 57B - Health Maintenance Organization Act [Recodified.]	31
Chapter 57C - North Carolina Limited Liability Company Act.	31
Chapter 58 - Insurance.	32
Chapter 58 - Insurance (Continuation)	33
Chapter 58 - Insurance (Continuation)	34
Chapter 58 - Insurance (Continuation)	35
Chapter 58 - Insurance (Continuation)	36
Chapter 58 - Insurance (Continuation)	37
Chapter 58 - Insurance (Continuation)	38
Chapter 58A - North Carolina Health Insurance Trust Commission [Recodified.]	38
Chapter 59 - Partnership.	39
Chapter 59B - Uniform Unincorporated Nonprofit Association Act.	39
Chapter 60 - Railroads and Other Carriers [Repealed and Transferred.]	39
Chapter 61 - Religious Societies	39
Chapter 62 - Public Utilities	39

Chapter 62 - Public Utilities (Continuation)	40
Chapter 62A - Public Safety Telephone Service And Wireless Telephone Service	40
Chapter 63 - Aeronautics	40
Chapter 63A - North Carolina Global TransPark Authority	40
Chapter 64 - Aliens	40
Chapter 65 – Cemeteries	40
Chapter 66 - Commerce and Business	41
Chapter 67 - Dogs	41
Chapter 68 - Fences and Stock Law	41
Chapter 69 - Fire Protection	41
Chapter 70 - Indian Antiquities, Archaeological Resources and Unmarked Human Skeletal Remains Protection	42
Chapter 71 - Indians [Repealed.]	42
Chapter 71A - Indians	42
Chapter 72 - Inns, Hotels and Restaurants	42
Chapter 73 - Mills	42
Chapter 74 - Mines and Quarries	42
Chapter 74A - Company Police [Repealed.]	42
Chapter 74B - Private Protective Services Act [Repealed.]	42
Chapter 74C - Private Protective Services	42
Chapter 74D - Alarm Systems	42
Chapter 74E - Company Police Act	42
Chapter 74F - Locksmith Licensing Act	42
Chapter 74G - Campus Police Act	42
Chapter 75 - Monopolies, Trusts and Consumer Protection	42
Chapter 75A - Boating and Water Safety	43
Chapter 75B - Discrimination in Business	43
Chapter 75C - Motion Picture Fair Competition Act	43
Chapter 75D - Racketeer Influenced and Corrupt Organizations	43
Chapter 75E - Unlawful Activities in Connection With Certain Corporate Transactions	43
Chapter 76 - Navigation	43
Chapter 76A - Navigation and Pilotage Commissions	43
Chapter 77 - Rivers, Creeks, and Coastal Waters	43
Chapter 78 - Securities Law [Repealed.]	43
Chapter 78A - North Carolina Securities Act	43
Chapter 78B - Tender Offer Disclosure Act [Repealed.]	43
Chapter 78C - Investment Advisers	43
Chapter 78D - Commodities Act	43
Chapter 79 - Strays [Repealed.]	43
Chapter 80 - Trademarks, Brands, etc.	44
Chapter 81 - Weights and Measures [Recodified.]	44
Chapter 81A - Weights and Measures Act of 1975.	44
Chapter 82 - Wrecks [Repealed.]	44
Chapter 83 - Architects [Recodified.]	44

Chapter 83A - Architects	44
Chapter 84 - Attorneys-at-Law	44
Chapter 84A - Foreign Legal Consultants	44
Chapter 85 - Auctions and Auctioneers [Repealed.]	44
Chapter 85A - Bail Bondsmen and Runners [Recodified.]	44
Chapter 85B - Auctions and Auctioneers	44
Chapter 85C - Bail Bondsmen and Runners [Recodified.]	44
Chapter 86 - Barbers [Recodified.]	44
Chapter 86A - Barbers	44
Chapter 87 - Contractors	44
Chapter 88 - Cosmetic Art [Repealed.]	44
Chapter 88A - Electrolysis Practice Act	44
Chapter 88B - Cosmetic Art	45
Chapter 89 - Engineering and Land Surveying [Recodified.]	45
Chapter 89A - Landscape Architects	45
Chapter 89B - Foresters	45
Chapter 89C - Engineering and Land Surveying	45
Chapter 89D - Landscape Contractors	45
Chapter 89E - Geologists Licensing Act	45
Chapter 89F - North Carolina Soil Scientist Licensing Act	45
Chapter 89G - Irrigation Contractors	45
Chapter 90 - Medicine and Allied Occupations	45
Chapter 90 - Medicine and Allied Occupations (Continuation)	46
Chapter 90 - Medicine and Allied Occupations (Continuation)	47
Chapter 90 - Medicine and Allied Occupations (Continuation)	48
Chapter 90A - Sanitarians and Water and Wastewater Treatment Facility Operators	48
Chapter 90B - Social Worker Certification and Licensure Act	48
Chapter 90C - North Carolina Recreational Therapy Licensure Act	48
Chapter 90D - Interpreters and Transliterators	48
Chapter 91 - Pawnbrokers [Repealed.]	48
Chapter 91A - Pawnbrokers Modernization Act of 1989	48
Chapter 92 - Photographers [Deleted.]	48
Chapter 93 - Certified Public Accountants	48
Chapter 93A - Real Estate License Law	49
Chapter 93B - Occupational Licensing Boards	49
Chapter 93C - Watchmakers [Repealed.]	49
Chapter 93D - North Carolina State Hearing Aid Dealers and Fitters Board.	49
Chapter 93E - North Carolina Appraisers Act	49
Chapter 94 - Apprenticeship	49
Chapter 95 - Department of Labor and Labor Regulations	49
Chapter 95 - Department of Labor and Labor Regulations (Continuation)	50
Chapter 96 - Employment Security	50
Chapter 97 - Workers' Compensation Act	50
Chapter 97 - Workers' Compensation Act (Continuation)	51

Chapter 98 - Burnt and Lost Records	51
Chapter 99 - Libel and Slander	51
Chapter 99A - Civil Remedies for Criminal Actions	51
Chapter 99B - Products Liability	51
Chapter 99C - Actions Relating to Winter Sports Safety and Accidents	51
Chapter 99D - Civil Rights	51
Chapter 99E - Special Liability Provisions	51
Chapter 100 - Monuments, Memorials and Parks	51
Chapter 101 - Names of Persons	51
Chapter 102 - Official Survey Base	51
Chapter 103 - Sundays, Holidays and Special Days	51
Chapter 104 - United States Lands	51
Chapter 104A - Degrees of Kinship	51
Chapter 104B - Hurricanes or Other Acts of Nature	51
Chapter 104C - Atomic Energy, Radioactivity and Ionizing Radiation [Repealed and Recodified.]	51
Chapter 104D - Southern States Energy Compact	51
Chapter 104E - North Carolina Radiation Protection Act	51
Chapter 104F - Southeast Interstate Low-Level Radioactive Waste Management Compact [Repealed]	51
Chapter 104G - North Carolina Low-Level Radioactive Waste Management Authority Act of 1987 [Repealed]	51
Chapter 105 - Taxation	51
Chapter 105 - Taxation (Continuation)	52
Chapter 105 - Taxation (Continuation)	53
Chapter 105 - Taxation (Continuation)	54
Chapter 105A - Setoff Debt Collection Act	55
Chapter 105B - Defaulted Student Loan Recovery Act	55
Chapter 106 - Agriculture	55
Chapter 106 - Agriculture (Continue)	56
Chapter 106 - Agriculture (Continue)	57
Chapter 107 - Agricultural Development Districts [Repealed.]	57
Chapter 108 - Social Services [Repealed and Recodified.]	57
Chapter 108A - Social Services	57
Chapter 108B - Community Action Programs	58
Chapter 108C Medicaid and Health Choice Provider Requirements.	58
Chapter 108D Medicaid Managed Care for Behavioral Health Services.	58
Chapter 109 - Bonds [Recodified.]	58
Chapter 110 - Child Welfare	58
Chapter 111 - Aid to the Blind	58
Chapter 112 - Confederate Homes and Pensions [Repealed.]	58
Chapter 113 - Conservation and Development	58
Chapter 113 - Conservation and Development (Continuation)	59

Chapter 113A - Pollution Control and Environment	59
Chapter 113A - Pollution Control and Environment (Continuation)	60
Chapter 113B - North Carolina Energy Policy Act of 1975	60
Chapter 114 - Department of Justice	60
Chapter 115 - Elementary and Secondary Education [Repealed.]	60
Chapter 115A - Community Colleges, Technical Institutes, and Industrial Education Centers [Repealed.]	60
Chapter 115B - Tuition and Fee Waivers	60
Chapter 115C - Elementary and Secondary Education	60
Chapter 115C - Elementary and Secondary Education (Continuation)	61
Chapter 115C - Elementary and Secondary Education (Continuation)	62
Chapter 115C - Elementary and Secondary Education (Continuation)	63
Chapter 115D - Community Colleges	63
Chapter 115E - Private Educational Facilities Finance Act [Recodified]	63
Chapter 116 - Higher Education	63
Chapter 116 - Higher Education (Continuation)	63
Chapter 116A - Escheats and Abandoned Property [Repealed.]	64
Chapter 116B - Escheats and Abandoned Property	64
Chapter 116C - Continuum of Education Programs	64
Chapter 116D - Higher Education Bonds	64
Chapter 116E -Education Longitudinal Data System	64
Chapter 117 - Electrification	64
Chapter 118 - Firemen's and Rescue Squad Workers' Relief and Pension Funds [Recodified.]	64
Chapter 118A - Firemen's Death Benefit Act [Repealed.]	64
Chapter 118B - Members of a Rescue Squad Death Benefit Act [Repealed.]	64
Chapter 119 - Gasoline and Oil Inspection and Regulation	64
Chapter 120 - General Assembly	65
Chapter 120 - General Assembly (Continuation)	66
Chapter 120 - General Assembly (Continuation)	67
Chapter 120C - Lobbying	67
Chapter 121 - Archives and History	67
Chapter 122 - Hospitals for the Mentally Disordered [Repealed.]	67
Chapter 122A - North Carolina Housing Finance Agency	67
Chapter 122B - North Carolina Agricultural Facilities Finance Act [Repealed.]	67
Chapter 122C - Mental Health, Developmental Disabilities, and Substance Abuse Act of 1985	67
Chapter 122C - Mental Health, Developmental Disabilities, and Substance Abuse Act of 1985 (Continuation)	68

Chapter 122D - North Carolina Agricultural Finance Act	68
Chapter 122E - North Carolina Housing Trust and Oil Overcharge Act	68
Chapter 123 - Impeachment	69
Chapter 123A - Industrial Development [Repealed.]	69
Chapter 124 - Internal Improvements	69
Chapter 125 - Libraries	69
Chapter 126 - State Personnel System	69
Chapter 127 - Militia [Repealed.]	69
Chapter 127A - Militia	69
Chapter 127B - Military Affairs	69
Chapter 127C - Advisory Commission on Military Affairs	69
Chapter 128 - Offices and Public Officers	69
Chapter 128 - Offices and Public Officers (Continuation)	70
Chapter 129 - Public Buildings and Grounds	70
Chapter 130 - Public Health [Repealed.]	70
Chapter 130A - Public Health	70
Chapter 130A - Public Health (Continuation)	71
Chapter 130A - Public Health (Continuation)	72
Chapter 130B - Hazardous Waste Management Commission [Repealed.]	72
Chapter 131 - Public Hospitals [Repealed.]	72
Chapter 131A - Health Care Facilities Finance Act	72
Chapter 131B - Licensing of Ambulatory Surgical Facilities [Repealed.]	72
Chapter 131C - Charitable Solicitation Licensure Act [Repealed.]	72
Chapter 131D - Inspection and Licensing of Facilities	72
Chapter 131E - Health Care Facilities and Services	72
Chapter 131E - Health Care Facilities and Services (Continuation)	73
Chapter 131F - Solicitation of Contributions	73
Chapter 132 - Public Records	73
Chapter 133 - Public Works	74
Chapter 134 - Youth Development [Recodified.]	74
Chapter 134A - Youth Services [Repealed.]	74
Chapter 135 - Retirement System for Teachers and State Employees; Social Security; Health Insurance Program for Children	74
Chapter 135 - Retirement System for Teachers and State Employees; Social Security; Health Insurance Program for Children	75
Chapter 136 - Transportation	75
Chapter 136 - Transportation (Continuation)	76
Chapter 137 - Rural Rehabilitation [Repealed.]	76
Chapter 138 - Salaries, Fees and Allowances	76
Chapter 138A - State Government Ethics Act	76

Chapter 139 - Soil and Water Conservation Districts	76
Chapter 140 - State Art Museum; Symphony and Art Societies	76
Chapter 140A - State Awards System	76
Chapter 141 - State Boundaries	76
Chapter 142 - State Debt	76
Chapter 143 - State Departments, Institutions, and Commissions	77
Chapter 143 - State Departments, Institutions, and Commissions (Continuation)	78
Chapter 143 - State Departments, Institutions, and Commissions (Continuation)	79
Chapter 143 - State Departments, Institutions, and Commissions (Continuation)	80
Chapter 143A - State Government Reorganization	80
Chapter 143B - Executive Organization Act of 1973	80
Chapter 143B - Executive Organization Act of 1973 (Continuation)	81
Chapter 143B - Executive Organization Act of 1973 (Continuation)	82
Chapter 143C - State Budget Act	83
Chapter 143D - The State Governmental Accountability and Internal Control Act	83
Chapter 144 - State Flag, Official Governmental Flags, Motto, and Colors	83
Chapter 145 - State Symbols and Other Official Adoptions.	83
Chapter 146 - State Lands	83
Chapter 147 - State Officers	83
Chapter 148 - State Prison System	84
Chapter 149 - State Song and Toast	84
Chapter 150 - Uniform Revocation of Licenses [Repealed.]	84
Chapter 150A - Administrative Procedure Act [Recodified.]	84
Chapter 150B - Administrative Procedure Act	84
Chapter 151 - Constables [Repealed.]	84
Chapter 152 - Coroners	84
Chapter 152A - County Medical Examiner [Repealed.]	84
Chapter 152A - County Medical Examiner [Repealed.] (Continuation)	84
Chapter 153 - Counties and County Commissioners [Repealed.]	84
Chapter 153A - Counties	84
Chapter 153A - Counties (Countinue)	85
Chapter 153B - Mountain Resources Planning Act	85
Chapter 153C - Uwharrie Regional Resources Act	85
Chapter 154 - County Surveyor [Repealed.]	85
Chapter 155 - County Treasurer [Repealed.]	85

Chapter 156 - Drainage	85
Chapter 156 – Drainage (Continuation)	86
Chapter 157 - Housing Authorities and Projects	86
Chapter 157A - Historic Properties Commissions [Transferred.]	86
Chapter 158 - Local Development	86
Chapter 159 - Local Government Finance	86
Chapter 159 - Local Government Finance (Continuation)	87
Chapter 159A - Pollution Abatement and Industrial Facilities Financing Act [Unconstitutional.]	87
Chapter 159B - Joint Municipal Electric Power and Energy Act	87
Chapter 159C - Industrial and Pollution Control Facilities Financing Act	87
Chapter 159D - The North Carolina Capital Facilities Financing Act	87
Chapter 159E - Registered Public Obligations Act	87
Chapter 159F - North Carolina Energy Development Authority [Repealed.]	87
Chapter 159G - Water Infrastructure	87
Chapter 159H - [Reserved.]	87
Chapter 159I - Solid Waste Management Loan Program and Local Government Special Obligation Bonds	87
Chapter 160 - Municipal Corporations [Repealed And Transferred.]	87
Chapter 160A - Cities and Towns	88
Chapter 160A - Cities and Towns (Continuation)	89
Chapter 160B - Consolidated City-County Act	89
Chapter 160C - Baseball Park Districts [Repealed.]	90
Chapter 161 - Register of Deeds	90
Chapter 162 - Sheriff	90
Chapter 162A - Water and Sewer Systems	90
Chapter 162B Continuity of Local Government in Emergency.	90
Chapter 163 Elections and Election Laws.	90
Chapter 163 Elections and Election Laws. (Continuation)	91
Chapter 164 Concerning the General Statutes of North Carolina.	92
Chapter 165 Veterans.	92
Chapter 166 Civil Preparedness Agencies [Repealed.]	92
Chapter 166A North Carolina Emergency Management Act.	92
Chapter 167 State Civil Air Patrol [Repealed.]	92
Chapter 168 Persons with Disabilities.	92
Chapter 168A Persons With Disabilities Protection Act.	92

§ 143-151.54. Miscellaneous license provisions.

(a) License as Property of the Board and Display of License. - A license issued by the Board is the property of the Board. If the Board suspends or revokes a license issued by it, the individual to whom it is issued must give it to the Board upon demand. An individual who is licensed by the Board must display the license certificate in the manner prescribed by the Board. A license holder whose address changes must report the change to the Board.

(b) Report Criminal Convictions and Disciplinary Actions. - A license holder who is convicted of any felony or misdemeanor or is disciplined by any governmental agency in connection with any other occupational or professional license shall file with the Board a written report of the conviction or disciplinary action within 60 days of the final judgment, order, or disposition of the case. (1993 (Reg. Sess., 1994), c. 724, s. 1; 2009-509, s. 5.1.)

§ 143-151.55. Renewal of license; inactive licenses; lapsed licenses.

(a) Renewal. - A license expires on September 30 of each year. A license may be renewed by filing an application for renewal with the Board and paying the required renewal fee. The Board must notify license holders at least 30 days before their licenses expire. The Board must renew the license of a person who files an application for renewal, pays the required renewal fee, has fulfilled the continuing education requirements set by the Board, and is not in violation of this Article when the application is filed. If the Board imposes a continuing education requirement as a condition of renewing a license, the Board must ensure that the courses needed to fulfill the requirement are available in all geographic areas of the State.

(b) Late Renewal. - The Board may provide for the late renewal of a license upon the payment of a late fee, but no late renewal of a license may be granted more than one year after the license expires.

(c) Inactive License. - A license holder may apply to the Board to be placed on inactive status. An applicant for inactive status must follow the procedure set by the Board. A license holder who is granted inactive status is not subject to the license renewal requirements during the period the license holder remains on inactive status.

A license holder whose application is granted and is placed on inactive status may apply to the Board to be reinstated to active status at any time. To change a license from inactive status to active status, the license holder must complete the same number of continuing education credit hours that would have been required of the license holder had the license holder maintained an active license. The number of continuing education credit hours required to return an inactive license to active status shall not exceed 24 credit hours. The Board may set conditions for reinstatement to active status. An individual who is on inactive status and applies to be reinstated to active status must comply with the conditions set by the Board.

(d) Lapsed License. - The license of a licensed home inspector shall lapse if the licensee fails to continuously maintain the [insurance] requirements provided in G.S. 143-151.58(b). (1993 (Reg. Sess., 1994), c. 724, s. 1; 1999-149, s. 1; 2009-509, ss. 2.3, 3.5, 5.2.)

§ 143-151.56. Suspension, revocation, and refusal to renew license.

(a) The Board may deny or refuse to issue or renew a license, may suspend or revoke a license, or may impose probationary conditions on a license if the license holder or applicant for licensure has engaged in any of the following conduct:

(1) Employed fraud, deceit, or misrepresentation in obtaining or attempting to obtain or renew a license.

(2) Committed an act of malpractice, gross negligence, or incompetence in the practice of home inspections.

(3) Without having a current license, either performed home inspections for compensation or claimed to be licensed.

(4) Engaged in conduct that could result in harm or injury to the public.

(5) Been convicted of or pled guilty or nolo contendere to any misdemeanor involving moral turpitude or to any felony.

(6) Been adjudicated incompetent.

(7) Engaged in any act or practice that violates any of the provisions of this Article or any rule issued by the Board, or aided, abetted, or assisted any person in a violation of any of the provisions of this Article.

(8) Failed to maintain the requirements provided in G.S. 143-151.58(b).

(b) A denial of licensure, refusal to renew, suspension, revocation, or imposition of probationary conditions upon a license holder may be ordered by the Board after a hearing held in accordance with Article 3A of Chapter 150B of the General Statutes and rules adopted by the Board. An application may be made to the Board for reinstatement of a revoked license if the revocation has been in effect for at least one year. (1993 (Reg. Sess., 1994), c. 724, s. 1; 1998-211, s. 36; 2009-509, s. 2.4.)

§ 143-151.57. Fees.

(a) Maximum Fees. - The Board may adopt fees that do not exceed the amounts set in the following table for administering this Article:

Item
Maximum Fee

Application for home inspector license
$35.00

Home inspector examination
80.00

Issuance or renewal of home inspector license
160.00

Late renewal of home inspector license
30.00

Application for course approval
150.00

Renewal of course approval
75.00

Course fee, per credit hour per licensee
5.00

Credit for unapproved continuing education course
50.00

Copies of Board rules or licensure standards		Cost
of printing

and mailing.

(b)		Subsequent Application. - An individual who applied for a license as a home inspector and who failed the home inspector examination is not required to pay an additional application fee if the individual submits another application for a license as a home inspector. The individual must pay the examination fee, however, to be eligible to take the examination again. An individual may take the examination only once every 180 days. (1993 (Reg. Sess., 1994), c. 724, s. 1; 1999-149, s. 2; 2000-140, s. 32; 2009-451, s. 21.8; 2009-509, ss. 3.6, 5.3.)

§ 143-151.58. Duties of licensed home inspector.

(a)		Home Inspection Report. - A licensed home inspector must give to each person for whom the inspector performs a home inspection for compensation a written report of the home inspection. The inspector must give the person the report by the date set in a written agreement by the parties to the home inspection. If the parties to the home inspection did not agree on a date in a written agreement, the inspector must give the person the report within three business days after the inspection was performed.

(a1)		Summary Page. - A written report provided under subsection (a) of this section for a prepurchase home inspection of three or more systems must include a summary page that contains the information required by this subsection. All other subject matters pertaining to the home inspection must appear in the body of the report. The summary page must contain the following statement: "This summary page is not the entire report. The complete report may include additional information of interest or concern to you. It is strongly recommended that you promptly read the complete report. For information regarding the negotiability of any item in this report under the real estate purchase contract, contact your North Carolina real estate agent or an attorney."

The summary page must describe any system or component of the home that does not function as intended, allowing for normal wear and tear that does not prevent the system or component from functioning as intended. The summary page must also describe any system or component that appears not to function as intended, based upon documented tangible evidence, and that requires either subsequent examination or further investigation by a specialist. The summary page may describe any system or component that poses a safety concern.

(a2)   State Building Code. - If a licensee includes a deficiency in the written report of a home inspection that is stated as a violation of the North Carolina State Residential Building Code, the licensee must do all of the following:

(1)   Determine the date of construction, renovation, and any subsequent installation or replacement of any system or component of the home.

(2)   Determine the State Building Code in effect at the time of construction, renovation, and any subsequent installation or replacement of any system or component of the home.

(3)   Conduct the home inspection using the building codes in effect at the time of the construction, renovation, and any subsequent installation or replacement of any system or component of the home.

In order to fully inform the client, if the licensee describes a deficiency as a violation of the State Building Code in the written report, then the report shall include the information described in subdivision (1) of this subsection and photocopies of the relevant provisions of the State Building Code used pursuant to subdivision (2) of this subsection to determine any violation stated in the report. The Board may adopt rules that are more restrictive on the use of the State Building Code by home inspectors.

(b)   Insurance, Net Assets, and Bond Requirements. - A licensed home inspector must continuously maintain general liability insurance and minimum net assets, a bond, or errors and omissions insurance as required in G.S. 143-151.51(b).

(c)   Repealed by Session Laws 2009-509, s. 3.3, effective October 1, 2013.

(d)   Record Keeping. - All licensees under this Article shall make and keep full and accurate records of business done under their licenses. Records shall include the written, signed contract and the written report required by subsection (a) of this section and the standards of practice referred to in G.S. 143-151.49(a)(2) and any other information the Board requires by rule. Records shall be retained by licensees for not less than three years. Licensees shall furnish their records to the Board on demand. (1993 (Reg. Sess., 1994), c. 724, s. 1; 1999-149, s. 3; 2009-509, ss. 2.5, 3.3, 3.7, 4.1, 4.2.)

§ 143-151.59. Violation is a misdemeanor.

A person who violates a provision of this Article is guilty of a Class 2 misdemeanor. Each unlawful act or practice constitutes a distinct and separate offense. (1993 (Reg. Sess., 1994), c. 724, s. 1.)

§ 143-151.60. Injunctions.

The Board may make application to any appropriate court for an order enjoining violations of this Article. Upon a showing by the Board that any person has violated or is about to violate this Article, the court may grant an injunction or a restraining order or take other appropriate action. (1993 (Reg. Sess., 1994), c. 724, s. 1.)

§ 143-151.61. (Repealed effective October 1, 2013) Certain applicants do not have to be licensed as an associate home inspector before being eligible for licensure as a home inspector.

The requirement that an applicant for licensure as a home inspector first have a license as an associate home inspector does not apply to a person who, prior to October 1, 1996, had been engaged in the business of performing home inspections for compensation for at least one year and had conducted at least 100 home inspections for compensation. All other requirements for licensure as a home inspector, including passing a licensing examination provided by the Board, apply to an applicant who is exempted by this section from the requirement of prior licensure as an associate home inspector. (1993 (Reg. Sess., 1994), c. 724, s. 1; 2009-509, s. 3.3.)

§ 143-151.62. Persons and practices not affected.

This Article does not apply to any of the following:

(1) A person who is employed as a code enforcement official by the State or a political subdivision of the State and is certified pursuant to Article 9C of Chapter 143 of the General Statutes, when acting within the scope of that employment.

(2) A plumbing or heating contractor who does not claim to be a home inspector and is licensed under Article 2 of Chapter 87 of the General Statutes, when acting pursuant to that Article.

(3) An electrical contractor who does not claim to be a home inspector and is licensed under Article 4 of Chapter 87 of the General Statutes, when acting pursuant to that Article.

(4) A real estate broker or a real estate sales representative who does not claim to be a home inspector and is licensed under Article 1 of Chapter 93A of the General Statutes, when acting pursuant to that Article.

(5) A structural pest control licensee licensed under the provisions of Article 4C of Chapter 106 of the General Statutes, an employee of the licensee, or a certified applicator licensed under the provisions of Article 4C of Chapter 106 of the General Statutes who does not claim to be a home inspector, while performing structural pest control activities pursuant to that Article. (1993 (Reg. Sess., 1994), c. 724, s. 1.)

§ 143-151.63. Administration.

(a) The Division of Engineering and Building Code in the Department of Insurance shall provide clerical and other staff services required by the Board, and shall administer and enforce all provisions of this Article and all rules adopted under this Article, subject to the direction of the Board. The Board shall reimburse the Division for its services to the Board.

(b) Any monies received by the Board pursuant to this Article shall be deposited in the State treasury to the account of the Board and shall be used to administer this Article.

(c) The books and records of the Board are subject to the oversight of the State Auditor, as provided in G.S. 93B-4. (1993 (Reg. Sess., 1994), c. 724, s. 1.)

§ 143-151.64. Continuing education requirements.

(a) Requirements. - The Board may establish programs of continuing education for licensees under this Article. A licensee subject to a program under this section shall present evidence to the Board upon the license renewal following initial licensure, and every renewal thereafter, that during the 12 months preceding the annual license expiration date the licensee has completed the required number of classroom hours of instruction in courses approved by the Board. Annual continuing education hour requirements shall be determined by the Board, but shall not be less than 12 credit hours and no more than 20 hours. No member of the Board shall provide or sponsor a continuing education course under this section while that person is serving on the Board.

(b) Fees. - The Board may establish a nonrefundable course application fee to be charged to a course sponsor for the review and approval of a proposed continuing education course. Approval of a continuing education course must be renewed annually. The Board may also require a course sponsor to pay a fee for each licensee completing an approved continuing education course conducted by the sponsor.

(c) Credit for Unapproved Course. - The Board may award continuing education credit for an unapproved course or related educational activity. The Board may prescribe procedures for a licensee to submit information on an unapproved course or related educational activity for continuing education credit. The Board may charge a fee to the licensee for each course or activity submitted.

(d) Extension of Time. - The Board may, for good cause shown, grant extensions of time to licensees to comply with these requirements. Any licensee who, after obtaining an extension under this subsection, offers evidence satisfactory to the Board that the licensee has satisfactorily completed the required continuing education courses, is in compliance with this section.

(e) Rules. - The Board may adopt rules governing continuing education requirements, including rules that govern:

(1)	The content and subject matter of continuing education courses.

(2)	The criteria, standards, and procedures for the approval of courses, course sponsors, and course instructors.

(3)	The methods of instruction.

(4)	The computation of course credit.

(5)	The ability to carry forward course credit from one year to another.

(6)	The waiver of or variance from the continuing education requirement for hardship or other reasons.

(7)	The procedures for compliance and sanctions for noncompliance. (1999-149, s. 4; 2001-421, s. 2.5; 2009-509, s. 1.1.)

§ 143-151.65: Reserved for future codification purposes.

§ 143-151.66: Reserved for future codification purposes.

§ 143-151.67: Reserved for future codification purposes.

§ 143-151.68: Reserved for future codification purposes.

§ 143-151.69: Reserved for future codification purposes.

Article 9G.

Military Lands Protection.

§ 143-151.70. Short title.

This Article shall be known as the Military Lands Protection Act of 2013. (2013-206, s. 1.)

§ 143-151.71. Definitions.

Within the meaning of this Article:

(1) "Area surrounding major military installations" is the area that extends five miles beyond the boundary of a major military installation and may include incorporated and unincorporated areas of counties and municipalities.

(2) "Building Code Council" means the Council created pursuant to Article 9 of Chapter 143 of the General Statutes.

(3) "Commissioner" means the Commissioner of Insurance.

(4) "Construction" includes reconstruction, alteration, or expansion.

(5) "Major military installation" means Fort Bragg, Pope Army Airfield, Camp Lejeune Marine Corps Air Base, New River Marine Corps Air Station, Cherry Point Marine Corps Air Station, Military Ocean Terminal at Sunny Point, the United States Coast Guard Air Station at Elizabeth City, Naval Support Activity Northwest, Air Route Surveillance Radar (ARSR-4) at Fort Fisher, and Seymour Johnson Air Force Base, in its own right and as the responsible entity for the Dare County Bombing Range, and any facility located within the State that is subject to the installations' oversight and control.

(6) "Person" means any individual, partnership, firm, association, joint venture, public or private corporation, trust, estate, commission, board, public or private institution, utility, cooperative, interstate body, the State of North Carolina and its agencies and political subdivisions, or other legal entity.

(7) "Tall buildings or structures" means any building, structure, or unit within a multiunit building with a vertical height of more than 200 feet measured from the top of the foundation of the building, structure, or unit and the uppermost point of the building, structure, or unit. "Tall buildings or structures" do not include buildings and structures listed individually or as contributing resources within a district listed in the National Register of Historic Places. (2013-206, s. 1.)

§ 143-151.72. Legislative findings.

North Carolina has a vested economic interest in preserving, maintaining, and sustaining land uses that are compatible with military activities at major installations. Development located proximate to military installations has been identified as a critical issue impacting the long-term viability of the military in this State. Additional concerns associated with development include loss of access to air space and coastal and marine areas and radio frequency encroachment. The construction of tall buildings or structures in areas surrounding major military installations is of utmost concern to the State as those buildings and structures may interfere with or impede the military's ability to carry out activities that are vital to its function and future presence in North Carolina. (2013-206, s. 1.)

§ 143-151.73. Certain buildings and structures prohibited without endorsement.

(a) No county or city may authorize the construction of and no person may construct a tall building or structure in any area surrounding a major military installation in this State, unless the county or city is in receipt of either a letter of endorsement issued to the person by the Building Code Council pursuant to G.S. 143-151.75 or proof of the Council's failure to act within the time allowed pursuant to G.S. 143-151.75.

(b) No county or city may authorize the provision of the following utility services to any building or structure constructed in violation of subsection (a) of this section: electricity, telephone, gas, water, sewer, or septic system. (2013-206, s. 1.)

§ 143-151.74. Exemptions from applicability.

(a) Wind energy facilities and wind energy facility expansions, as those terms are defined in Chapter 143 of the General Statutes, that are subject to the applicable permit requirements of that Chapter shall be exempt from obtaining the endorsement required by this Article.

(b) Cellular, radio, and television towers erected to temporarily replace cellular, radio, and television towers that are damaged or destroyed due to a natural disaster shall be exempt from obtaining the endorsement required by this Article provided all of the following conditions are met:

(1) The height of the cellular, radio, or television tower that is erected to temporarily replace the cellular, radio, or television tower that is damaged or destroyed does not exceed the height of the original cellular, radio, or television tower.

(2) A disaster has been declared pursuant to Chapter 166A of the General Statutes for the area in which the damaged or destroyed cellular, radio, or television tower is located.

(3) The temporary cellular, radio, or television tower shall only remain in place until the expiration of the declared disaster.

(c) The modification, replacement, removal, or addition of antennas on cellular, radio, or television towers in an area surrounding a major military installation shall be exempt from obtaining the endorsement required by this Article provided the modification, replacement, removal, or addition does not increase the vertical height of the structure. (2013-206, s. 1; 2013-413, s. 47.)

§ 143-151.75. Endorsement for proposed tall buildings or structures required.

(a) No person shall undertake construction of a tall building or structure in any area surrounding a major military installation in this State without either first obtaining the endorsement from the Building Code Council or proof of the Council's failure to act within the time allowed.

(b) A person seeking endorsement for a proposed tall building or structure in any area surrounding a major military installation in this State shall provide written notice of the intent to seek endorsement to the base commander of the major military installation that is located within five miles of the proposed tall building or structure and shall provide all of the following to the Building Code Council:

(1) Identification of the major military installation and the base commander of the installation that is located within five miles of the proposed tall building or structure.

(2) A copy of the written notice sent to the base commander of the installation identified in subdivision (1) of this subsection that is located within five miles of the proposed tall building or structure.

(3) A written "Determination of No Hazard to Air Navigation" issued by the Federal Aviation Administration pursuant to Subpart D of Part 77 of Title 14 of the Code of Federal Regulations (January 1, 2012, Edition) for the proposed tall building or structure.

(c) After receipt of the information provided by the applicant pursuant to subsection (b) of this section, the Building Code Council shall, in writing, request a written statement concerning the proposed tall building or structure from the base commander of the major military installation identified in subdivision (1) of subsection (b) of this section. The Building Code Council shall request that the following information be included in the written statement from the base commander:

(1) A determination whether the location of the proposed tall building or structure is within a protected area that surrounds the installation.

(2) A determination whether any activities of the installation may be adversely affected by the proposed tall building or structure. A detailed description of the potential adverse effects, including frequency disturbances and physical obstructions, shall accompany the determination required by this subdivision.

(d) The Building Code Council shall not endorse a tall building or structure if the Council finds any one or more of the following:

(1) The proposed tall building or structure would encroach upon or otherwise interfere with the mission, training, or operations of any major military installation in North Carolina and result in a detriment to continued military presence in the State. In its evaluation, the Building Code Council may consider whether the proposed tall building or structure would cause interference with air navigation routes, air traffic control areas, military training routes, or radar based on the written statement received from a base commander as provided in subsection (c) of this section and written comments received by members of affected communities. Provided, however, if the Building Code Council does not receive a written statement requested pursuant to subsection (c) of this section within 45 days of issuance of the request to the base commander, the Building Code Council shall deem the tall building or structure as endorsed by the base commander.

(2) The Council is not in receipt of the written "Determination of No Hazard to Air Navigation" issued to the person by the Federal Aviation Administration required pursuant to subdivision (3) of subsection (b) of this section.

(e) The Building Code Council shall make a final decision on the request for endorsement of a tall building or structure within 90 days from the date on which the Council requested the written statement from the base commander of the major military installation identified in subdivision (1) of subsection (b) of this section. If the Council determines that a request for a tall building or structure fails to meet the requirements for endorsement under this section, the Council shall deny the request. The Council shall notify the person of the denial, and the notice shall include a written statement of the reasons for the denial. If the Council fails to act within any time period set forth in this section, the person may treat the failure to act as a decision to endorse the tall building or structure.

(f) The Building Code Council may meet by telephone, video, or Internet conference, so long as consistent with applicable law regarding public meetings, to make a decision on a request for endorsement for a tall building or structure pursuant to subsection (e) of this section. (2013-206, s. 1.)

§ 143-151.76. Application to existing tall buildings and structures.

G.S. 143-151.73 applies to tall buildings or structures that existed in an area surrounding major military installations upon the effective date of this Article as follows:

(1) No reconstruction, alteration, or expansion may aggravate or intensify a violation by an existing building or structure that did not comply with G.S. 143-151.73 upon its effective date.

(2) No reconstruction, alteration, or expansion may cause or create a violation by an existing building or structure that did comply with G.S. 143-151.73 upon its effective date. (2013-206, s. 1.)

§ 143-151.77. Enforcement and penalties.

(a) In addition to injunctive relief, the Commissioner may assess and collect a civil penalty against any person who violates any of the provisions of this Article or rules adopted pursuant to this Article, as provided in this subsection [section]. The maximum civil penalty for a violation is five thousand dollars ($5,000). A civil penalty may be assessed from the date of the violation. Each day of a continuing violation may constitute a separate violation.

(b) The Commissioner shall determine the amount of the civil penalty and shall notify the person who is assessed the civil penalty of the amount of the penalty and the reason for assessing the penalty. The notice of assessment shall be served by any means authorized under Rule 4 of G.S. 1A-1 and shall direct the violator to either pay the assessment or contest the assessment within 30 calendar days by filing a petition for a contested case under Article 3 of Chapter 150B of the General Statutes. If a violator does not pay a civil penalty assessed by the Commissioner within 30 calendar days after it is due, the Commissioner shall request that the Attorney General institute a civil action to recover the amount of the assessment. The civil action may be brought in the superior court of any county where the violation occurred. A civil action must be filed within one year of the date the assessment was due. An assessment that is not contested is due when the violator is served with a notice of assessment. An assessment that is contested is due at the conclusion of the administrative and judicial review of the assessment.

(c) In determining the amount of the penalty, the Commissioner shall consider the degree and extent of harm caused by the violation, the cost of rectifying the damage, the amount of money the violator saved by noncompliance, whether the violation was committed willfully, the prior record of the violator in complying or failing to comply with this Article, and the action of the person to remedy the violation.

(d) The clear proceeds of civil penalties collected by the Commissioner under this subsection shall be remitted to the Civil Penalty and Forfeiture Fund in accordance with G.S. 115C-457.2. (2013-206, s. 1.)

Article 10.

Various Powers and Regulations.

§ 143-152. Injury to water supply misdemeanor.

If any person shall in any way intentionally or maliciously damage or obstruct any waterline of any public institution, or in any way contaminate or render the water impure or injurious, he shall be guilty of a Class 1 misdemeanor. (1893, c. 63, s. 3; Rev., s. 3458; C.S., s. 7526; 1993, c. 539, s. 1014; 1994, Ex. Sess., c. 24, s. 14(c).)

§ 143-153. Keeping swine near State institutions; penalty.

On the petition of a majority of the legal voters living within a radius of one quarter of a mile of the administrative building of any State educational or charitable institution, it shall be unlawful for any person to keep swine or swine pens within such radius of one quarter of a mile. Any person violating this section shall be guilty of a Class 3 misdemeanor and shall be subject to only a fine of not less than ten dollars ($10.00) nor more than fifty dollars ($50.00). (1909, c. 706; C.S., s. 7527; 1993, c. 539, s. 1015; 1994, Ex. Sess., c. 14, s. 62, c. 24, s. 14(c).)

§ 143-154. Expenditures for departments and institutions; accounting and warrants.

All expenditures of any character allowed by the General Assembly in making appropriations and not covered in the appropriations named shall be charged against the department or institution for which the expense is incurred, and the warrant shall be made to show clearly for what purpose the expenditure is made. The warrant shall be charged against the department or institution, thereby showing the total amount expended for the maintenance and expenses of such department or institution. (1917, c. 289; C.S., s. 7528; 1983, c. 913, s. 35.)

§ 143-155. Repealed by Session Laws 1983, c. 913, s. 36, effective July 22, 1983.

§ 143-156. Certain institutions to report to Governor and General Assembly.

It shall be the duty of the boards of directors, managers, or trustees of the several State institutions for the insane, or the several institutions for the deaf, dumb, and blind, and of the State Prison to submit their respective reports to the Governor, to be transmitted by him with his message to the General Assembly. (1883, c. 60, ss. 2, 4; Rev., s. 5373; C.S., s. 7530.)

§ 143-157. Reports of departments and institutions; investigations and audits.

All State departments and State institutions shall make reports to the Governor from time to time as may be required by him, and the Governor is empowered to have all departments of the State government and State institutions examined and audited from time to time, and shall employ such experts to make audits and examinations and to analyze the reports of such institutions and departments as he may deem to be necessary. (1917, c. 58, s. 7; C.S., s. 7531.)

§ 143-157.1. Reports on gender-proportionate appointments to statutorily created decision-making regulatory bodies.

(a) Appointments. - In appointing members to public bodies set forth in subsections (c) and (d) of this section, the appointing authority should select, from among the most qualified persons, those persons whose appointment would promote membership on the body that accurately reflects the proportion that each gender represents in the population of the State as a whole or, in the case of a local body, in the population of the area represented by the or body, as determined pursuant to the most recent federal decennial census, unless the law regulating such appointment requires otherwise. If there are multiple appointing authorities for the body, they may consult with each other to accomplish the purposes of this section.

(b) Reports Generally. - Each appointing authority described in subsection (a) shall submit a report to the Secretary of State annually which discloses the number of appointments made during the preceding year and the number of appointments of each gender made, expressed both in numerical terms and as a percentage of the total membership of the body. In addition, each appointing authority shall designate a person responsible for retaining all applications for appointment, who shall ensure that information describing each applicant's gender and qualifications is available for public inspection during reasonable hours. Nothing in this section requires disclosure of an applicant's identity or of any other information made confidential by law. The Secretary of State shall prescribe the form used to report these appointments and may accept these reports by electronic means. Reports by appointing authorities shall be due in the Department of the Secretary of State on or before September 1. From these reports, the Secretary of State shall generate an annual composite report that shall be published by December 1. Copies of the report shall be submitted to the Governor, the Speaker of the House of Representatives, and the President Pro Tempore of the Senate.

(c) State Reporting. - Each State appointing authority that makes appointments to a statutorily created public body, however denominated, except those having only advisory authority, shall file a report with the Secretary of State as prescribed in subsection (b) of this section. The Secretary shall submit to the Governor, the Speaker of the House of Representatives, and the President Pro Tempore by July 1 of each year the names of all State bodies that an appointing authority must report on pursuant to this section.

(d) Reporting by Local Units of Government. - In those cases where a county or a city is the appointing authority, the reporting required by subsection (b) of this section shall be submitted to the Secretary of State by the clerk of that appointing authority. Appointments to the following local, municipal, or county public bodies, or to public bodies however denominated that have the functions of the following public bodies, must be reported:

(1) City or county ABC board, or local board created pursuant to G.S. 18B-703.

(2) Adult Care Home Community Advisory Committee.

(3) Airport Authority.

(4) Community Child Protection Team or a Child Fatality Prevention Team.

(5) Civil Service Board or similarly named board established by local act.

(6) Community Relations Committee.

(7) Council of Governments.

(8) Criminal Justice Partnership Task Force.

(9) Emergency Planning Committee.

(10) Board of Equalization and Review.

(11) Local Board of Health.

(12) Hospital Authority.

(13) Housing Authority.

(14) Human Relations Commission.

(15) County Industrial Facilities and Pollution Control Financing Authority.

(16) Juvenile Crime Prevention Council.

(17) Library Board of Trustees.

(18) Community College Board of Trustees.

(19) Economic development commission.

(20) Area mental health, developmental disabilities, and substance abuse board.

(21) Adult care home community advisory committee.

(22) Local partnership for children.

(23) Planning Board.

(24) Recreation Board.

(25) County board of social services.

(26) A public transportation authority created pursuant to Article 25 of Chapter 160A of the General Statutes, a regional public transportation authority created pursuant to Article 26 of Chapter 160A of the General Statutes, or a regional transportation authority created pursuant to Article 27 of Chapter 160A of the General Statutes.

(27) Local tourism development authority.

(28) Water and sewer authority.

(29) Workforce Development Board.

(30) Zoning Board of Adjustment.

(31) Planning and Zoning Board.

(32) Board of Adjustment.

(33) Historic Preservation Commission.

(34) Redevelopment Commission.

(35) City board of education (if appointive).

(36) Metropolitan Planning Organization.

(37) Rural Planning Organization. (1999, c. 457, s. 1(b), (c); 2007-167, s. 1.)

§ 143-158. Special investigations.

At any time, upon complaint made to him or upon his own motion, the Governor may appoint a special commission to investigate any State department or State institution, which commission shall have power to subpoena witnesses, require the production of books and papers, and to do all things necessary to a full and thorough investigation, and shall submit its findings to the Governor. The members of such special commission shall, while engaged in the performance of their duties, receive their actual expenses and a per diem of four dollars ($4.00). (1917, c. 58, s. 8; C.S., s. 7532.)

§ 143-159. Governor given authority to direct investigation.

The Governor is hereby authorized and empowered to call upon and direct the Attorney General to investigate the management of or condition within any department, agency, bureau, division or institution of the State, or any other matters pertaining to the administration of the Executive Department, when the

Governor shall determine that such an investigation shall be necessary. (1927, c. 234, s. 1.)

§ 143-160. Conduct of investigation.

Whenever called upon and requested by the Governor as set out in G.S. 143-159, the Attorney General shall conduct such investigation at such reasonable time and place as may be determined by him. He shall have power to issue subpoenas, administer oaths, compel the attendance of witnesses and the production of papers necessary and material in such investigation. All subpoenas issued by him shall be served by the sheriff or other officer of any county to which they may be directed. Parties interested in such investigation may appear at the hearing and be represented by counsel, who shall have the right to examine or cross-examine witnesses.

All persons subpoenaed to attend any hearing before the Attorney General shall, for a failure so to attend and testify, be subject to the same penalties as prescribed by law for such failure in the superior court. (1927, c. 234, s. 2.)

§ 143-161. Stenographic record of proceedings.

A stenographic record of the proceedings had in such investigation shall be taken and copy thereof forwarded by the Attorney General to the Governor with his report. (1927, c. 234, s. 3.)

§ 143-162: Repealed by Session Laws 1955, c. 984.

§ 143-162.1. First menu operator access.

(a) The General Assembly finds that:

(1) Some telephone systems operated by State government agencies require callers to proceed through several menus to finally reach an individual extension, an arrangement that can be intimidating to the caller;

(2) Many State telephone systems also make it difficult to reach an attendant or operator at the agency; and

(3) While automated telephone systems and voice mail are intended to improve the efficiency of government, the first duty of government is to serve the people, and efficiency should not impede the average citizen in attempting to contact a State agency for service or information.

(b) State agency telephone systems routing calls to multiple extensions shall be reprogrammed by September 1, 1997, to minimize the number of menus that a caller must go through to reach the desired extension, and to allow the caller to reach an attendant or operator after accessing not more than two menus from the first menu when calling during normal business hours. As used in this section, the term "menu" refers to the first point in the call at which the caller is asked to choose from two or more options, regardless of whether that choice is referred to as a menu, router, or other term within the telephone industry itself.

This act shall be implemented by State agencies with existing personnel at no additional cost to the State.

(c) All State agencies shall include the agency's telephone number or numbers in a prominent place on all agency letterhead.

(d) The provisions of subsection (b) of this section shall not apply to any "511" traveler information system operated by the Department of Transportation. (1997-351, ss. 1, 2; 1999-429, ss. 1, 2; 2003-184, s. 4.)

§ 143-162.2. Use of public property by production companies.

If a State agency makes real property available to a production company for a production, it shall not charge any fee other than reimbursement of actual costs incurred and actual revenues lost by the agency. As used in this section, the term "production company" has the meaning provided in G.S. 105-164.3. This section does not require a State agency to make real property available to a production company for a production. (2000-153, s. 3.)

Article 11.

Revenue Bonds and Governmental Aid.

§ 143-163. State agencies may issue bonds to finance certain public undertakings.

The several departments, institutions, agencies and commissions of the State of North Carolina, acting at the suggestion of the Governor of North Carolina, with the approval of the Council of State, are hereby authorized to issue bonds of the several departments, agencies or commissions of the State, in such sum or sums, not to exceed in the aggregate two million dollars ($2,000,000), at such time or times, in such denominations as may be determined, and at such rate of interest as may be most advantageous to the several departments, institutions, agencies and commissions of the State, the said bonds to run for a period not exceeding 30 years from date, which bonds may be sold and delivered as other like bonds of the State of North Carolina: Provided, however, that the credit of the State of North Carolina, or any of its departments, institutions, agencies or commissions, shall not be pledged further in the payment of such bonds, except with respect to the rentals, profits and proceeds received in connection with the undertaking, for which said bonds are issued, and said bonds and interest so issued shall be payable solely out of the receipts from the undertaking for which they were issued, without further obligation on the part of the State of North Carolina, or any of its departments, institutions, agencies or commissions, provided that no State department or institution issuing any of said bonds shall be allowed to pledge any of its appropriations received from the State as security for these bonds; provided, further, that no State department, institution, agency or commission of the State shall make application for or issue any bonds, as provided in this section, after June 1, 1941. (1935, c. 479, s. 1; Ex. Sess. 1936, c. 2, s. 1; 1937, c. 323; 1939, c. 391.)

§ 143-164. Acceptance of federal loans and grants permitted.

The State of North Carolina, and its several departments, institutions, agencies and commissions, are hereby authorized to accept and receive loans, grants, and other assistance from the United States government, departments and/or agencies thereof, for its use, and to receive like financial and other aid from other agencies in carrying out any undertaking which has been authorized by the Governor of North Carolina, with the approval of the Council of State. (1935, c. 479, s. 2.)

§ 143-165. Approval by Governor and Council of State necessary; covenants in resolutions authorizing bonds.

The several departments, institutions, agencies and commissions of the State of North Carolina, before issuing any revenue bonds as herein provided for any undertaking, shall first receive the approval of the undertaking from the Governor of North Carolina, which action shall be approved by the Council of State before such undertaking shall be entered into and revenue bonds issued in payment therefor in whole or in part.

Any resolution or resolutions heretofore or hereafter adopted authorizing the issuance of bonds under this Article may contain covenants which shall have the force of contract so long as any of said bonds and interest thereon remain outstanding and unpaid as to

(1) The use and disposition of revenue of the undertaking for which the said bonds are to be issued,

(2) The pledging of all the gross receipts or any part thereof derived from the operation of the undertaking to the payment of the principal and interest of said bonds including reserves therefor,

(3) The operation and maintenance of such undertaking,

(4) The insurance to be carried thereon and the use and disposition of the insurance moneys,

(5) The fixing and collection of rates, fees and charges for the services, facilities and commodities furnished by such undertaking sufficient to pay said bonds and interest as the same shall become due, and for the creation and maintenance of reasonable reserve therefor,

(6) Provisions that the undertaking shall not be conveyed, leased or mortgaged so long as any of the bonds and interest thereon remain outstanding and unpaid.

Provided, however, that the credit of the State of North Carolina or any of its departments, institutions, agencies or commissions shall not be pledged to the payment of such bonds except with respect to the rentals, profits and proceeds received in connection with the undertaking for which the said bonds are issued, and that none of the appropriations received from the State shall be pledged as security for said bonds. (1935, c. 479, s. 3; Ex. Sess. 1936, c. 2, s. 2.)

Article 12.

Law-Enforcement Officers' Retirement System.

§§ 143-166 through 143-166.04: Repealed by Session Laws 1985, c. 479, s. 196(t).

Article 12A.

Law-Enforcement Officers', Firemen's, Rescue Squad Workers' and Civil Air Patrol Members' Death Benefits Act.

§ 143-166.1. Purpose.

In consideration of hazardous public service rendered to the people of this State, there is hereby provided a system of benefits for dependents of law-enforcement officers, firemen, rescue squad workers and senior Civil Air Patrol members killed in the discharge of their official duties. (1959, c. 1323, s. 1; 1965, c. 937; 1973, c. 634, s. 2; 1975, c. 284, s. 6; 1977, c. 797; 1983, c. 761, s. 236.)

§ 143-166.2. Definitions.

(a)   The term "dependent child" shall mean any unmarried child of the deceased officer, fireman, rescue squad worker or senior member of the Civil Air Patrol whether natural, adopted, posthumously born or whether a child born out of wedlock as entitled to inherit under the Intestate Succession Act, who is under 18 years of age and dependent upon and receiving his chief support from said officer or fireman or rescue squad worker or senior member of the Civil Air Patrol at the time of his death; provided, however, that if a dependent child is entitled to receive benefits at the time of the officer's or fireman's or rescue squad worker's or senior Civil Air Patrol member's death as hereinafter provided, he shall continue to be eligible to receive such benefits regardless of his age thereafter; and further provided that any child over 18 years of age who is physically or mentally incapable of earning a living and any child over 18 years of age who was enrolled as a full-time student at the time of the officer's, the fireman's, the rescue squad worker's or the senior Civil Air Patrol member's death shall so long as he remains a full-time student as defined in the Social Security Act be regarded as a dependent child and eligible to receive benefits under the provisions of this Article.

(b) The term "dependent parent" shall mean the parent of the deceased officer, fireman, rescue squad worker or senior member of the Civil Air Patrol, whether natural or adoptive, who was dependent upon and receiving his total and entire support from the officer, fireman, rescue squad worker or senior member of the Civil Air Patrol at the time of the injury which resulted in his death.

(c) The term "killed in the line of duty" shall apply to any law-enforcement officer, fireman, rescue squad worker who is killed or dies as a result of bodily injuries sustained or of extreme exercise or extreme activity experienced in the course and scope of his official duties while in the discharge of his official duty or duties. When applied to a senior member of the Civil Air Patrol as defined in this Article, "killed in the line of duty" shall mean any such senior member of the North Carolina Wing-Civil Air Patrol who is killed or dies as a result of bodily injuries sustained or of extreme exercise or extreme activity experienced in the course and scope of his official duties while engaged in a State requested and approved mission pursuant to Article 13 of Chapter 143B of the General Statutes. For purposes of this Article, when a law enforcement officer, fireman, rescue squad worker, or senior Civil Air Patrol member dies as the direct and proximate result of a myocardial infarction suffered while on duty or within 24 hours after participating in a training exercise or responding to an emergency situation, the law enforcement officer, fireman, rescue squad worker, or senior Civil Air Patrol member is presumed to have been killed in the line of duty.

(d) The term "law-enforcement officer", "officer", or "fireman" shall mean a sheriff and all law-enforcement officers employed full-time, permanent part-time, or temporarily by a sheriff, the State of North Carolina or any county or municipality thereof, whether paid or unpaid; and all full-time custodial employees and probation and parole officers of the Division of Adult Correction of the Department of Public Safety; and all full time institutional and full-time, permanent part-time, and temporary detention employees of the Division of Juvenile Justice of the Department of Public Safety and full-time, permanent part-time, and temporary detention officers employed by any sheriff, county or municipality, whether paid or unpaid. The term "firemen" shall mean both "eligible firemen" as defined in Article 86 of Chapter 58 of the General Statutes, notwithstanding any age requirements set out in that Article, and all full-time, permanent part-time and temporary employees of the North Carolina Forest Service of the Department of Agriculture and Consumer Services during the time they are actively engaged in firefighting activities; or engaged in emergency response activities pursuant to G.S. 166A-19.77; and shall mean all full-time employees of the North Carolina Department of Insurance during the time they are actively engaged in firefighting activities, during the time they are training firefighters or rescue squad workers, and during the time they are engaged in activities as members of the State Emergency Response Team, when the Team has been activated; and shall mean all otherwise eligible persons who, while actively engaged as firefighters or rescue squad workers, are acting in the capacity of a fire or rescue instructor outside their own department or squad. The term "rescue squad worker" shall mean a person who is dedicated to the purpose of alleviating human suffering and assisting anyone who is in difficulty or who is injured or becomes suddenly ill by providing the proper and efficient care or emergency medical services. In addition, this person must belong to an organized rescue squad which is eligible for membership in the North Carolina Association of Rescue and Emergency Medical Services, Inc., and the person must have attended a minimum of 36 hours of training in the last calendar year. Each rescue squad belonging to the North Carolina Association of Rescue and Emergency Medical Services, Inc., must file a roster of those members meeting the above requirements with the State Treasurer on or about January 31 of each year, and this roster must be certified to by the secretary of said association. In addition, the term "rescue squad worker" shall mean a member of an ambulance service certified by the Department of Health and Human Services pursuant to Article 7 of Chapter 131E of the General Statutes. The Department of Health and Human Services shall furnish a list of ambulance service members to the State Treasurer on or about January 31 of each year. The term "Civil Air Patrol members" shall mean those senior members of the North Carolina Wing-Civil Air Patrol 18 years of age or older and currently certified pursuant to G.S. 143B-1031. The term "fireman" shall also mean county fire marshals when engaged in the performance of their county duties. The term "rescue squad worker" shall also mean county emergency services coordinators when engaged in the performance of their county duties.

(e) The term "spouse" shall mean the wife or husband of the deceased officer, fireman, rescue squad worker or senior Civil Air Patrol member who survives him and who was residing with such officer, fireman, rescue squad worker, or senior Civil Air Patrol member at the time of and during the six months next preceding the date of injury to such officer, fireman, rescue squad worker or senior Civil Air Patrol member which resulted in his death and who also resided with such officer, fireman, rescue squad worker or senior Civil Air Patrol member from that date of injury up to and at the time of his death and who remains unmarried during the time benefits are forthcoming; provided, however, the part of this section requiring the spouse to have been residing with the deceased officer, fireman, rescue squad worker or senior Civil Air Patrol member for six months next preceding the date of the injury which resulted in his death shall not apply where marriage occurred during this six-month period or where the officer, fireman, rescue squad worker or senior Civil Air Patrol member was absent during this six-month period due to service in the Armed Forces of the United States.

(f) The term "official duties" means those duties performed while en route to, engaged in, or returning from training, or in the course of responding to, engaged in or returning from a call by the department of which he is a member, or from a call for assistance from any department or such organization within the State of North Carolina or within a service area contiguous to the borders of the State of North Carolina, when served or aided by a department from within the State of North Carolina. While within the State of North Carolina, any eligible person, as defined in this section or in G.S. 58-86-25, who renders service or assistance, of his own volition, at the scene of an emergency, is performing his official duties when:

(1) Reasonably apparent circumstances require prompt decisions and actions to protect persons and property; and

(2) The necessity of immediate action is so reasonably apparent that any delay in acting would seriously worsen the property damage or endanger any person's life. (1959, c. 1323, s. 1; 1965, c. 937; 1969, c. 1025; 1973, c. 634, s. 2; c. 955, ss. 1, 2; 1975, c. 19, s. 49; c. 284, s. 7; 1977, c. 1048; 1979, c. 516, ss. 2, 3; c. 869; 1981, c. 944, s. 1; 1983, c. 761, s. 237; 1987, c. 812; 1987 (Reg. Sess., 1988), c. 1050, s. 1; 1989, c. 727, s. 218(97); 1989 (Reg. Sess., 1990), c. 1024, s. 32; 1991 (Reg. Sess., 1992), c. 833, s. 5; 1997-443, ss. 11A.118(a), 11A.119(a); 2000-137, s. 4(y); 2003-284, s. 30.18A(b); 2004-124, s. 31.18C(a); 2005-276, s. 29.30C; 2005-376, s. 1; 2008-163, s. 1; 2011-145, ss.

13.25(ss), 19.1(h), (l); 2011-183, s. 104; 2012-83, s. 46; 2013-155, s. 20; 2013-198, s. 27; 2013-288, s. 10.)

§ 143-166.3. Payments; determination.

(a) When any law-enforcement officer, fireman, rescue squad worker or senior Civil Air Patrol member shall be killed in the line of duty, the Industrial Commission shall award a death benefit to be paid in the amounts set forth in subsection (b) to the following:

(1) The spouse of such officer, fireman, rescue squad worker or senior Civil Air Patrol member if there be a surviving spouse; or

(2) If there be no spouse qualifying under the provisions of this Article, then payments shall be made to any surviving dependent child of such officer, fireman, rescue squad worker or senior Civil Air Patrol member and if there be more than one surviving dependent child, then said payment shall be made to and equally divided among all surviving dependent children; or

(3) If there be no spouse and no dependent child or children qualifying under the provisions of this Article, then payments shall be made to the surviving dependent parent of such officer, fireman, rescue squad worker or senior Civil Air Patrol member and if there be more than one surviving dependent parent then said payments shall be made to and equally divided between the surviving dependent parents of said officer, fireman, rescue squad worker or senior Civil Air Patrol member.

(b) Payment shall be made to the person or persons qualifying therefor under subsection (a) in the following amounts:

(1) At the time of the death of an officer, fireman, rescue squad worker or senior Civil Air Patrol member, twenty thousand dollars ($20,000) shall be paid to the person or persons entitled thereto.

(2) Thereafter, ten thousand dollars ($10,000) shall be paid annually to the person or persons entitled thereto until the sum of the initial payment and each annual payment reaches fifty thousand dollars ($50,000).

(3) In the event there is no person qualifying under subsection (a) of this section, fifty thousand dollars ($50,000) shall be paid to the estate of the

deceased officer, fireman, rescue squad worker or senior Civil Air Patrol member at the time of death.

(c) In the event that any person or persons eligible for payments under subsection (a) of this section shall become ineligible, and other eligible person or persons qualify for said death benefit payments under subsection (a), then they shall receive the remainder of any payments up to the limit of fifty thousand dollars ($50,000) in the manner set forth in subsection (b) of this section.

(d) In the event any person or persons eligible for payments under subsection (a) of this section shall become ineligible and no other person or persons qualify for payments under that subsection and where the sum of the initial payment of twenty thousand dollars ($20,000) and each subsequent annual payment of ten thousand dollars ($10,000) does not total fifty thousand dollars ($50,000), then the difference between the total of the payments made and fifty thousand dollars ($50,000) shall immediately be payable to the estate of the deceased officer, fireman, rescue squad worker, or senior Civil Air Patrol member. (1959, c. 1323, s. 1; 1965, c. 937; 1971, c. 960; 1973, c. 634, s. 2; 1975, c. 284, s. 8; 2003-284, s. 30.18A(a).)

§ 143-166.4. Funds; conclusiveness of award.

Such award of benefits as is provided for by this Article shall be paid from the Contingency and Emergency Fund and such amounts as may be required to pay benefits provided for by this Article are hereby appropriated from said fund for this special purpose.

The Industrial Commission shall have power to make necessary rules and regulations for the administration of the provisions of this Article. It shall be vested with power to make all determinations necessary for the administration of this Article and all of its decisions and determinations shall be final and conclusive and not subject to review or reversal except by the Industrial Commission itself. The Industrial Commission shall keep a record of all proceedings conducted under this Article and shall have the right to subpoena any persons and records which it may deem necessary in making its determinations, and the Industrial Commission shall further have the power to require all persons called as witnesses to testify under oath or affirmation, and any member of the Industrial Commission may administer oaths. If any person shall refuse to comply with any subpoena issued hereunder or to testify with respect to any matter relevant to proceedings conducted under this Article, the Superior Court of Wake County, on application of the Industrial Commission, may issue an order requiring such person to comply with the subpoena and to testify; and any failure to obey any such order of the court may be punished by the court as for contempt. (1959, c. 1323, s. 1; 1965, c. 937.)

§ 143-166.5. Other benefits not affected.

None of the other benefits now provided for law-enforcement officers, or other persons covered by this Article, or their dependents by the Workers' Compensation Act or other laws shall be affected by the provisions of this Article, and the benefits provided for herein shall not be diminished, abated or otherwise affected by such other provisions of law. (1959, c. 1323, s. 1; 1965, c. 937; 1979, c. 245; c. 714, s. 2.)

§ 143-166.6. Awards exempt from taxes.

Any award made under the provisions of this Article shall be exempt from taxation by the State or any political subdivision. The Industrial Commission shall not be responsible for any determination of the validity of any claims against said awards and shall distribute the death benefit awards directly to the dependent or dependents entitled thereto under the provisions of this Article. (1959, c. 1323, s. 1; 1965, c. 937.)

§ 143-166.7. Applicability of Article.

The provisions of this Article shall apply and be in full force and effect with respect to any law-enforcement officer, fireman, rescue squad worker or senior Civil Air Patrol member killed in the line of duty on or after May 13, 1975. The provisions of this Article shall apply with respect to full-time, permanent part-time and temporary employees of [the] North Carolina Forest Service of the Department of Agriculture and Consumer Services killed in [the] line of duty on or after July 1, 1975. The provisions of this Article shall apply to county fire marshals and emergency services coordinators killed in the line of duty on and after July 1, 1988. (1965, c. 937; 1973, c. 634, s. 3; 1975, c. 284, s. 9; 1981, c.

944, s. 2; 1987 (Reg. Sess., 1988), c. 1050, s. 2; 1989, c. 727, s. 218(98); 1997-443, s. 11A.119(a); 2011-145, s. 13.25(tt); 2013-155, s. 21.)

§§ 143-166.8 through 143-166.12. Reserved for future codification purposes.

Article 12B.

Salary Continuation Plan for Certain State Law-Enforcement Officers.

§ 143-166.13. Persons entitled to benefits under Article.

(a) The following persons who are subject to the Criminal Justice Training and Standards Act are entitled to benefits under this Article:

(1) State Government Security Officers, Department of Administration;

(2) State Correctional Officers, Division of Adult Correction of the Department of Public Safety;

(3) State Probation and Parole Officers, Division of Adult Correction of the Department of Public Safety;

(4) Sworn State Law-Enforcement Officers with the power of arrest, Division of Adult Correction of the Department of Public Safety;

(5) Alcohol Law-Enforcement Agents, Department of Public Safety;

(6) State Highway Patrol Officers, Department of Public Safety;

(7) General Assembly Special Police, General Assembly;

(8) Sworn State Law-Enforcement Officers with the power of arrest, Department of Health and Human Services;

(9) Juvenile Justice Officers, Division of Juvenile Justice of the Department of Public Safety;

(10) Insurance Investigators, Department of Insurance;

(11) State Bureau of Investigation Officers and Agents, Department of Justice;

(12) Director and Assistant Director, License and Theft Enforcement Section, Division of Motor Vehicles, Department of Transportation;

(13) Members of License and Theft Enforcement Section, Division of Motor Vehicles, Department of Transportation, designated by the Commissioner of Motor Vehicles as either "inspectors" or uniformed weigh station personnel;

(14) Utilities Commission Transportation Inspectors and Special Investigators;

(15) North Carolina Ports Authority Police, Department of Transportation;

(16) Sworn State Law-Enforcement Officers with the power of arrest, Department of Environment and Natural Resources;

(17) Sworn State Law-Enforcement Officers with the power of arrest, Department of Public Safety.

(18) Sworn State Law-Enforcement Officers with the power of arrest, Department of Revenue.

(19) Sworn State Law-Enforcement Officers with the power of arrest, University System.

(b) The following persons are entitled to benefits under this Article regardless of whether they are subject to the Criminal Justice Training and Standards Act:

(1) Driver License Examiners injured by accident arising out of and in the course of giving a road test, Division of Motor Vehicles, Department of Transportation;

(2) Employees of the Division of Adult Correction of the Department of Public Safety injured by a direct and deliberate act of an offender supervised by the Division or while performing supervisory duties over offenders which place the employees at risk of such injury. (1979, 2nd Sess., c. 1272, s. 1; 1981, c. 348, s. 1; c. 964, s. 19; 1989, c. 727, s. 218(99), c. 751, s. 7(15); 1991 (Reg. Sess., 1992), c. 959, s. 34; 1996, 2nd Ex. Sess., c. 18, s. 20.7(a); 1997-443, ss.

11A.118(a), 11A.119(a); 1997-503, s. 3; 1998-212, s. 28.25(a); 2001-487, s. 89; 2005-359, s. 3; 2011-145, ss. 14.6(d), 19.1(g), (h), (l).)

§ 143-166.14. Payment of salary notwithstanding incapacity; Workers' Compensation Act applicable after two years; duration of payment.

The salary of any of the above listed persons shall be paid as long as his employment in that position continues, notwithstanding his total or partial incapacity to perform any duties to which he may be lawfully assigned, if that incapacity is the result of an injury by accident or an occupational disease arising out of and in the course of the performance by him of his official duties, except if that incapacity continues for more than two years from its inception, the person shall, during the further continuance of that incapacity, be subject to the provisions of Chapter 97 of the General Statutes pertaining to workers' compensation. Salary paid to a person pursuant to this Article shall cease upon the resumption of his regularly assigned duties, retirement, resignation, or death, whichever first occurs, except that temporary return to duty shall not prohibit payment of salary for a subsequent period of incapacity which can be shown to be directly related to the original injury. (1979, 2nd Sess., c. 1272, s. 1.)

§ 143-166.15. Application of § 97-27; how payments made.

Notwithstanding the provisions of G.S. 143-166.14 of this Article, the persons entitled to benefits shall be subject to the provisions of G.S. 97-27 during the two-year period of payment of full salary. All payments of salary shall be made at the same time and in the same manner as other salaries are paid to other persons in the same department. (1979, 2nd Sess., c. 1272, s. 1.)

§ 143-166.16. Effect on workers' compensation and other benefits; application of § 97-24.

The provisions of G.S. 143-166.14 shall be in lieu of all compensation provided for the first two years of incapacity by G.S. 97-29 and 97-30, but shall be in addition to any other benefits or compensation to which such person shall be entitled under the provisions of the Workers' Compensation Act. The provisions of G.S. 97-24 will commence at the end of the two-year period for which salary is paid pursuant to G.S. 143-166.14. (1979, 2nd Sess., c. 1272, s. 1.)

§ 143-166.17. Period of incapacity not charged against sick leave or other leave.

The period for which the salary of any person is paid pursuant to G.S. 143-166.14 while he is incapacitated as a result of an injury by accident or an occupational disease arising out of and in the course of the performance by him of his official duties, shall not be charged against any sick or other leave to which he shall be entitled under any other provision of law. (1979, 2nd Sess., c. 1272, s. 1.)

§ 143-166.18. Report of incapacity.

Any person designated in G.S. 143-166.13, who, as a result of an injury by accident arising out of and in the course of the performance by him of his official duties, is totally or partially incapacitated to perform any duties to which he may be lawfully assigned, shall report the incapacity as soon as practicable in the manner required by the secretary or other head of the department to which the agency is assigned by statute. (1979, 2nd Sess., c. 1272, s. 1; 1981, c. 348, s. 2.)

§ 143-166.19. Determination of cause and extent of incapacity; hearing before Industrial Commission; appeal; effect of refusal to perform duties.

Upon the filing of the report, the secretary or other head of the department or, in the case of the General Assembly, the Legislative Services Officer, shall determine the cause of the incapacity and to what extent the claimant may be assigned to other than his normal duties. The finding of the secretary or other head of the department shall determine the right of the claimant to benefits under this Article. Notice of the finding shall be filed with the North Carolina Industrial Commission. Unless the claimant, within 30 days after he receives notice, files with the North Carolina Industrial Commission, upon the form it shall require, a request for a hearing, the finding of the secretary or other department head shall be final. Upon the filing of a request, the North Carolina Industrial Commission shall proceed to hear the matter in accordance with its regularly established procedure for hearing claims filed under the Worker's Compensation Act, and shall report its findings to the secretary or other head of the department. From the decision of the North Carolina Industrial Commission, an appeal shall lie as in other matters heard and determined by the Commission. Any person who refuses to perform any duties to which he may be properly assigned as a result of the finding of the secretary, other head of the department or of the North Carolina Industrial Commission shall be entitled to no benefits pursuant to this Article as long as the refusal continues. (1979, 2nd Sess., c. 1272, s. 1; 1981, c. 348, s. 3.)

§ 143-166.20. Subrogation.

The same rights and remedies set forth in G.S. 97-10.2 shall apply in all third party liability cases occurring under this Article, including cases involving the right of the affected State agency to recover the salary paid to an injured officer during his period of disability. (1981, c. 348, s. 4.)

§§ 143-166.21 through 143-166.29. Reserved for future codification purposes.

Article 12C.

Retirement Benefits for State Law-Enforcement Officers.

§ 143-166.30. Retirement benefits for State law-enforcement officers.

(a) Definitions. - The following words and phrases as used in this Article, unless a different meaning is plainly required by the context, shall have the following meanings:

(1) "Beneficiary" means any person in receipt of a retirement allowance or other benefit from a Retirement System.

(2) "Creditable service" means membership service plus prior service plus military service allowable with a Retirement System.

(3) "Employer" means the State of North Carolina and its departments, agencies and institutions.

(4) "Law-enforcement officer" means a full-time paid employee of an employer who is actively serving in a position with assigned primary duties and responsibilities for prevention and detection of crime or the general enforcement of the criminal laws of the State or serving civil processes, and who possesses the power of arrest by virtue of an oath administered under the authority of the State.

(5) "Member" means an officer included in the membership of a retirement system including former officers no longer employed who also elected to leave their accumulated contributions on deposit with a Retirement System.

(6) "Officer" means a "law-enforcement officer."

(7) "Participant" means an officer with an individual account with the Supplemental Retirement Income Plan.

(8) "Regular accumulated contributions" means the sum of all contributions of a member made to the Retirement System, together with regular interest thereon, pursuant to G.S. 143-166 as the same appeared prior to January 1, 1985.

(9) "Retirement allowance" means annual payments for life payable in monthly installments continuing until the death of a beneficiary.

(10) "Law-Enforcement Officers' Retirement System" means the system provided for under G.S. 143-166.

(11) "Special annuity account accumulated contributions" means the sum of all contributions of a member or an employer made to the Special Annuity Accounts for Members of the Law-Enforcement Officers' Retirement System, together with regular interest thereon, pursuant to G.S. 143-166.03 as the same appeared prior to January 1, 1985.

(12) "Special Annuity Accounts" means the supplemental defined contribution provisions of the Law-Enforcement Officers' Retirement System,

provided for under G.S. 143-166.03 as the same appeared prior to January 1, 1985.

(13) "State" means the State of North Carolina.

(14) "State Retirement System" means the Teachers' and State Employees' Retirement System of North Carolina provided for under Article 1 of Chapter 135 of the General Statutes.

(15) "Supplemental Retirement Income Plan" means a plan created in conformance with Section 401(a), 401(k), or any other section of the Internal Revenue Code of 1954 as amended.

(b) Basic Retirement System. - On and after January 1, 1985, law-enforcement officers employed by the State shall be members of the Teachers' and State Employees' Retirement System and beneficiaries who were last employed as officers by the State, or who are surviving beneficiaries of officers last employed by the State, shall be beneficiaries of the State Retirement System and paid in benefit amounts then in effect. All members of the Law-Enforcement Officers' Retirement System last employed and paid by the State shall be members of the State Retirement System.

(c) Transfers of Assets and Liabilities to Other Retirement Systems. - As of January 1, 1985, certain assets and liabilities of the Law-Enforcement Officers' Retirement System shall be transferred to the Teachers' and State Employees' Retirement System and the Supplemental Retirement Income Plan in the amounts calculated and in the order of precedence enumerated as follows:

(1) The regular accumulated contributions of members of the Law-Enforcement Officers' Retirement System employed by the State or last employed by the State shall be transferred from the annuity savings fund of the Law-Enforcement Officers' Retirement System to the annuity savings fund of the State Retirement System to the credit of each individual officer.

(2) An amount equal to the present value of the liabilities on account of the retirement allowances payable to beneficiaries last employed as officers by the State and the surviving beneficiaries of officers last employed by the State, as calculated by the Retirement System's consulting actuary, shall be transferred from the pension accumulation fund of the Law-Enforcement Officers' Retirement System to the pension accumulation fund of the State Retirement System.

(3) After the transfers provided for above, additional assets in the pension accumulation fund of the Law-Enforcement Officers' Retirement System shall be transferred to the pension accumulation fund of the State Retirement System, in an amount equal to the ratio of the accrued liabilities on account of members of the Law-Enforcement Officers' Retirement System employed by the State or last employed by the State to the total accrued liabilities on account of all members of the Law-Enforcement Officers' Retirement System.

(4) The special annuity account accumulated contributions shall be transferred from the special annuity savings fund of the Law-Enforcement Officers' Retirement System to the Supplemental Retirement Income Plan pursuant to subsection (d) of this section to the credit of individual officers.

(d) Supplemental Retirement Income Plan for State Law-Enforcement Officers. - As of January 1, 1985, there shall be created a Supplemental Retirement Income Plan, hereinafter called the "Plan," established for the benefit of all law-enforcement officers employed by the State, who shall be participants. The Board of Trustees of the State Retirement System shall administer the Plan and shall, under the terms and conditions otherwise appearing herein, provide Plan benefits either (i) by establishing a separate trust fund in conformance with Section 401(a), Section 401(k) or other sections of the Internal Revenue Code of 1954 as amended or, (ii) by causing the Plan to affiliate with some master trust fund providing the same benefits for participants. The Plan shall be separate and apart from any retirement systems.

In addition to the contributions transferred from the Law-Enforcement Officers' Retirement System and the contributions otherwise provided for in this Article, participants may make voluntary contributions to the Plan to be credited to the designated individual accounts of participants.

All contributions to the Plan shall be credited to the individual accounts of participants, and except as provided in subsection (g1) of this section, shall be fully and immediately vested in the name of the participant, and shall be invested according to each participant's election, as provided by the Board of Trustees, including but not limited to time deposits, and both fixed and variable investments. The Plan may provide for loans to participants, at reasonable rates of interest to be charged, from participants' individual accounts, and may provide for withdrawal of contributions on account of hardship.

The benefit to a participant in the Plan shall be either a lump-sum distribution or a distribution in periodic installments of the participant's account payable under retirement, disability, or termination of employment. Upon the death of a participant there shall be paid the same lump-sum distribution or periodic installments to the surviving spouse of the participant or otherwise to the participant's estate; provided, should a participant instruct the Board of Trustees in writing that he does not wish these benefits to be paid to his spouse or estate, then the benefits shall be paid to the person or persons as the participant may name for this purpose.

Upon retirement, a participant in the Plan may elect to transfer any portion of his eligible accumulated contributions, not including any Roth after-tax contributions and the earnings thereon, to the Teachers' and State Employees' Retirement System and receive, in addition to his basic service, early or disability retirement allowance a special retirement allowance which shall be based on his eligible accumulated account balance at the date of the transfer of the assets.

(e) State Contributions to the Supplemental Retirement Income Plan. - Under all other restrictions as are herein provided, the State shall contribute monthly to the individual accounts of participants who are employed by the State an amount equal to five percent (5%) of the compensation of each participant. The contributions so paid shall be in addition to the contributions on account of court cost assessments as hereinafter provided.

Contributions shall be made to the individual accounts of all participants in the Plan on a per capita basis in equal shares, equal to the sum of the one-half dollar ($0.50) for each cost of court assessed and collected under G.S. 7A-304.

(e1) Rights of Participants under the Uniformed Services Employment and Reemployment Rights Act. - A participant whose employment is interrupted by reason of service in the Uniformed Services, as that term is defined in section 4303(16) of the Uniformed Services Employment and Reemployment Rights Act, Public Law 103-353, hereafter referred to as "USERRA", shall be entitled to all rights and benefits that the participant would have been entitled to under this section had the participant's employment not been interrupted, provided that the participant returns to service as a law enforcement officer while the participant's reemployment rights are protected under the provisions of USERRA.

(f) Administration. - The provisions of the State Retirement System pertaining to administration and management of funds under G.S. 135-6 and 7 are made applicable to the Plan.

(g) Exemption from Garnishment and Attachment. - Except as provided in subsection (g1) of this section, the right of a participant in the Supplemental Retirement Income Plan to the benefits provided under this Article is nonforfeitable and exempt from levy, sale, and garnishment.

(g1) Forfeiture of Benefits for Certain Felonies. - Participants in the Supplemental Retirement Income Plan for State Law-Enforcement Officers whose benefits are forfeited under G.S. 135-18.10A shall also forfeit contributions paid on or after December 1, 2012, on behalf of the participant by the State to the Supplemental Retirement Income Plan. Any funds forfeited shall be deposited in the Supplemental Retirement Income Plan.

(h) Notwithstanding any other provisions of law, any pending or inchoate rights of a member of the Law-Enforcement Officers' Retirement System as of their transfer to the State Retirement System on January 1, 1985, including the rights to a vested deferred retirement allowance and to commence retirement at certain ages with required years of service as a law-enforcement officer, shall in no way be diminished; provided, however, in no event may a member commence retirement and continue membership service with the same Retirement System.

No eligible officer shall be precluded from exercising that officer's pending or inchoate rights under this section, should the officer elect to make Roth after-tax contributions to the Supplemental Retirement Income Plan, except that these Roth after-tax contributions and the earnings thereon shall not be subsequently transferred to the Teachers' and State Employees' Retirement System. (1983 (Reg. Sess., 1984), c. 1034, s. 248; 1985, c. 479, s. 196(s); 1989, c. 792, s. 2.7; 1995, c. 361, s. 5; 2006-141, s. 1; 2007-384, s. 10.5; 2010-72, s. 11(a); 2012-193, s. 13; 2013-288, s. 1(a).)

§§ 143-166.31 through 143-166.39. Reserved for future codification purposes.

Article 12D.

Separation Allowances for Law-Enforcement Officers.

§ 143-166.40. Rules for selection and retention of law-enforcement officers; rules exempt from Administrative Procedure Act.

(a) Except as otherwise provided by State and federal law, the head of each principal State department may establish rules and procedures for the selection and retention of sworn law-enforcement officers to ensure that they are physically, emotionally, and intellectually qualified to perform their duties. These rules and procedures shall not establish any mandatory age limit for service as a law-enforcement officer that conflicts with a federal statute.

(b) These rules and procedures are exempt from the provisions of Chapter 150B of the General Statutes. (1983 (Reg. Sess., 1984), c. 1034, s. 104; 1987, c. 827, s. 1.)

§ 143-166.41. Special separation allowance.

(a) Notwithstanding any other provision of law, every sworn law-enforcement officer as defined by G.S. 135-1(11c) or G.S. 143-166.30(a)(4) employed by a State department, agency, or institution prior to August 1, 2011, and who qualifies under this section shall receive, beginning in the month in which he retires on a basic service retirement under the provisions of G.S. 135-5(a), an annual separation allowance equal to eighty-five hundredths percent (0.85%) of the annual equivalent of the base rate of compensation most recently applicable to him for each year of creditable service. The allowance shall be paid in equal installments on the payroll frequency used by the employer. To qualify for the allowance the officer shall:

(1) Have (i) completed 30 or more years of creditable service or, (ii) have attained 55 years of age and completed five or more years of creditable service; and

(2) Not have attained 62 years of age; and

(3) Have completed at least five years of continuous service as a law enforcement officer as herein defined immediately preceding a service retirement. Any break in the continuous service required by this subsection because of disability retirement or disability salary continuation benefits shall not adversely affect an officer's qualification to receive the allowance, provided the officer returns to service within 45 days after the disability benefits cease and is otherwise qualified to receive the allowance.

(a1) Notwithstanding any other provision of law, every sworn law-enforcement officer as defined by G.S. 135-1(11c) or G.S. 143-166.30(a)(4) employed by a State department, agency, or institution on or after August 1, 2011, and who qualifies under this section shall receive, beginning in the month in which the member retires on a basic service retirement under the provisions of G.S. 135-5(a), an annual separation allowance equal to eighty-five hundredths percent (0.85%) of the annual equivalent of the base rate of compensation most recently applicable to him for each year of creditable service. The allowance shall be paid in equal installments on the payroll frequency used by the employer. To qualify for the allowance, the officer shall:

(1) Have (i) completed 30 or more years of creditable service or (ii) attained 55 years of age and completed 10 or more years of creditable service; and

(2) Not have attained 62 years of age; and

(3) Have completed at least 10 years of continuous service as a law enforcement officer as herein defined immediately preceding a service retirement. Any break in the continuous service required by this subsection because of disability retirement or disability salary continuation benefits shall not adversely affect an officer's qualification to receive the allowance, provided the officer returns to service within 45 days after the disability benefits cease and is otherwise qualified to receive the allowance.

(b) As used in this section, "creditable service" means the service for which credit is allowed under the retirement system of which the officer is a member, provided that at least fifty percent (50%) of the service is as a law enforcement officer as herein defined.

(c) Payment to a retired officer under the provisions of this section shall cease at the first of:

(1) The death of the officer;

(2) The last day of the month in which the officer attains 62 years of age; or

(3) The first day of reemployment by any State department, agency, or institution, except that this subdivision does not apply to an officer returning to State employment in a position exempt from the North Carolina Human Resources Act in an agency other than the agency from which that officer retired.

(d) This section does not affect the benefits to which an individual may be entitled from State, federal, or private retirement systems. The benefits payable under this section shall not be subject to any increases in salary or retirement allowances that may be authorized by the General Assembly for employees of the State or retired employees of the State.

(e) The head of each State department, agency, or institution shall determine the eligibility of employees for the benefits provided herein.

(f) The Director of the Budget may authorize from time to time the transfer of funds within the budgets of each State department, agency, or institution necessary to carry out the purposes of this Article. These funds shall be taken from those appropriated to the department, agency, or institution for salaries and related fringe benefits.

(g) The head of each State department, agency, or institution shall make the payments set forth in subsection (a) to those persons certified under subsection (e) from funds available under subsection (f). (1983 (Reg. Sess., 1984), c. 1034, s. 104; 1985, c. 479, s. 143; 1985 (Reg. Sess., 1986), c. 1014, ss. 51, 52; 2002-126, s. 28.14; 2007-69, s. 1; 2011-232, s. 9; 2013-382, s. 9.1(c).)

§ 143-166.42. Special separation allowances for local officers.

(a) On and after January 1, 1987, every sworn law enforcement officer as defined by G.S. 128-21(11d) or G.S. 143-166.50(a)(3) employed by a local government employer who qualifies under this section shall receive, beginning in the month in which the officer retires on a basic service retirement under the provisions of G.S. 128-27(a), an annual separation allowance equal to eighty-five hundredths percent (0.85%) of the annual equivalent of the base rate of compensation most recently applicable to the officer for each year of creditable service. The allowance shall be paid in equal installments on the payroll frequency used by the employer. To qualify for the allowance, the officer shall:

(1) Have (i) completed 30 or more years of creditable service or (ii) have attained 55 years of age and completed five or more years of creditable service; and

(2) Not have attained 62 years of age; and

(3) Have completed at least five years of continuous service as a law enforcement officer as herein defined immediately preceding a service retirement. Any break in the continuous service required by this subsection because of disability retirement or disability salary continuation benefits shall not adversely affect an officer's qualification to receive the allowance, provided the officer returns to service within 45 days after the disability benefits cease and is otherwise qualified to receive the allowance.

(b) As used in this section, "creditable service" means the service for which credit is allowed under the retirement system of which the officer is a member, provided that at least fifty percent (50%) of the service is as a law enforcement officer as herein defined.

(c) Payment to a retired officer under the provisions of this section shall cease at the first of:

(1) The death of the officer;

(2) The last day of the month in which the officer attains 62 years of age; or

(3) The first day of reemployment by a local government employer in any capacity.

Notwithstanding the provisions of subdivision (3) of this subsection, a local government employer may employ retired officers in a public safety position in a capacity not requiring participation in the Local Governmental Employees' Retirement System, and doing so shall not cause payment to cease to those officers under the provisions of this section.

(d) This section does not affect the benefits to which an individual may be entitled from State, local, federal, or private retirement systems. The benefits payable under this section shall not be subject to any increases in salary or retirement allowances that may be authorized by local government employers or for retired employees of local governments.

(e) The governing body of each local employer shall determine the eligibility of employees for the benefits provided herein.

(f) The governing body of each local employer shall make the payments set forth in subsection (a) of this section to those persons certified under subsection

(e) of this section from funds available. (1985 (Reg. Sess., 1986), c. 1019, s. 2; 2009-396, s. 1.)

§§ 143-166.43 through 143-166.49. Reserved for future codification purposes.

§ 143-166.50. Retirement benefits for local governmental law-enforcement officers.

(a) Definitions. - The following words and phrases as used in this Article, unless a different meaning is plainly required by the context, have the following meaning:

(1) "Beneficiary" means any person in receipt of a retirement allowance or other benefit from a Retirement System.

(2) "Employer" means a county, city, town or other political subdivision of the State.

(3) "Law-enforcement officer" means a full-time paid employee of an employer, who possesses the power of arrest, who has taken the law enforcement oath administered under the authority of the State as prescribed by G.S. 11-11, and who is certified as a law enforcement officer under the provisions of Chapter 17C of the General Statutes or certified as a deputy sheriff under the provisions of Chapter 17E of the General Statutes. "Law enforcement officer" also means the sheriff of the county. The number of paid personnel employed as law enforcement officers by a law enforcement agency may not exceed the number of law enforcement positions approved by the applicable local governing board.

(4) "Law-Enforcement Officers' Retirement System" means the system provided for under Article 12 of Chapter 143 of the General Statutes, as it existed prior to January 1, 1986.

(5) "Local Governmental Employees' Retirement System" means the Local Governmental Employees' Retirement System of North Carolina provided for under Article 3 of Chapter 128 of the General Statutes.

(6) "Member" means an officer included in the membership of a retirement system, including former officers no longer employed who also elected to leave their accumulated contributions on deposit with a Retirement System.

(7) "Officer" means a "law-enforcement officer."

(8) "State" means the State of North Carolina.

(b) Basic Retirement System. - On and after January 1, 1986, law-enforcement officers employed by an employer shall be members of the Local Government Employees' Retirement System, and beneficiaries who were last employed as officers by an employer, or who are surviving beneficiaries of officers last employed by an employer, are beneficiaries of the Local Governmental Employees' Retirement System and paid in benefit amounts then in effect. All members of the Law-Enforcement Officers' Retirement System last employed and paid by an employer are members of the Local Retirement System.

(c) Rights. - Notwithstanding any other provisions of law, any accrued or inchoate rights of a member of the Law-Enforcement Officers' Retirement System as of his transfer to the Local Governmental Employees' Retirement System on January 1, 1986, including the rights to a vested deferred retirement allowance and to commence retirement at certain ages with required years of service as a law-enforcement officer, may in no way be diminished; provided, however, in no event may a member commence retirement and continue membership service with the same Retirement System after January 1, 1986.

No eligible officer shall be precluded from exercising that officer's pending or inchoate rights under this section, should the officer elect to make Roth after-tax contributions to the Supplemental Retirement Income Plan, except that these Roth after-tax contributions and the earnings thereon shall not be subsequently transferred to the Local Governmental Employees' Retirement System.

(d) Court Cost Receipts. - Of the sum derived from the cost of court provided for in G.S. 7A-304(a)(3), the amount designated for this Article, except for the amount designated for the provisions of G.S. 143-166.50(e), shall be paid over to the pension accumulation fund of the Local Governmental Employees' Retirement System and shall offset, to the extent of these receipts, the employers' normal contribution rate required in G.S. 128-30(d)(2) as it pertains to law enforcement officers.

(e) Supplemental Retirement Income Plan for Local Governmental Law-Enforcement Officers. - As of January 1, 1986, all law-enforcement officers employed by a local government employer, are participating members of the Supplemental Retirement Income Plan as provided by Article 5 of Chapter 135 of the General Statutes. In addition to the contributions transferred from the Law-Enforcement Officers' Retirement System, participants may make voluntary contributions to the Supplemental Retirement Income Plan to be credited to the designated individual accounts of participants. From July 1, 1987, until July 1, 1988, local government employers of law enforcement officers shall contribute an amount equal to at least two percent (2%) of participating local officers' monthly compensation to the Supplemental Retirement Income Plan to be credited to the designated individual accounts of participating local officers; and on and after July 1, 1988, local government employers of law enforcement officers shall contribute an amount equal to five percent (5%) of participating local officers' monthly compensation to the Supplemental Retirement Income Plan to be credited to the designated individual accounts of participating local officers.

Additional contributions shall also be made to the individual accounts of all participants in the Plan, except for Sheriffs, on a per capita equal-share basis from the sum of one dollar and twenty-five cents ($1.25) for each cost of court collected under G.S. 7A-304.

Upon retirement, a participant in the Plan may elect to transfer any portion of his eligible accumulated contributions, not including any Roth after-tax contributions and the earnings thereon, to the Local Governmental Employees' Retirement System and receive, in addition to his basic service, early or disability retirement allowance a special retirement allowance which shall be based on his eligible accumulated account balance at the date of the transfer of the assets.

(e1) Rights of Participants under the Uniformed Services Employment and Reemployment Rights Act. - A participant whose employment is interrupted by reason of service in the Uniformed Services, as that term is defined in section 4303(16) of the Uniformed Services Employment and Reemployment Rights Act, Public Law 103-353, hereafter referred to as "USERRA", shall be entitled to all rights and benefits that the participant would have been entitled to under this section had the participant's employment not been interrupted, provided that the participant returns to service as a law enforcement officer while the participant's reemployment rights are protected under the provisions of USERRA.

(e2) Forfeiture of Benefits for Certain Felonies. - Participants in the Supplemental Retirement Income Plan for Local Governmental Law-Enforcement Officers whose benefits are forfeited under G.S. 128-38.4A shall also forfeit contributions paid on or after December 1, 2012, on behalf of the participant by local government employers of law enforcement officers to the Supplemental Retirement Income Plan for Local Governmental Law-Enforcement Officers. Any funds forfeited shall be deposited in the Supplemental Retirement Income Plan. (1985, c. 479, s. 196(t); c. 729, ss. 6, 7; 1985 (Reg. Sess., 1986), c. 1015, s. 2; c. 1019, s. 1; 1995, c. 361, s. 6; 1997-144, s. 2; 2006-141, s. 2; 2007-384, s. 10.6; 2010-72, s. 11(b); 2012-193, s. 14; 2013-288, s. 1(b).)

§§ 143-166.51 through 143-166.59. Reserved for future codification purposes.

Article 12F.

Separate Insurance Benefits Plan for State and Local Governmental Law-Enforcement Officers.

§ 143-166.60. Separate insurance benefits plan for law-enforcement officers.

(a) A Separate Insurance Benefits Plan, hereinafter called the "Plan", is to be an employee welfare benefit plan, established for the benefit of (i) all law enforcement officers, as defined in G.S. 135-1(11c) and G.S. 128-21(11d) employed by the State and local governments and (ii) all former law-enforcement officers previously employed by the State and local governments, who had 20 or more years of service as an officer or are in receipt of a disability retirement allowance from any State-administered retirement system or are in receipt of a benefit from the Disability Income Plan of North Carolina, who shall be participants.

(b) The Boards of Trustees of the Teachers' and State Employees' Retirement System and the Local Governmental Employees' Retirement System shall jointly administer the Plan and shall, under the terms and conditions otherwise appearing in this Article, provide Plan benefits either (i) by establishing a separate trust fund in conformance with Section 501(c)(9) of the Internal Revenue Code of 1954 as amended or, (ii) by causing the Plan to affiliate with a master trust providing the same benefits for participants.

(c) The initial assets of the Plan are the assets of the former Separate Benefit Plan established under G.S. 143-166.04 as it existed prior to January 1, 1986, which shall be transferred to the Plan on January 1, 1986. The Plan shall be separate and apart from any retirement systems or plans.

(d) The Boards of Trustees shall promulgate rules and regulations as are necessary to establish benefits under the Plan, within the availability of funds, to provide:

(1) An accident and sickness disability insurance benefit;

(2) A group life insurance benefit for participants employed by an employer at the time of death, not to exceed five thousand dollars ($5,000);

(3) A group life insurance benefit for participants who are eligible former officers, not to exceed four thousand dollars ($4,000); and

(4) An accidental line-of-duty insurance death benefit not to exceed two thousand one hundred dollars ($2,100) in total on account of the death of a participant caused by an accident while in the actual performance of duty as an officer.

(d1) In addition to the benefits provided under subsection (d) of this section, the assets of the Plan may be used to pay the employer health insurance contributions and contribution rates on behalf of law enforcement officers, as defined in G.S. 135-1(11c), employed by the State and former law enforcement officers receiving a retirement allowance from the Teachers' and State Employees' Retirement System.

(e) The insurance benefit of the Plan on account of the death of a participant shall be payable to the surviving spouse of the participant or otherwise to the participant's estate; provided, should a participant instruct the Board of Trustees in writing that he does not wish these benefits to be paid to his spouse or estate, then the benefits shall be paid to the person or persons as the participant may name for this purpose. The life insurance benefits shall be payable only on account of participants in the Plan for six or more months or, if an actively employed officer, at any time after employment if death results from an accident. The accident and sickness disability insurance benefits shall be payable to a participant at any time after becoming a participant in the Plan.

(f) Should amounts in the trust fund of the Plan be insufficient at any time to enable the Boards of Trustees to pay benefits due in full, then an equitable graded percentage of the payment shall be made.

(g) The provisions of the State and Local Retirement Systems pertaining to administration and management of funds under G.S. 128-28, G.S. 128-29, G.S. 135-6 and G.S. 135-7 are made applicable to the Plan.

(h) Exemption from Garnishment and Attachment. - The right of a participant in the Separate Insurance Benefits Plan to the benefits provided under this Article is nonforfeitable and exempt from levy, sale, and garnishment. (1985, c. 479, s. 196(t); 1987, c. 738, s. 29(p); 1989, c. 792, s. 2.8; 2003-284, s. 30.19B(b); 2013-360, s. 35.17(a).)

§§ 143-166.61 through 143-166.69. Reserved for future codification purposes.

Article 12G.

Transfers of Assets of Law-Enforcement Officers' Retirement System to Other Retirement Systems.

§ 143-166.70. Transfers of assets of Law-Enforcement Officers' Retirement System to other retirement systems.

As of January 1, 1986, assets of the Law-Enforcement Officers' Retirement System, provided for under Article 12 of Chapter 143 of the General Statutes, as it existed prior to January 1, 1986, shall be transferred to the Local Governmental Employees' Retirement System provided for under Article 3 of Chapter 128 of the General Statutes, and the Supplemental Retirement Income Plan of North Carolina, provided for under Article 5 of Chapter 135 of the General Statutes, in the amounts calculated and in the order of precedence enumerated as follows:

(1) The regular accumulated contributions of members of the Law-Enforcement Officers' Retirement System shall be transferred from the annuity savings fund of the Law-Enforcement Officers' Retirement System to the annuity savings fund of the Local Governmental Employees' Retirement System to the credit of each individual member.

(2) An amount equal to the present value of the liabilities on account of the retirement allowances payable to beneficiaries of the Law-Enforcement Officers' Retirement System, as calculated by the Retirement System's consulting actuary, shall be transferred from the pension accumulation fund of the Law-Enforcement Officers' Retirement System to the pension accumulation fund of the Local Governmental Employees' Retirement System.

(3) After the transfer provided for above, the remaining assets in the pension accumulation fund of the Law-Enforcement Officers' Retirement System shall be transferred to the pension accumulation fund of the Local Governmental Employees' Retirement System with the amount of such assets to be taken into account by the Retirement System's consulting actuary in determining the employers' rates of contribution under G.S. 128-30(d)(9).

(4) The special annuity account accumulated contributions shall be transferred from the special annuity savings fund of the Law-Enforcement Officers' Retirement System to the Supplemental Retirement Income Plan of North Carolina, or some other employer-sponsored trust qualified under Sections 401(a) and 401(k) of the Internal Revenue Code of 1954 as amended.

(5) The separate trust fund reserves held under the death benefit plan provided for in G.S. 143-166.02, as it existed prior to January 1, 1986, shall be transferred to the separate trust fund for the death benefit plan provided for in G.S. 128-27(1) [128-27(l)]. (1985, c. 479, s. 196(u).)

§§ 143-166.71 through 143-166.79. Reserved for future codification purposes.

Article 12H.

Sheriffs' Supplemental Pension Fund Act of 1985.

§ 143-166.80. Short title and purpose.

(a) This Article shall be known and may be cited as the "Sheriffs' Supplemental Pension Fund Act of 1985".

(b) The purpose of this Article is to create a pension fund to supplement local government retirement benefits which will attract the most highly qualified talent available within the State to the position of sheriff and to fully recognize that sheriffs are constitutional officials elected by the people and are also officers of the court enforcing the laws of the State of North Carolina. (1985, c. 729, s. 1.)

§ 143-166.81. Scope.

(a) This Article provides supplemental pension benefits for all county sheriffs who are retired from the Local Governmental Employees' Retirement System or an equivalent locally sponsored plan as herein described.

(b) The North Carolina Department of Justice shall administer the provisions of this Article.

(c) The provisions of this Article shall be subject to future legislative change or revision, and no person is deemed to have acquired any vested right to a pension payment provided by this Article. (1985, c. 729, s. 1.)

§ 143-166.82. Assets.

(a) On and after July 1, 1985, each Clerk of Superior Court shall remit to the Department of Justice the monthly receipts collected pursuant to G.S. 7A-304 (a)(3a) to be deposited to the credit of the Sheriffs' Supplemental Pension Fund, hereinafter referred to as the Fund, to be used in making monthly pension payments to eligible retired sheriffs under the provisions of this Article and to pay the cost of administering the provisions of this Article.

(b) The State Treasurer shall be the custodian of the Sheriffs' Supplemental Pension Fund and shall invest its assets in accordance with the provisions of G.S. 147-69.2 and G.S. 147-69.3. (1985, c. 729, s. 1.)

§ 143-166.83. Disbursements.

(a) Repealed by Session Laws 1991 (Reg. Sess., 1992), c. 900, s. 54, effective January 1, 1993.

(b) Immediately following January 1, 1993, and the first of January of each succeeding calendar year thereafter, the Department of Justice shall divide an amount equal to ninety percent (90%) of the assets of the Fund at the end of the preceding calendar year and shall add to that amount any assets remaining pursuant to subsection (f) of this section and disburse the same as monthly payments in accordance with the provisions of this Article.

(c) Ten percent (10%) of the Fund's assets as of January 1, 1993, and at the beginning of each calendar year thereafter, may be used by the Department of Justice in administering the provisions of this Article. This ten percent (10%) is to be derived from the Fund's assets prior to the addition of assets remaining pursuant to subsection (f) of this section.

(d) All the Fund's disbursements shall be conducted in the same manner as disbursements are conducted for other special funds of the State.

(e) If, for any reason, the Fund shall be insufficient to pay any pension benefits or other charges, then all benefits or payments shall be reduced pro rata for as long as the deficiency in amount exists. No claim shall accrue with respect to any amount by which a pension payment shall have been reduced.

(f) Any assets remaining after reserving an amount equal to the disbursements required under subsections (b) and (c) of this section shall be accrued and included in disbursements for pensioners in succeeding years. (1985, c. 729, s. 1; 1985 (Reg. Sess., 1986), c. 1030, ss. 1, 2; 1991 (Reg. Sess., 1992), c. 900, s. 54(a).)

§ 143-166.84. Eligibility.

(a) Each county sheriff who has retired from the Local Governmental Employees' Retirement System, and who has attained the age of 55 years or attained 30 years of creditable service regardless of age, and who has completed at least 10 years of eligible service as sheriff, is entitled to receive a monthly pension under this Article.

(a1) Each county sheriff who withdrew any service standing to his credit in the Local Governmental Employees' Retirement System prior to July 1, 1986, and who has attained the age of 55 or attained 30 creditable years of service regardless of age, and who has completed at least 10 years of eligible service as sheriff, is entitled to receive a monthly pension under this Article provided the sheriff is not eligible to receive any retirement benefit from any State or locally sponsored plan.

(a2) Each county sheriff who has been approved for disability benefits from the Local Governmental Employees' Retirement System is eligible to receive benefits from the Fund based on years of creditable service as sheriff, regardless of age, provided the retiree has at least 10 years of eligible service as sheriff.

(b) Each eligible retired sheriff as defined in subsections (a), (a1), and (a2) of this section relating to age and service shall be entitled to receive a monthly pension under this Article beginning with the month immediately following the effective date of retirement. (1985, c. 729, s. 1; 1985 (Reg. Sess., 1986), c. 1030, ss. 3, 5(a); 1987, c. 177, s. 3; 1989 (Reg. Sess., 1990) c. 1079, s. 1; 1991 (Reg. Sess., 1992), c. 900, s. 54(b).)

§ 143-166.85. Benefits.

(a) An eligible retired sheriff shall be entitled to and receive an annual pension benefit, payable in equal monthly installments, equal to one share for each full year of eligible service as sheriff multiplied by his total number of years of eligible service. The amount of each share shall be determined by dividing the total number of years of eligible service for all eligible retired sheriffs on December 31 of each calendar year into the amount to be disbursed as monthly pension payments in accordance with the provisions of G.S. 143-166.83(b). In no event however shall a monthly pension under this Article exceed an amount, which when added to a retired allowance at retirement from the Local Governmental Employees' Retirement System or to the amount he would have been eligible to receive if service had not been forfeited by the withdrawal of accumulated contributions, is greater than seventy-five percent (75%) of a sheriff's equivalent annual salary immediately preceding retirement computed on the latest monthly base rate, to a maximum amount of one thousand five hundred dollars ($1,500).

(b) All monthly pensions payable under this Article shall be paid on the last business day of each month.

(c) At the death of the pensioner, benefits for the current calendar year will continue and be paid in monthly installments to the decedent's spouse or estate, in accordance with the provisions of Chapter 28A of the General Statutes. Benefits will cease upon the last payment being made in December of the current year.

(d) Monthly pensions payable under this Article will cease upon the full-time reemployment of a pensioner with an employer participating in the Local Governmental Employees' Retirement System for as long as the pensioner is so reemployed.

(e) Repealed by Session Laws 1989, c. 792, s. 2.9.

(f) Nothing contained in this Article shall preclude or in any way affect the benefits that a pensioner may be entitled to from any state, federal or private pension, retirement or other deferred compensation plan. (1985, c. 729, s. 1; 1985 (Reg. Sess., 1986), c. 1030, ss. 4, 5(b); 1987, c. 177, s. 4; 1989, c. 792, s. 2.9; 1989 (Reg. Sess., 1990), c. 1079, s. 2; 1991 (Reg. Sess., 1992), c. 900, s. 54(c); 2005-276, s. 29.30(a).)

Article 13.

Publications.

§ 143-167. Transferred to G.S. 147-54.1 by Session Laws 1943, c. 543.

§ 143-168. Reports; conciseness.

The annual or biennial reports now authorized or required to be printed by the several State agencies and institutions shall be as compact and concise as is consistent with an intelligent understanding of the work of those agencies and institutions. The details of the work of the agencies and institutions shall not be printed when not necessary to an intelligent understanding of such work, but totals and results may be tabulated and printed in their reports. (1911, c. 211, s. 2; 1917, c. 202, s. 2; C.S., s. 7294; 1931, c. 261, s. 3; 1955, c. 983; 1961, c. 243, s. 2; 1983, c. 866, s. 1.)

§ 143-169. Limitations on publications.

(a) Repealed by Session Laws 1983, c. 866, s. 2.

(b) Repealed by Session Laws 2007-234, s. 1, effective July 18, 2007.

(c) Every publication published at State expense shall be prepared in accordance with the recycling and reuse requirements set forth in G.S. 130A-309.14(j). (1911, c. 211, s. 2; C.S., s. 7302; 1931, c. 261, s. 3; c. 312, ss. 14, 15; 1955, c. 1203; 1961, c. 243, s. 3; 1973, c. 1262, s. 86; 1977, c. 771, s. 4; 1983, c. 866, s. 2; 1989, c. 727, s. 218(100); 1993, c. 448, s. 4; 1997-443, s. 11A.119(a); 2007-234, s. 1.)

§ 143-169.1. State agency public document mailing lists to be updated.

(a) On or before July 1 of each year, beginning with July 1, 1976, the head of every agency of this State shall certify to the Director of the Budget that the mailing lists for each public document issued by his agency have been carefully reviewed, updated and corrected within the previous 12 months. The above date may be extended by the Director of the Budget for 90 days for good cause shown. The reviewed, updated and corrected mailing lists shall be comprised only of those persons and organizations who, within the previous 12 months, have either requested that they be included in such a mailing list or have renewed a request that they be so included, or are recipients contemplated for receipt of the pertinent public document by express provision of statute or judicial order, but this sentence does not apply to mailing lists of alumni of a constituent institution of The University of North Carolina, used or maintained by the constituent institution.

(b), (c) Repealed by Session Laws 1989, c. 715, s. 2. (1975, c. 362, s. 1; 1983, c. 866, ss. 3-5; 1989, c. 715, s. 2; 1993, c. 448, s. 5.)

§ 143-169.2. Definitions.

(a) For the purposes of this Article, the term "public document" shall mean any annual, biennial, regular or special report or publication of which at least

200 copies are printed, but shall not include intra-agency communications nor agency correspondence.

(b)   For the purposes of this Article, the term "agency" shall mean and include, as the context may require, State department, institution, university, commission, committee, board, licensing board, division, bureau, officer or official; provided, however, the provisions of G.S. 143-169.1 shall not apply to the General Assembly, the Department of Revenue, the Department of Commerce, or to the Administrative Office of the Courts and the court system, nor shall the provisions of G.S. 143-170.2 and 143-170.3 apply to the General Assembly or to the Administrative Office of the Courts and the courts system. (1989, c. 715, s. 3; c. 751, ss. 7(16), 18; 1991 (Reg. Sess., 1992), c. 959, s. 35.)

§ 143-170. Repealed by Session Laws 1955, c. 986.

§ 143-170.1. Statement of cost of public documents; chief administrator charged with compliance.

(a)   Every agency of this State publishing a public document, other than one published for the principal purpose of sale to the public, shall cause the following statement to be printed adjacent to the identification of the agency responsible for the publication:

"(Number of copies) copies of this public document were printed at a cost of $____, or $____ per copy."

For the purposes of this Article the term "cost" shall include printing costs in the form of labor and materials, and other identifiable design, typesetting, and binding costs.

(a1)   Any public document without a statement of cost shall not be mailed or distributed at public expense.

(a2)   Whenever a public document that is published by an agency of this State is printed on recycled paper, the document shall contain a printed statement or symbol indicating that the document was printed on recycled paper.

(a3) If an agency fails to comply with this section, then the agency's printing budget for the fiscal year following the violation shall be reduced by ten percent (10%).

(b) The chief administrator of the agency authorizing the printing is charged with agency compliance with the provisions of this Article. (1983, c. 866, ss. 6, 7; 1989, c. 34; 1993, c. 256, s. 4; 1995, c. 324, s. 6.10.)

§ 143-170.2. Publication procedure manuals.

(a) The State Librarian in consultation with the State Auditor shall administer and periodically revise guidelines to be used by all State agencies and community colleges in developing publication procedures manuals for public documents. The initial guidelines developed by the Department of Administration shall be released no later than December 1, 1989 and shall address at least the following elements of publication production for public documents:

(1) Bibliographic style, substantially in accord with a recognized style manual approved by the State Librarian; provided, however, the Department shall not develop guidelines concerning the design, layout, size or appearance of publications except as otherwise permitted herein;

(2) Procedures for the notification of the State Library for title changes in serial publications;

(3) Pricing of documents for resale;

(4) Use of publication services at State-operated printing facilities;

(5) Purchase of commercial publication services; and

(6) The distribution of publications.

The Department of Administration shall submit the initial guidelines to State agencies for review and comment for a period of 60 days; provided, however, that submission to the University of North Carolina General Administration shall satisfy this requirement with respect to universities. The Department, in consultation with at least the State Librarian and the State Auditor, shall consider the comments of the State agencies before adopting final guidelines. The Department of Administration shall adopt and release the final guidelines no later than four months after the release of the initial guidelines.

(b)   Upon the adoption and release of final guidelines by the Department of Administration, each State agency and community college shall within four months thereafter adopt a publication procedures manual for public documents consistent with the guidelines established pursuant to subsection (a) of this section and an administrative review and approval process to ensure appropriate review and approval of its public documents.

(c)   Each State agency and community college shall submit to the State Library for review and retention a copy of its publication procedures manual and its administrative review procedure for public documents. Any revisions made by an agency shall also be submitted to the State Library within 30 days of adoption by the agency.

(d)   Repealed by Session Laws 1991, c. 757. s. 1.

(d1)   The State Library may revise the final statewide guidelines, originally issued April 1, 1990, by the Department of Administration, at any time after July 1, 1990, provided that there be distribution of any proposed revisions to all agencies and institutions subject to these provisions, and that there be a 30-day review period for these agencies to comment. (1989, c. 715, s. 1; 1991, c. 757. s. 1.)

§ 143-170.3. Reports; audits.

(a)   The Department of Administration shall report to the Joint Legislative Commission on Governmental Operations each State agency and community college that fails to timely adopt and submit to the Department the information required by G.S. 143-170.2. The initial report shall be made by January 1, 1991.

(b)   Upon the determination of the State Auditor that a State agency or community college has failed to substantially comply with its publications procedure manual or its administrative review and approval process for public documents, the State Auditor shall report the noncompliance to the Joint Legislative Commission on Governmental Operations within 60 days if the

General Assembly is not in session, and to the President Pro Tempore of the Senate, the Speaker of the House, and the Senate and House Appropriations Committee Chairmen within 30 days if the General Assembly is in session.

(c) The State Librarian and the University Librarian of the University of North Carolina at Chapel Hill shall identify the types of publications for which the use of acid-free paper is desirable and, with the assistance of the Department of Administration, shall study the availability of acid-free paper and the costs associated with purchasing and using acid-free paper. The State Librarian and the University Librarian of the University of North Carolina at Chapel Hill shall report to the Joint Legislative Commission on Governmental Operations no later than November 1, 1990 the information required by this subsection. (1989, c. 715, s. 1.)

§ 143-170.4. Administrative Office of the Courts; publications procedures manual; reports.

Not later than June 1, 1990, the Administrative Office of the Courts, after review of the Department of Administration's state publications procedures guidelines and after consultation with the State Librarian and State Auditor, shall adopt (i) a publications procedures manual for public documents, other than the official reports of the North Carolina Supreme Court and the North Carolina Court of Appeals and official forms published by the Administrative Office of the Courts pursuant to G.S. 7A-343, that addresses the elements of publication production described in G.S. 143-170.2 and (ii) an administrative review and approval process to ensure appropriate review and approval of its public documents. The initial guidelines and the administrative review and approval process shall be reported to the Joint Legislative Commission on Governmental Operations by January 1, 1991. (1989, c. 715, s. 1; 2001-424, s. 22.6(b).)

§ 143-170.5. Designated public documents to be printed on alkaline paper.

The State Librarian and the University Librarian at the University of North Carolina at Chapel Hill shall designate annually as provided by G.S. 125-11.13 those State documents that must be printed on alkaline paper. Each agency publishing a State document designated by the State Librarian and the University Librarian at the University of North Carolina at Chapel Hill as one that must be printed on alkaline paper shall comply with that publication requirement. (1991, c. 224, s. 2; 1993, c. 553, s. 4.)

Article 14.

North Carolina Zoological Authority.

§§ 143-171 through 143-176.1: Repealed by Session Laws 1973, c. 1262, s. 85.

§ 143-177. Right to receive gifts.

In order to carry out the purposes of this Article, the Board is authorized to acquire by gift or will, absolutely or in trust, from individuals, corporations, or any other source money or other property, or any interests in property, which may be retained, sold or otherwise used to promote the purposes of this Article. The use of gifts shall be subject to such limitations as may be imposed thereon by donors, notwithstanding any other provisions of this Article. (1969, c. 1104, s. 8.)

§ 143-177.1. North Carolina Zoological Park Fund.

All gifts made to the North Carolina Zoological Park for the purposes of this Article shall be exempt from every form of taxation including, but not by the way of limitation, ad valorem, intangible, gift, inheritance and income taxation. Proceeds from the sale of any property acquired under the provisions of this Article shall be deposited in the North Carolina State treasury and shall be credited to the North Carolina Zoological Park. (1969, c. 1104, s. 9; 1973, c. 1262, s. 85.)

§ 143-177.2. Cities and counties.

Cities and counties are hereby authorized to expend funds derived from nontax sources and to make gifts of surplus property, to assist in carrying out the purposes of this Article. (1969, c. 1104, s. 10.)

§ 143-177.3. Sources of funds.

(a) It is the intent of this Article that the funds for the creation, establishment, construction, operation and maintenance of the North Carolina Zoological Park shall be obtained primarily from private sources; however, the Council under the supervision and approval and with the assistance of the Secretary of Environment and Natural Resources is hereby authorized to receive and expend such funds as may from time to time become available by appropriation or otherwise from the State of North Carolina; provided, that the North Carolina Zoological Park Council shall not in any manner pledge the faith and credit of the State of North Carolina for any of its purposes.

(b) The Council with the approval of the Secretary of Environment and Natural Resources is authorized to establish and set admission fees which are reasonable and consistent with the purpose and function of the North Carolina Zoological Park. (1969, c. 1104, s. 11; 1973, c. 1262, s. 85; 1977, c. 771, s. 4; 1981, c. 278, s. 1; 1989, c. 727, s. 218(101); 1997-443, s. 11A.119(a).)

Article 15.

Council of State Governments.

§§ 143-178 through 143-185: Repealed by Session Laws 1975, c. 879, s. 25.

§ 143-186. Council of State Governments a joint governmental agency.

The Council of State Governments is hereby declared to be a joint governmental agency of this State and of the other states which cooperate through it. (1937, c. 374, s. 10; 1959, c. 137, s. 4.)

§ 143-187. Transferred to G.S. 143-186 by Session Laws 1959, c. 137, s. 4.

§ 143-188: Repealed by Session Laws 1959, c. 137, s. 1.

Article 16.

Spanish-American War Relief Fund.

§§ 143-189 through 143-190: Repealed by Session Laws 1961, c. 481.

Article 17.

State Post-War Reserve Fund.

§ 143-191. Appropriation for fund.

There is hereby appropriated from the general fund of the State the sum of twenty million dollars ($20,000,000), the said sum, together with the investments and income therefrom, to be hereafter known and designated as the State Post-War Reserve Fund. (1943, c. 6, s. 1.)

§ 143-192. Fund to be invested by Governor and Council of State; State Treasurer custodian.

The Governor and Council of State are hereby fully authorized and directed to invest the said fund exclusively in bonds of the United States of America, of such series as may be readily converted into money and notes or certificates of indebtedness of the United States of America, or in bonds, notes or other obligations of any agency or instrumentality of the United States of America, when the payment of principal and interest thereof is fully guaranteed by the United States of America, and in bonds or notes of the State of North Carolina. The interest and revenues received from such investments, or profits realized in the sale thereof, shall become a part of the said State Post-War Reserve Fund and shall be likewise invested. Bonds of the State of North Carolina purchased for the said fund shall not be cancelled or retired but shall remain in full force and the income therefrom reinvested as hereinbefore provided. The State Treasurer shall be custodian of all securities and investments made under authority of this Article. (1943, c. 6, s. 2.)

§ 143-193. Fund to be held for such use as directed by General Assembly.

The said State Post-War Reserve Fund shall be held for such use as shall hereafter be directed by an act of the General Assembly of North Carolina, and no other use thereof whatsoever shall be made. (1943, c. 6, s. 3.)

§ 143-194. Report to General Assembly.

The Governor and Council of State shall make a report in writing to the General Assembly, not later than the tenth day of each regular or special session thereof, stating the nature and amount of all receipts and disbursements from the said fund and the amount contained in said fund, and giving an itemized statement of all investments made as herein authorized, which report shall be spread upon the journals of the Senate and House of Representatives. (1943, c. 6, s. 4.)

Article 18.

Rules and Regulations Filed with Secretary of State.

§§ 143-195 through 143-198.1. Repealed by Session Laws 1973, c. 1331, s. 2.

Article 19.

Roanoke Island Historical Association.

§ 143-199. Association under patronage and control of State.

Roanoke Island Historical Association, Incorporated is hereby permanently placed under the patronage and control of the State. (1945, c. 953, s. 1.)

§ 143-200. Members of board of directors; terms; appointment.

The governing body of the Association shall be a board of directors consisting of the Governor of the State, the Attorney General, the Superintendent of Public Instruction, the Chair of the Dare County Board of Commissioners, and the Secretary of Cultural Resources, or their designees, as ex officio members, and the following 21 members: J. Spencer Love, Greensboro; Miles Clark, Elizabeth City; Mrs. Richard J. Reynolds, Winston-Salem; D. Hiden Ramsey, Asheville; Mrs. Charles A. Cannon, Concord; Dr. Fred Hanes, Durham; Mrs. Frank P. Graham, Chapel Hill; Bishop Thomas C. Darst, Wilmington; W. Dorsey Pruden, Edenton; John A. Buchanan, Durham; William B. Rodman, Jr., Washington; J. Melville Broughton, Raleigh; Melvin R. Daniels, Manteo; Paul Green, Chapel Hill; Samuel Selden, Chapel Hill; R. Bruce Etheridge, Manteo; Theodore S. Meekins, Manteo; Roy L. Davis, Manteo; M. K. Fearing, Manteo; A. R. Newsome, Chapel Hill. The members of the board of directors herein named other than the ex officio members, shall serve for a term of three years and until their successors are appointed. Appointments thereafter shall be made by the membership of the Association in regular annual meeting or special meeting called for such purpose. In the event the Association through its membership should fail to make such appointments, then the appointments shall be made by the Governor of the State. If a vacancy occurs between annual meetings, the board of directors may fill the vacancy until the next annual meeting. All vacancies occurring on the board of directors not filled by the board of directors within 30 days of the vacancy shall be filled by the Governor of the State. (1945, c. 953, s. 2; 1973, c. 476, s. 48; 1996, 2nd Ex. Sess., c. 18, s. 11.1(a); 1999-32, s. 1; 1999-431, s. 3.1.)

§ 143-201. Bylaws; officers of board.

The said board of directors when organized under the terms of this Article shall have authority to adopt bylaws for the organization and said bylaws shall thereafter be subject to change only by three-fifths vote of a quorum of said board of directors; the board of directors shall choose from its membership or from the membership of the Association a chairman, a vice-chairman, a secretary and a treasurer, which offices in the discretion of the board may be combined in one, and also a historian and a general counsel. The board also in its discretion may choose one or more honorary vice-chairmen. The duly elected officers of the Association shall serve as an advisory committee to the Secretary of Cultural Resources concerning matters relating to "The Lost Colony" historical drama. (1945, c. 953, s. 3; 1973, c. 476, s. 87.)

§ 143-202. Exempt from taxation; gifts and donations.

The said Association is and shall be an educational and charitable association within the meaning of the laws of the State of North Carolina, and the property and income of such Association, real and personal, shall be exempt from all taxation. The said Association is authorized and empowered to receive gifts and donations and administer the same for the charitable and educational purposes for which the Association is formed and in keeping with the will of the donors, and such gifts and donations to the extent permitted by law shall be exempted from the purpose of income taxes and gift taxes. (1945, c. 953, s. 4.)

§ 143-203. Repealed by Session Laws 1983, c. 913, s. 39, effective July 22, 1983.

§ 143-204. Repealed by Session Laws 1977, c. 996, s. 3.

Article 19A.

Governor Richard Caswell Memorial Commission.

§§ 143-204.1 through 143-204.4. Repealed by Session Laws 1973, c. 476, s. 116.

Article 19B.

Historic Swansboro Commission.

§§ 143-204.5 through 143-204.7. Repealed by Session Laws 1973, c. 476, s. 116.

Article 19C.

Outdoor Historical Dramas.

§ 143-204.8. Allotments to outdoor historical dramas.

(a) Upon the application of an outdoor historical drama corporation or trust, approved by the Secretary of Cultural Resources, the Governor and the Council of State may order an allotment from the Contingency and Emergency Fund of the State not to exceed fifteen thousand dollars ($15,000) a year to that outdoor historical drama corporation or trust to aid in the production of an outdoor historical drama if the provisions of subsection (b) of this section are met.

(b) An allotment shall only be made under this section upon evidence submitted to the Governor and Council of State by the Secretary of Cultural Resources that during the immediately preceding season of production, the drama was operated at a deficit because of inclement weather or other circumstances beyond the control of the corporation or trust and that contributions or gifts made to the corporation or trust are deductible for income tax purposes under the Internal Revenue Code.

(c) For purposes of this section, an "outdoor historical drama corporation or trust," means only the following corporations or trusts presenting outdoor historical dramas:

Corporation or Trust	Outdoor Historical Drama
Cherokee Historical Association, Incorporated	"Unto These Hills"
The Committee for an Outdoor Drama at Bath, Incorporated	"Blackbeard - The Knight of the Black Flag"
The Duplin Outdoor Drama Society, A Incorporated	"The Liberty Cart: Duplin Story"
Eastern Stage, Inc.	"First for Freedom"
The Moore County Historical	"The House in the

Association, Incorporated	Horseshoe"
The Outdoor Theatre Fund Forward"	"From This Day
Charitable Trust	
"Revolution!", Incorporated	"Revolution!"
Roanoke Island Historical Association, Incorporated	"The Lost Colony"
Robeson Historical Drama, Wind" Incorporated	"Strike at the
Snow Camp Historical Drama Society, Incorporated	"Sword of Peace"
Southern Appalachian Historical Association, Incorporated	"Horn in the West"
The Waxhaws Historical Festival Remember" and Drama Association	"Listen and

The above listing of dramas is for informational purposes only and shall not be construed to limit the eligibility of the specified outdoor historical drama corporation or trust to receive allotments under this section.

(d) An outdoor historical drama corporation or trust which has applied for or received an allotment under this section shall permit the State Auditor to inspect and audit its financial records. (1977, c. 996, s. 1; 1987 (Reg. Sess., 1988), c. 1086, s. 44; 1989, c. 752, s. 21; 1991, c. 636, s. 16.)

Article 20.

Recreation Commission.

§§ 143-205 through 143-210.1: Repealed by Session Laws 1969, c. 1145, s. 4.

Article 21.

Water and Air Resources.

Part 1. Organization and Powers Generally; Control of Pollution.

§ 143-211. Declaration of public policy.

(a) It is hereby declared to be the public policy of this State to provide for the conservation of its water and air resources. Furthermore, it is the intent of the General Assembly, within the context of this Article and Articles 21A and 21B of this Chapter, to achieve and to maintain for the citizens of the State a total environment of superior quality. Recognizing that the water and air resources of the State belong to the people, the General Assembly affirms the State's ultimate responsibility for the preservation and development of these resources in the best interest of all its citizens and declares the prudent utilization of these resources to be essential to the general welfare.

(b) It is the public policy of the State to maintain, protect, and enhance water quality within North Carolina. Further, it is the public policy of the State that the cumulative impact of transfers from a source river basin shall not result in a violation of the antidegradation policy set out in 40 Code of Federal Regulations § 131.12 (l July 1997 Edition) and the statewide antidegradation policy adopted pursuant thereto.

(c) It is the purpose of this Article to create an agency which shall administer a program of water and air pollution control and water resource management. It is the intent of the General Assembly, through the duties and powers defined herein, to confer such authority upon the Department of Environment and Natural Resources as shall be necessary to administer a complete program of water and air conservation, pollution abatement and control and to achieve a coordinated effort of pollution abatement and control with other jurisdictions. Standards of water and air purity shall be designed to protect human health, to prevent injury to plant and animal life, to prevent damage to public and private property, to insure the continued enjoyment of the natural attractions of the State, to encourage the expansion of employment opportunities, to provide a permanent foundation for healthy industrial development and to secure for the people of North Carolina, now and in the future, the beneficial uses of these great natural resources. It is the intent of the General Assembly that the powers and duties of the Environmental Management Commission and the Department of Environment and Natural Resources be construed so as to enable the Department and the Commission to qualify to administer federally mandated programs of environmental management and to qualify to accept and administer funds from the federal government for such programs. (1951, c. 606; 1967, c. 892, s. 1; 1973, c. 1262, s. 23; 1977, c. 771, s. 4; 1979, 2nd Sess., c. 1158, s. 2; 1989, c. 135, s. 1; c. 727, s. 218(102); 1997-443, s. 11A.119(a); 1998-168, s. 1.)

§ 143-212. Definitions.

Unless a different meaning is required by the context, the following definitions apply to this Article and Articles 21A and 21B of this Chapter:

(1)   "Area of the State" means a municipality, a county, a portion of a county or a municipality, or other substantial geographic area of the State designated by the Commission.

(2)   "Commission" means the North Carolina Environmental Management Commission.

(3)   "Department" means the Department of Environment and Natural Resources.

(4)   "Person" includes individuals, firms, partnerships, associations, institutions, corporations, municipalities and other political subdivisions, and governmental agencies.

(5)   "Secretary" means the Secretary of Environment and Natural Resources.

(6)   "Waters" means any stream, river, brook, swamp, lake, sound, tidal estuary, bay, creek, reservoir, waterway, or other body or accumulation of

water, whether surface or underground, public or private, or natural or artificial, that is contained in, flows through, or borders upon any portion of this State, including any portion of the Atlantic Ocean over which the State has jurisdiction. (1987, c. 827, s. 152A; 1989, c. 727, s. 218(103); 1989 (Reg. Sess., 1990), c. 1004, s. 19(b); 1991 (Reg. Sess., 1992), c. 1028, s. 1; 1997-443, s. 11A.119(a).)

§ 143-213. Definitions.

Unless the context otherwise requires, the following terms as used in this Article and Articles 21A and 21B of this Chapter are defined as follows:

(1)   The term "air cleaning device" means any method, process or equipment which removes, reduces, or renders less noxious air contaminants discharged into the atmosphere.

(2)   The term "air contaminant" means particulate matter, dust, fumes, gas, mist, smoke, or vapor or any combination thereof.

(3)   The term "air contamination" means the presence in the outdoor atmosphere of one or more air contaminants which contribute to a condition of air pollution.

(4)   The term "air contamination source" means any source at, from, or by reason of which there is emitted into the atmosphere any air contaminant.

(5)   The term "air pollution" shall mean the presence in the outdoor atmosphere of one or more air contaminants in such quantities and duration as is or tends to be injurious to human health or welfare, to animal or plant life or to property or that interferes with the enjoyment of life or property.

(6)   to (8) Repealed by Session Laws 1987, c. 827, s. 153.

(9)   Whenever reference is made in this Article to "discharge" or the "discharge of waste," it shall be interpreted to include discharge, spillage, leakage, pumping, placement, emptying, or dumping into waters of the State, or into any unified sewer system or arrangement for sewage disposal, which system or arrangement in turn discharges the waste into the waters of the State. A reference to "discharge" or the "discharge of waste" shall not be interpreted to include "emission" as defined in subdivision (12) of this section.

(10)   The term "disposal system" means a system for disposing of waste, and including sewer systems and treatment works.

(11)   Repealed by Session Laws 1987, c. 827, s. 153.

(12)   The term "emission" means a release into the outdoor atmosphere of air contaminants.

(13)   The term "outlet" means the terminus of a sewer system, or the point of emergence of any waste or the effluent therefrom, into the waters of the State.

(14)   Repealed by Session Laws 1987, c. 827, s. 153.

(15)   The term "sewer system" means pipelines or conduits, pumping stations, and force mains, and all other construction, devices, and appliances appurtenant thereto, used for conducting wastes to a point of ultimate disposal.

(16)   The term "standard" or "standards" means such measure or measures of the quality of water and air as are established by the Commission pursuant to G.S. 143-214.1 and G.S. 143-215.

(16a)   "Stormwater" means the flow of water which results from precipitation and which occurs immediately following rainfall or a snowmelt.

(17)   The term "treatment works" means any plant, septic tank disposal field, lagoon, pumping station, constructed drainage ditch or surface water intercepting ditch, incinerator, area devoted to sanitary landfill, or other works not specifically mentioned herein, installed for the purpose of treating, equalizing, neutralizing, stabilizing or disposing of waste.

(18)   "Waste" shall mean and include the following:

a.   "Sewage," which shall mean water-carried human waste discharged, transmitted, and collected from residences, buildings, industrial establishments, or other places into a unified sewerage system or an arrangement for sewage disposal or a group of such sewerage arrangements or systems, together with such ground, surface, storm, or other water as may be present.

b.   "Industrial waste" shall mean any liquid, solid, gaseous, or other waste substance or a combination thereof resulting from any process of industry, manufacture, trade or business, or from the development of any natural resource.

c. "Other waste" means sawdust, shavings, lime, refuse, offal, oil, tar chemicals, dissolved and suspended solids, sediment, and all other substances, except industrial waste, sewage, and toxic chemicals which may be discharged into or placed in such proximity to the water that drainage therefrom may reach the water.

d. "Toxic waste" means that waste, or combinations of wastes, including disease-causing agents, which after discharge and upon exposure, ingestion, inhalation, or assimilation into any organism, either directly from the environment or indirectly by ingestion through food chains, will cause death, disease, behavioral abnormalities, cancer, genetic mutations, physiological malfunctions (including malfunctions in reproduction) or physical deformities, in such organisms or their offspring.

(19) The term "water pollution" means the man-made or man-induced alteration of the chemical, physical, biological, or radiological integrity of the waters of the State, including, but specifically not limited to, alterations resulting from the concentration or increase of natural pollutants caused by man-related activities.

(20) Repealed by Session Laws 1987, c. 827, s. 153.

(21) The term "watershed" means a natural area of drainage, including all tributaries contributing to the supply of at least one major waterway within the State, the specific limits of each separate watershed to be designated by the Commission.

(22) The term "complex sources" means any facility which is or may be an air pollution source or which will induce or tend to induce development or activities which will or may be air pollution sources, and which shall include, but not be limited to, shopping centers; sports complexes; drive-in theaters; parking lots and garages; residential, commercial, industrial or institutional developments; amusement parks and recreation areas; highways; and any other facilities which will result in increased emissions from motor vehicles or stationary sources.

(23) The term "effluent standards or limitations" means any restrictions established pursuant to this Article on quantities, rates, characteristics and concentrations of chemical, physical, biological and other constituents of wastes

which are discharged from any pretreatment facility or from any outlet or point source to the waters of the State.

(24) The term "point source" means any discernible, confined, and discrete conveyance, including, but specifically not limited to, any pipe, ditch, channel, tunnel, conduit, well, discrete fissure, container, rolling stock, or concentrated animal-feeding operation from which wastes are or may be discharged to the waters of the State.

(25) The term "pretreatment facility" means any treatment works installed for the purpose of treating, equalizing, neutralizing or stabilizing waste from any source prior to discharge to any disposal system subject to effluent standards or limitations.

(26) The term "pretreatment standards" means effluent standards or limitations applicable to waste discharged from a pretreatment facility.

(27) The term "Clean Air Act" refers to the federal Clean Air Act, as amended, codified generally at 42 U.S.C. § 7401 et seq.

(28) The term "nonattainment area" refers to an area which is shown to exceed any national ambient air quality standard for such pollutant.

(29) The term "prevention of significant deterioration" refers to the statutory and regulatory requirements arising from the Clean Air Act designed to prevent the significant deterioration of air quality in areas with air quality better than required by the national ambient air quality standards.

(29a) Reserved.

(29b) "Title II" means Title II of the 1990 amendments to the federal Clean Air Act and the National Emission Standards Act (Pub. L. 101-549, 104 Stat. 2471, 42 U.S.C. § 7521 et seq.).

(29c) "Title III" means Title III of the 1990 amendments to the federal Clean Air Act (Pub. L. 101-549, 104 Stat. 2531, 42 U.S.C. § 7412 et seq.).

(29d) "Title IV" means Title IV of the 1990 amendments to the federal Clean Air Act (Pub. L. 101-549, 104 Stat. 2584, 42 U.S.C. § 7651 et seq.).

(29e) "Title V" means Title V of the 1990 amendments to the federal Clean Air Act (Pub. L. 101-549, 104 Stat. 2635, 42 U.S.C. § 7661 et seq.).

(29f) through (29o) Reserved.

(29p) "Title V Account" means the Account established in G.S. 143-215.3A(b).

(30) The term "waste treatment management practice" means any method, measure or practice to control plant site runoff, spillage or leaks, sludge or waste disposal and drainage from raw material storage which are associated with, or ancillary to the industrial manufacturing or treatment process of the class or category of point sources to which the management practice is applied. Waste treatment management practices may only be imposed, supplemental to effluent limitations, for a class or category of point sources, for any specific pollutant which has been designated as toxic or hazardous pursuant to sections 307(a)(1) or 311 of the Federal Water Pollution Control Act. (1951, c. 606; 1957, c. 1275, s. 1; 1959, c. 779, s. 8; 1967, c. 892, s. 1; 1971, c. 1167, s. 4; 1973, c. 821, ss. 1-3; c. 1262, s. 23; 1977, c. 771, s. 4; 1979, c. 545, ss. 8-10; c. 633, s. 1; 1987, c. 827, ss. 153, 154; 1989, c. 135, s. 2; c. 447, s. 1; c. 742, s. 7; 1991, c. 287, s. 1; c. 403, s. 1; c. 552, s. 1; 1991 (Reg. Sess., 1992), c. 889, ss. 1, 2; c. 1028, s. 2; c. 1039, s. 13; 1993, c. 400, ss. 1(a)-(c); 2012-187, s. 11.)

§ 143-214. Repealed by Session Laws 1973, c. 1262, s. 23.

§ 143-214.1. Water; water quality standards and classifications; duties of Commission.

(a) Development and Adoption of Classifications and Standards. - The Commission is hereby directed and empowered, as rapidly as possible within the limits of funds and facilities available to it, and subject to the procedural requirements of this Article:

(1) To develop and adopt, after proper study, a series of classifications and the standards applicable to each such classification, which will be appropriate for the purpose of classifying each of the waters of the State in such a way as to promote the policy and purposes of this Article most effectively;

(2) To survey all the waters of the State and to separately identify all such waters as the Commission believes ought to be classified separately in order to promote the policy and purposes of this Article, omitting only such waters, as in the opinion of the Commission, are insufficiently important to justify classification or control under this Article; and

(3) To assign to each identified water of the State such classification, from the series adopted as specified above, as the Commission deems proper in order to promote the policy and purposes of this Article most effectively.

(b) Criteria for Classification. - In developing and adopting classifications, and the standards applicable to each, the Commission shall recognize that a number of different classifications should be provided for (with different standards applicable to each) so as to give effect to the need for balancing conflicting considerations as to usage and other variable factors; that different classifications with different standards applicable thereto may frequently be appropriate for different segments of the same water; and that each classification and the standards applicable thereto should be adopted with primary reference to the best usage to be made of the waters to which such classification will be assigned.

(c) Criteria for Standards. - In establishing the standards applicable to each classification, the Commission shall consider and the standards when finally adopted and published shall state: the extent to which any physical, chemical, or biological properties should be prescribed as essential to the contemplated best usage.

(d) Criteria for Assignment of Classifications. - In assigning to each identified water the appropriate classifications (with its accompanying standards), the Commission shall consider, and the decision of the Commission when finally adopted and published shall contain its conclusions with respect to the following factors as related to such identified waters:

(1) The size, depth, surface area covered, volume, direction and rate of flow, stream gradient and temperature of the water;

(2) The character of the district bordering said water, including any peculiar suitability such district may have or any dominant economic interest or development which has become established in relation to or by reason of any particular use of such water;

(3) The uses and extent thereof which have been made, are being made, or may in the future be made, of such water for domestic consumption, bathing, fish or wildlife and their culture, industrial consumption, transportation, fire prevention, power generation, scientific or research uses, the disposal of sewage, industrial wastes and other wastes, or any other uses;

(4) In revising existing or adopting new water quality classifications or standards, the Commission shall consider the use and value of State waters for public water supply, propagation of fish and wildlife, recreation, agriculture, industrial and other purposes, use and value for navigation, and shall take into consideration, among other things, an estimate as prepared under section 305(b)(1) of the Federal Water Pollution Control Act amendments of 1972 of the environmental impact, the economic and social costs necessary to achieve the proposed standards, the economic and social benefits of such achievement and an estimate of the date of such achievement;

(5) With regard to the groundwaters, the factors to be considered shall include the natural quality of the water below land surface and the condition of occurrences, recharge, movement and discharge, the vulnerability to pollution from wastewaters and other substances, and the potential for improvement of the quality and quantity of the water.

(e) Chapter 150B of the General Statutes governs the adoption and publication of rules under this Article.

(f), (g) Repealed by Session Laws 1987, c. 827, s. 156.

(1951, c. 606; 1957, c. 1275, s. 2; 1967, c. 892, s. 1; 1969, c. 822, s. 1; 1973, c. 1262, s. 23; 1975, c. 19, s. 50; c. 583, s. 8; c. 655, s. 5; 1977, c. 771, s. 4; 1979, c. 633, s. 6; 1979, 2nd Sess., c. 1199; 1983, c. 296, s. 1; 1987, c. 827, ss. 154, 156.)

§ 143-214.2. Prohibited discharges.

(a) The discharge of any radiological, chemical or biological warfare agent or high-level radioactive waste to the waters of the State is prohibited.

(b) The discharge of any wastes to the subsurface or groundwaters of the State by means of wells is prohibited. This section shall not be construed to prohibit (i) the operation of closed-loop groundwater remediation systems in accordance with G.S. 143-215.1A or (ii) injection of hydraulic fracturing fluid for the exploration or development of natural gas resources.

(c)   Unless permitted by a rule of the Commission, the discharge of wastes, including thermal discharges, to the open waters of the Atlantic Ocean over which the State has jurisdiction are prohibited. (1973, c. 698, s. 2; c. 1262, s. 23; 1987, c. 827, ss. 154, 157; 1991 (Reg. Sess., 1992), c. 786, s. 2; 2012-143, s. 3(b).)

§ 143-214.2A. Prohibited disposal of medical waste.

(a)   Violation. - It is unlawful for any person to engage in conduct which causes or results in the dumping, discharging, or disposal directly or indirectly, of any medical waste as defined in G.S. 130A-290 to the open waters of the Atlantic Ocean over which the State has jurisdiction or to any waters of the State.

(b)   Civil Penalty. -

(1)   A civil penalty of not more than twenty-five thousand dollars ($25,000) may be assessed by the Secretary against any person for a first violation of this section and an additional penalty of twenty-five thousand dollars ($25,000) may be assessed for each day during which the violation continues. A civil penalty of not more than fifty thousand dollars ($50,000) may be assessed by the Secretary for a second or further violation and an additional penalty of fifty thousand dollars ($50,000) may be assessed for each day during which the violation continues.

(2)   In determining the amount of the penalty the Secretary shall consider the factors set out in G.S. 143B-282.1(b). The procedures set out in G.S. 143B-282.1 shall apply to civil penalty assessments that are presented to the Commission for final agency decision.

(3)   The Secretary shall notify any person assessed a civil penalty of the assessment and the specific reasons therefor by registered or certified mail, or by any means authorized by G.S. 1A-1, Rule 4. Contested case petitions shall be filed within 30 days of receipt of the notice of assessment.

(4) Requests for remission of civil penalties shall be filed with the Secretary. Remission requests shall not be considered unless made within 30 days of receipt of the notice of assessment. Remission requests must be accompanied by a waiver of the right to a contested case hearing pursuant to Chapter 150B and a stipulation of the facts on which the assessment was based. Consistent with the limitations in G.S. 143B-282.1(c) and (d), remission requests may be resolved by the Secretary and the violator. If the Secretary and the violator are unable to resolve the request, the Secretary shall deliver remission requests and his recommended action to the Committee on Civil Penalty Remissions of the Environmental Management Commission appointed pursuant to G.S. 143B-282.1(c).

(5) If any civil penalty has not been paid within 30 days after notice of assessment has been served on the violator, the Secretary shall request the Attorney General to institute a civil action in the Superior Court of any county in which the violator resides or has his or its principal place of business to recover the amount of the assessment, unless the violator contests the assessment as provided in subdivision (3) of this subsection, or requests remission of the assessment in whole or in part as provided in subdivision (4) of this subsection. If any civil penalty has not been paid within 30 days after the final agency decision or court order has been served on the violator, the Secretary shall request the Attorney General to institute a civil action in the Superior Court of any county in which the violator resides or has his or its principal place of business to recover the amount of the assessment.

(6) Repealed by Session Laws 1995 (Regular Session, 1996).

(7) The clear proceeds of civil penalties assessed pursuant to this subsection shall be remitted to the Civil Penalty and Forfeiture Fund in accordance with G.S. 115C-457.2.

(c) Criminal Penalties. -

(1) A person who willfully violates this section is guilty of a Class 1 misdemeanor.

(2) A person who willfully violates this section and in so doing releases medical waste that creates a substantial risk of physical injury to any person who is not a participant in the offense is guilty of a Class F felony which may include a fine not to exceed fifty thousand dollars ($50,000) per day of violation.

(d) Restoration. -

(1) Any person having control over medical waste discharged in violation of this section shall immediately undertake to collect, remove, and dispose of the medical waste discharged and to restore the area affected by the discharge as nearly as may be to the condition existing prior to the discharge. If it is not feasible to collect and remove the medical waste, the person responsible shall take all practicable actions and measures to otherwise contain, treat, and disperse the medical waste; but no chemical or other dispersants or treatment materials shall be used for such purposes unless they shall have been previously approved by the Department.

(2) Notwithstanding the requirements of subdivision (1), the Department is authorized and empowered to utilize any staff, equipment and materials under its control or supplied by other cooperating State or local agencies, and to contract with any agent or contractor that it deems appropriate to take such actions as are necessary, to collect, investigate, perform surveillance over, remove, contain, treat or disperse or dispose of medical waste discharged into the waters of the State in violation of this section, and to perform any necessary restoration. The Secretary shall keep a record of all expenses incurred in carrying out any project or activity authorized under this section, including actual expenses incurred for services performed by the State's personnel and for use of the State's equipment and material.

(3) Every person owning or having control over medical waste discharged in violation of, or in circumstances likely to constitute a violation of this section, upon discovery that the discharge of medical waste has occurred, shall immediately notify the Department, or any of its agents or employees, of the nature, location and time of the discharge and of the measures which are being taken or are proposed to be taken to contain, remove, treat and dispose of the medical waste. The agent or employee of the department receiving the notification shall immediately notify the Secretary or such member of the permanent staff of the Department as the Secretary may designate.

(4) Any person who discharges medical waste in violation of this section or violates any order or rule of the Commission regarding the prohibitions concerning medical waste, or fails to perform any duty imposed regarding medical waste, and in the course thereof causes the death of, or injury to fish, animals, vegetation or other resources of the State, or otherwise causes a reduction in the quality of the waters of the State below the standards set by the Commission, or causes the incurring of costs by the State for the containment,

removal, treatment, or dispersal, or disposal of such medical waste, shall be liable to pay the State damages. Such damages shall be an amount equal to the cost of all reasonable and necessary investigations made or caused to be made by the State in connection with such violation and the sum of money necessary to restock such waters, replenish such resources, contain, remove, treat, or disperse, or dispose of such medical waste, or otherwise restore such waters and adjacent lands prior to the injury as such condition is determined by the Commission in conference with the Wildlife Resources Commission, the Marine Fisheries Commission, and any other State agencies having an interest affected by such violation (or by the designees of any such boards, commissions, and agencies).

(5) Upon receipt of the estimate of damages caused, the Department shall give written notice by registered or certified mail to the person responsible for the death, killing, or injury to fish, animals, vegetation, or other resources of the State, or any reduction in quality of the waters of the State, or the costs of the removal, treatment or disposal of such discharge, describing the damages and their causes with reasonable specificity, and shall request payment from such person. Damages shall become due and payable upon receipt of such notice. The Environmental Management Commission, if collection or other settlement of the damages is not obtained within a reasonable time, shall bring a civil action to recover such damages in the superior court in the county in which the discharge of waste or the damages to resources occurred, or in Wake County if the discharge or resource damage occurs in the open waters of the Atlantic Ocean. The assessment of damages is not a contested case under G.S. 150B-23.

(6) "Person having control over medical waste" shall mean, but shall not be limited to, any person using, storing, or transporting medical waste immediately prior to a discharge of such waste into the waters of the State, and specifically shall include carriers and bailees of such medical waste. (1989, c. 742, s. 8; 1989 (Reg. Sess., 1990), c. 1036, s. 9; 1993, c. 539, ss. 1016, 1312; 1994, Ex. Sess., c. 24, s. 14(c); 1995 (Reg. Sess., 1996), c. 743, s. 12; 1998-215, s. 60.)

§ 143-214.2B. Storage of waste on vessels.

The operator of a vessel in the State's waters shall take precautions to ensure that certain items do not enter and contaminate the waters. The operator shall store fuel, oil, paint, varnish, solvent, pesticide, insecticide, fungicide, algicide, or any other hazardous liquid in one or more closed containers that are adequate to prevent the release of the items into the waters of the State. (1993, c. 466, s. 5.)

§ 143-214.3. Revision to water quality standard.

(a) Any person subject to the provisions of G.S. 143-215.1 may petition the Commission for a hearing pursuant to G.S. 143-215.4 for a revision to water quality standards adopted pursuant to G.S. 143-214.1 as such water quality standards may apply to a specific stream segment into which the petitioner discharges or proposes to discharge.

(b) Upon a finding by the Commission that:

(1) Natural background conditions in the stream segment preclude the attainment of the applicable water quality standards; or

(2) Irretrievable and uncontrollable man-induced conditions preclude the attainment of the applicable water quality standards; or

(3) Application of effluent limitations for existing sources established or proposed pursuant to G.S. 143-215.1 more restrictive than those effluent standards and limitations determined or promulgated by the United States Environmental Protection Agency pursuant to section 301 of the Federal Water Pollution Control Act in order to achieve and maintain applicable water quality standards would result in adverse social and economic impact, disproportionate to the benefits to the public health, safety or welfare as a result of maintaining the standards; and

(4) There exists no reasonable relationship between the cost to the petitioner of achieving the effluent limitations necessary to comply with applicable water quality standards to the benefits, including the incremental benefits to the receiving waters, to be obtained from the application of the said effluent limitations;

Then the Commission shall revise the standard or standards, as such standard may apply to the petitioner, provided that such revised standards shall be no less stringent than that which can be achieved by the application of the highest level of treatment which will result in benefits, including the incremental benefits to the receiving waters, having a reasonable relationship to the cost to the petitioner to apply such treatment, as determined by the evidence; provided, however, in no event shall these standards be less stringent than the level attainable with the application by the petitioner of those effluent standards and limitations determined or promulgated by the United States Environmental Protection Agency pursuant to section 301 of the Federal Water Pollution Control Act; provided, further, that no revision shall be granted which would endanger human health or safety. (1979, c. 929; 1987, c. 827, s. 154.)

§ 143-214.4. Certain cleaning agents containing phosphorus prohibited.

(a)   No person may manufacture, store, sell, use, or distribute for sale or use any cleaning agent containing phosphorus in the State, except as otherwise provided in this section.

(b)   As used in this section, "cleaning agent" means a laundry detergent, dishwashing compound, household cleaner, metal cleaner or polish, industrial cleaner, or other substance that is used or intended for use for cleaning purposes.

(c)   This section shall not apply to cleaning agents which are used:

(1)   In agricultural or dairy production;

(2)   To clean commercial food or beverage processing equipment or containers;

(3)   As industrial sanitizers, metal brighteners, or acid cleaners, including those containing phosphoric acid or trisodium phosphate;

(4)   In industrial processes for metal, fabric or fiber cleaning and conditioning;

(5)   In hospitals, clinics, nursing homes, other health care facilities, or veterinary hospitals or clinics;

(6)   By a commercial laundry or textile rental service company or any other commercial entity: (i) to provide laundry service to hospitals, clinics, nursing homes, other health care facilities, or veterinary hospitals or clinics; (ii) to clean

textile products supplied to industrial or commercial users of the products on a rental basis; or (iii) to clean professional, industrial or commercial work uniforms;

(7) In the manufacture of health care or veterinary supplies;

(8) In any medical, biological, chemical, engineering or other such laboratory, including those associated with any academic or research facility;

(9) As water softeners, antiscale agents, or corrosion inhibitors, where such use is in a closed system such as a boiler, air conditioner, cooling tower, or hot water heating system;

(10) To clean hard surfaces including windows, sinks, counters, floors, ovens, food preparation surfaces, and plumbing fixtures.

(d) This section shall not apply to cleaning agents which:

(1) Contain phosphorus in an amount not exceeding five-tenths of one percent (0.5%) by weight which is incidental to manufacturing;

(2) Contain phosphorus in an amount not exceeding eight and seven-tenths percent (8.7%) by weight and which are intended for use in a commercial or household dishwashing machine;

(3) Are manufactured, stored, sold, or distributed for use solely outside the State.

(e) The Commission may permit the use of a cleaning agent which contains phosphorus in an amount exceeding five-tenths of one percent (0.5%) but not exceeding eight and seven-tenths percent (8.7%) by weight upon a finding that there is no adequate substitute for such cleaning agent, or that compliance with this section would otherwise be unreasonable or create a significant hardship on the user. The Commission shall adopt rules to administer this subsection.

(f) Any person who manufactures, sells or distributes any cleaning agent in violation of this section shall be guilty of a Class 3 misdemeanor punishable only by a fine not to exceed fifty dollars ($50.00).

(g) Any person who uses any cleaning agent in violation of the provisions of this section shall be responsible for an infraction for which the sanction is a penalty of not more than ten dollars ($10.00). Notwithstanding G.S. 14-3.1(a), the clear proceeds of infractions pursuant to this section shall be remitted to the Civil Penalty and Forfeiture Fund in accordance with G.S. 115C-457.2. (1987, c. 111, s. 1; c. 817; c. 827, s. 154; 1993, c. 539, s. 1017; 1994, Ex. Sess., c. 24, s. 14(c); 1998-215, s. 61; 2006-203, s. 88.)

§ 143-214.5. Water supply watershed protection.

(a)   Policy Statement. - This section provides for a cooperative program of water supply watershed management and protection to be administered by local governments consistent with minimum statewide management requirements established by the Commission. If a local government fails to adopt a water supply watershed protection program or does not adequately carry out its responsibility to enforce the minimum water supply watershed management requirements of its approved program, the Commission shall administer and enforce the minimum statewide requirements. The reduction of agricultural nonpoint source discharges shall be accomplished primarily through the Agriculture Cost Share Program for Nonpoint Source Pollution Control.

(b)   Development and Adoption of Water Supply Watershed Classifications and Management Requirements. - The Commission shall adopt rules for the classification of water supply watersheds and that establish minimum statewide water supply watershed protection requirements applicable to each classification to protect surface water supplies by (i) controlling development density, (ii) providing for performance-based alternatives to development density controls that are based on sound engineering principles, or (iii) a combination of both (i) and (ii). The Commission may designate water supply watersheds or portions thereof as critical water supply watersheds and impose management requirements that are more stringent than the minimum statewide water supply watershed management requirements. The Commission may adopt rules that require that any permit issued by a local government for a development or construction activity conducted by that local government within a designated water supply watershed be approved by the Department prior to issuance. Any variance from the minimum statewide water supply watershed management requirements must be approved by the Commission prior to the issuance of a permit by a local government. Except as provided by G.S. 153A-347 and G.S. 160A-392, the power to implement this section with respect to development or construction activities that are conducted by State agencies is vested exclusively in the Commission.

(c) Classification of Water Supply Watersheds. - The Commission shall assign to each water supply watershed in the State the appropriate classification with the applicable minimum management requirements. The Commission may reclassify water supply watersheds as necessary to protect future water supplies or improve protection at existing water supplies. A local government shall not be required to submit a revised water supply watershed protection program to the Commission earlier than 270 days after it receives notice of a reclassification from the Commission.

(d) Mandatory Local Programs. - The Department shall assist local governments to develop water supply watershed protection programs that comply with this section. Local government compliance programs shall include an implementing local ordinance and shall provide for maintenance, inspection, and enforcement procedures. As part of its assistance to local governments, the Commission shall approve and make available a model local water supply watershed management and protection ordinance. The model management and protection ordinance adopted by the Commission shall, at a minimum, include as options (i) controlling development density, (ii) providing for performance-based alternatives to development density controls that are based on sound engineering principles, and (iii) a combination of both (i) and (ii). Local governments shall administer and enforce the minimum management requirements. Every local government that has within its jurisdiction all or a portion of a water supply watershed shall submit a local water supply watershed management and protection ordinance to the Commission for approval. Local governments may adopt such ordinances pursuant to their general police power, power to regulate the subdivision of land, zoning power, or any combination of such powers. In adopting a local ordinance that imposes water supply watershed management requirements that are more stringent than those adopted by the Commission, a county must comply with the notice provisions of G.S. 153A-343 and a municipality must comply with the notice provisions of G.S. 160A-384. This section shall not be construed to affect the validity of any local ordinance adopted for the protection of water supply watersheds prior to completion of the review of the ordinance by the Commission or prior to the assumption by the Commission of responsibility for a local water supply watershed protection program. Local governments may create or designate agencies to administer and enforce such programs. The Commission shall approve a local program only if it determines that the requirements of the program equal or exceed the minimum statewide water supply watershed management requirements adopted pursuant to this section.

(d1) A local ordinance adopted to implement the minimum statewide water supply watershed management requirements applicable to agriculture and silviculture activities shall be no more restrictive than those adopted by the Commission. In adopting minimum statewide water supply watershed management requirements applicable to agriculture activities, the Commission shall consider the policy regarding agricultural nonpoint source discharges set out in subsection (a) of this section. The Commission may by rule designate another State agency to administer the minimum statewide water supply watershed management requirements applicable to agriculture and silviculture activities. If the Commission designates another State agency to administer the minimum statewide water supply watershed management requirements applicable to agriculture and silviculture activities, management requirements adopted by local governments shall not apply to such activities.

(d2) A local government implementing a water supply watershed program shall allow an applicant to average development density on up to two noncontiguous properties for purposes of achieving compliance with the water supply watershed development standards if all of the following circumstances exist:

(1) The properties are within the same water supply watershed. If one of the properties is located in the critical area of the watershed, the critical area property shall not be developed beyond the applicable density requirements for its classification.

(2) Overall project density meets applicable density or stormwater control requirements under 15A NCAC 2B .0200.

(3) Vegetated buffers on both properties meet the minimum statewide water supply watershed protection requirements.

(4) Built upon areas are designed and located to minimize stormwater runoff impact to the receiving waters, minimize concentrated stormwater flow, maximize the use of sheet flow through vegetated areas, and maximize the flow length through vegetated areas.

(5) Areas of concentrated density development are located in upland areas and, to the maximum extent practicable, away from surface waters and drainageways.

(6) The property or portions of the properties that are not being developed will remain in a vegetated or natural state and will be managed by a homeowners' association as common area, conveyed to a local government as a park or greenway, or placed under a permanent conservation or farmland preservation easement unless it can be demonstrated that the local government can ensure long-term compliance through deed restrictions and an electronic permitting mechanism. A metes and bounds description of the areas to remain vegetated and limits on use shall be recorded on the subdivision plat, in homeowners' covenants, and on individual deed and shall be irrevocable.

(7) Development permitted under density averaging and meeting applicable low density requirements shall transport stormwater runoff by vegetated conveyances to the maximum extent practicable.

(8) A special use permit or other such permit or certificate shall be obtained from the local Watershed Review Board or Board of Adjustment to ensure that both properties considered together meet the standards of the watershed ordinance and that potential owners have record of how the watershed regulations were applied to the properties.

(e) Assumption of Local Programs. - The Commission shall assume responsibility for water supply watershed protection, within all or the affected portion of a water supply watershed, if a local government fails to adopt a program that meets the requirements of this section or whenever a local government fails to adequately administer and enforce the provisions of its program. The Commission shall not assume responsibility for an approved local water supply watershed protection program until it or its designee notifies the local government in writing by certified mail, return receipt requested, of local program deficiencies, recommendations for changes and improvements in the local program, and the deadline for compliance. The Commission shall allow a local government a minimum of 120 days to bring its program into compliance. The Commission shall order assumption of an approved local program if it finds that the local government has made no substantial progress toward compliance. The Commission may make such finding at any time between 120 days and 365 days after receipt of notice under this subsection by the local government, with no further notice. Proceedings to review such orders by the Commission shall be conducted by the superior court pursuant to Article 4 of Chapter 150B of the General Statutes based on the agency record submitted to the Commission by the Secretary.

(f) State Enforcement Authority. - The Commission may take any appropriate preventive or remedial enforcement action authorized by this Part against any person who violates any minimum statewide water supply watershed management requirement.

(g) Civil Penalties. - A local government that fails to adopt a local water supply watershed protection program as required by this section or willfully fails to administer or enforce the provisions of its program in substantial compliance with the minimum statewide water supply watershed management requirements shall be subject to a civil penalty pursuant to G.S. 143-215.6A(e). In any area of the State that is not covered by an approved local water supply watershed protection program, any person who violates or fails to act in accordance with any minimum statewide water supply watershed management requirement or more stringent management requirement adopted by the Commission for a critical water supply watershed established pursuant to this section shall be subject to a civil penalty as specified in G.S. 143-215.6A(a)(7).

The clear proceeds of civil penalties provided for in this section shall be remitted to the Civil Penalty and Forfeiture Fund in accordance with G.S. 115C-457.2.

(h) Planning Grants to Local Governments. - The Secretary may make annual grants to local governments for the purpose of assisting in the development of local water supply watershed protection programs. The Secretary shall develop and administer generally applicable criteria under which local governments may qualify for such assistance. Such criteria shall give priority to local governments that are not then administering zoning ordinances in affected water supply watershed areas.

(i) Every State agency shall act in a manner consistent with the policies and purposes of this section, and shall comply with the minimum statewide water supply watershed management requirements adopted by the Commission and with all water supply watershed management and protection ordinances adopted by local governments. (1989, c. 426, s. 1; 1991, c. 342, s. 9; c. 471, s. 2; c. 579, s. 1; 1991 (Reg. Sess., 1992), c. 890, s. 14; 1998-215, s. 62; 2012-200, s. 7.)

§ 143-214.6: Repealed by Session Laws 2004-195, s. 3.1, effective August 17, 2004.

§ 143-214.7. Stormwater runoff rules and programs.

(a) Policy, Purpose and Intent. - The Commission shall undertake a continuing planning process to develop and adopt a statewide plan with regard to establishing and enforcing stormwater rules for the purpose of protecting the surface waters of the State. It is the purpose and intent of this section that, in developing stormwater runoff rules and programs, the Commission may utilize stormwater rules established by the Commission to protect classified shellfish waters, water supply watersheds, and outstanding resource waters; and to control stormwater runoff disposal in coastal counties and other nonpoint sources. Further, it is the intent of this section that the Commission phase in the stormwater rules on a priority basis for all sources of pollution to the water. The plan shall be applied evenhandedly throughout the State to address the State's water quality needs. The Commission shall continually monitor water quality in the State and shall revise stormwater runoff rules as necessary to protect water quality. As necessary, the stormwater rules shall be modified to comply with federal regulations.

(b) The Commission shall implement stormwater runoff rules and programs for point and nonpoint sources on a phased-in statewide basis. The Commission shall consider standards and best management practices for the protection of the State's water resources in the following order of priority:

(1) Classified shellfish waters.

(2) Water supply watersheds.

(3) Outstanding resource waters.

(4) High quality waters.

(5) All other waters of the State to the extent that the Commission finds control of stormwater is needed to meet the purposes of this Article.

(b1) The Commission shall develop model practices for incorporation of stormwater capture and reuse into stormwater management programs and shall make information on those model practices available to State agencies and local governments.

(b2) For purposes of implementing stormwater programs, "built-upon area" means impervious surface and partially impervious surface to the extent that the partially impervious surface does not allow water to infiltrate through the surface and into the subsoil. "Built-upon area" does not include a wooden slatted deck, the water area of a swimming pool, or gravel.

(c) The Commission shall develop model stormwater management programs that may be implemented by State agencies and units of local government. Model stormwater management programs shall be developed to protect existing water uses and assure compliance with water quality standards and classifications. A State agency or unit of local government may submit to the Commission for its approval a stormwater control program for implementation within its jurisdiction. To this end, State agencies may adopt rules, and units of local government are authorized to adopt ordinances and regulations necessary to establish and enforce stormwater control programs. Units of local government are authorized to create or designate agencies or subdivisions to administer and enforce the programs. Two or more units of local government are authorized to establish a joint program and to enter into any agreements that are necessary for the proper administration and enforcement of the program.

(c1) Any land-use restriction providing for the maintenance of stormwater best management practices or site consistency with approved stormwater project plans filed pursuant to a rule of the Commission, local ordinance, or permit approved by the Commission shall be enforced by any owner of the land on which the best management practice or project is located, any adjacent property owners, any downstream property owners who would be injured by failure to enforce the land-use restriction, any local government having jurisdiction over any part of the land on which the best management practice or project is located, or the Department through the remedies provided by any provision of law that is implemented or enforced by the Department or by means of a civil action, without first having exhausted any available administrative remedies. A land-use restriction providing for the maintenance of stormwater best management practices or site consistency with approved stormwater project plans filed pursuant to a rule of the Commission, local ordinance, or permit approved by the Commission shall not be declared unenforceable due to lack of privity of estate or contract, due to lack of benefit to particular land, or due to lack of any property interest in particular land. Any person who owns or leases a property subject to a land-use restriction under this section shall abide by the land-use restriction.

(c2) The Department shall transfer a permit issued under this section for a stormwater management system from the declarant of a condominium or a planned community to the unit owners association, owners association, or other management entity identified in the condominium or planned community's declaration upon request of a permittee if the Department finds that (i) common areas related to the operation and maintenance of the stormwater management system have been conveyed to the unit owners association or owners association in accordance with the declaration; (ii) the declarant has conveyed at least fifty percent (50%) of the units or lots to owners other than a declarant; and (iii) the stormwater management system is in substantial compliance with the stormwater permit issued to the permittee by the Department. In support of a request made pursuant to this subsection, a permittee shall submit documentation to the Department sufficient to demonstrate that ownership of the common area related to the operation and maintenance of the stormwater management system has been conveyed from the declarant to the association and that the declarant has conveyed at least fifty percent (50%) of the units or lots to owners other than a declarant. For purposes of this subsection, declarant of a condominium shall have the same meaning as provided in Chapter 47C of the General Statutes, and declarant of a planned community shall have the same meaning as provided in Chapter 47F of the General Statutes.

(c3) In accordance with the Federal Aviation Administration August 28, 2007, Advisory Circular No. 150/5200-33B (Hazardous Wildlife Attractants on or Near Airports), the Department shall not require the use of stormwater retention ponds, stormwater detention ponds, or any other stormwater control measure that promotes standing water in order to comply with this section at public airports that support commercial air carriers or general aviation services. Development projects located within five statute miles from the farthest edge of an airport air operations area, as that term is defined in 14 C.F.R. § 153.3 (July 2011 Edition), shall not be required to use stormwater retention ponds, stormwater detention ponds, or any other stormwater control measure that promotes standing water in order to comply with this section. Existing stormwater retention ponds, stormwater detention ponds, or any other stormwater control measure that promotes standing water in order to comply with this section located at public airports or that are within five statute miles from the farthest edge of an airport operations area may be replaced with alternative measures included in the Division of Water Resources' Best Management Practice Manual chapter on airports. In order to be approved by the Department, alternative measures or management designs that are not expressly included in the Division of Water Resources' Best Management Practice Manual shall provide for equal or better stormwater control based on the pre- and post-development hydrograph. Any replacement of existing stormwater retention ponds, stormwater detention ponds, or any other stormwater control measure that promotes standing water shall be considered a minor modification to the State general stormwater permit.

(c4) The Department shall deem runways, taxiways, and any other areas that provide for overland stormwater flow that promote infiltration and treatment of stormwater into grassed buffers, shoulders, and grass swales permitted pursuant to the State post-construction stormwater requirements.

(c5) The Department may transfer a permit issued pursuant to this section without the consent of the permit holder to a successor-owner of the property on which the permitted activity is occurring or will occur as provided in this subsection:

(1) The Department may transfer a permit if all of the following conditions are met:

a. The successor-owner of the property submits to the Department a written request for the transfer of the permit.

b. The Department finds all of the following:

1. The permit holder is one of the following:

I. A natural person who is deceased.

II. A partnership, limited liability corporation, corporation, or any other business association that has been dissolved.

III. A person who has been lawfully and finally divested of title to the property on which the permitted activity is occurring or will occur.

IV. A person who has sold the property on which the permitted activity is occurring or will occur.

2. The successor-owner holds title to the property on which the permitted activity is occurring or will occur.

3. The successor-owner is the sole claimant of the right to engage in the permitted activity.

4. There will be no substantial change in the permitted activity.

(2) The permit holder shall comply with all terms and conditions of the permit until such time as the permit is transferred.

(3) The successor-owner shall comply with all terms and conditions of the permit once the permit has been transferred.

(4) Notwithstanding changes to law made after the original issuance of the permit, the Department may not impose new or different terms and conditions in the permit without the prior express consent of the successor-owner.

(d) The Commission shall review each stormwater management program submitted by a State agency or unit of local government and shall notify the State agency or unit of local government that submitted the program that the program has been approved, approved with modifications, or disapproved. The Commission shall approve a program only if it finds that the standards of the program equal or exceed those of the model program adopted by the Commission pursuant to this section.

(d1) Repealed by Session Laws 2013-265, s. 19, effective July 17, 2013.

(d2) Repealed by Session Laws 2008-198, s. 8(a), effective August 8, 2008.

(e) On or before October 1 of each year, the Commission shall report to the Environmental Review Commission on the implementation of this section, including the status of any stormwater control programs administered by State agencies and units of local government. The status report shall include information on any integration of stormwater capture and reuse into stormwater control programs administered by State agencies and units of local government. (1989, c. 447, s. 2; 1995, c. 507, s. 27.8(q); 1997-458, s. 7.1; 2004-124, s. 6.29(a); 2006-246, s. 16(b); 2007-323, s. 6.22(a); 2008-198, s. 8(a); 2011-256, s. 1; 2011-394, s. 6; 2012-200, ss. 1, 6; 2013-121, s. 1; 2013-265, s. 19; 2013-413, ss. 51(a), 57(h).)

§ 143-214.7A. Stormwater control best management practices.

(a) The Department of Environment and Natural Resources shall establish standard stormwater control best management practices and standard process water treatment processes or equivalent performance standards for composting operations that are required to be permitted by the Division of Water Resources in the Department and the Division of Waste Management in the Department. These practices, processes, and standards shall be developed for the purpose of protecting water quality by controlling and containing stormwater that is associated with composting operations, by reducing the pollutant levels of process water from composting operations, and by reducing the opportunities for generation of such waters.

(b) Unless otherwise provided in this subsection, the Division of Water Resources shall clarify that stormwater is water that does not contact anything considered a feedstock, intermediate product, or final product of composting operations. Unless otherwise provided in this subsection, the Division of Water Resources shall clarify that wastewater is leachate and water that contacts feedstocks, intermediate products, or final product, of composting operations. The clarifications shall incorporate available scientifically valid information obtained from sampling and analyses of North Carolina composting facilities and from valid representative data from other states. In addition, the Division of Water Resources shall establish threshold quantities of feedstocks, intermediate products, and final products above which water quality permitting will be required. A Type 1 solid waste compost facility shall be subject only to applicable State stormwater requirements and federal stormwater requirements established pursuant to 33 U.S.C. § 1342(p)(3)(B). A Type 1 solid waste compost facility shall not be required to obtain a National Pollutant Discharge Elimination System (NPDES) permit for discharge of process wastewater based solely on the discharge of stormwater that has come into contact with feedstock, intermediate product, or final product at the facility. For purposes of this section, "Type 1 solid waste compost facilities" are facilities that may receive yard and garden waste, silvicultural waste, untreated and unpainted wood waste, or any combination thereof.

(c) The Department shall establish revised water quality permitting procedures for the composting industry. The revised permitting procedures shall identify the various circumstances that determine which water quality permit is required for various composting activities. The Department shall determine whether selected low-risk subsets of the composting industry may be suitable for expedited or reduced water quality permitting procedures. The determination shall include consideration of the economic impact of regulatory decisions.

(d) In developing the practices, processes, and standards and the revised water quality permitting procedures required by this section, the Department shall review practices, processes, and standards and permitting procedures adopted by other states and similar federal programs.

(e) The Department shall form a Compost Operation Stakeholder Advisory Group composed of representatives from the North Carolina Chapter of the United States Composting Council, the North Carolina Association of County Commissioners, the North Carolina League of Municipalities, the North Carolina State Agricultural Extension Service, the North Carolina Chapter of the American Water Works Association-Water Environment Federation, the North Carolina Pumper Group, the North Carolina Chapter of the Solid Waste Association of North America, the North Carolina Septic Tank Association, and any individual or group commenting to the Department on issues related to water quality at composting operations. The Compost Operation Stakeholder Advisory Group shall be convened periodically to provide input and assistance to the Department.

(f) The practices, processes, and standards and the revised permitting procedures shall address the site size of an operation, the nature of the feedstocks composted, the type of compost production method employed, the quantity and water quality of the stormwater or process water associated with composting facilities, the water quality of the receiving waters, as well as operation and maintenance requirements for the resulting standard stormwater control best management practices and standard process water treatment processes. (2009-322, s. 1(a)-(f); 2011-394, s. 7; 2012-200, s. 5; 2013-413, s. 57(i), (bb).)

§ 143-214.7B. Fast-track permitting for stormwater management systems.

The Commission shall adopt rules to establish a fast-track permitting process that allows for the issuance of stormwater management system permits without a technical review when the permit applicant (i) complies with the Minimum Design Criteria for stormwater management developed by the Department and (ii) submits a permit application prepared by a qualified professional. In developing the rules, the Commission shall consult with a technical working group that consists of industry experts, engineers, environmental consultants, relevant faculty from The University of North Carolina, and other interested stakeholders. The rules shall, at a minimum, provide for all of the following:

(1) A process for permit application, review, and determination.

(2)   The types of professionals that are qualified to prepare a permit application submitted pursuant to this section and the types of qualifications such professionals must have.

(3)   A process for ensuring compliance with the Minimum Design Criteria.

(4)   That permits issued pursuant to the fast-track permitting process comply with State water quality standards adopted pursuant to G.S. 143-214.1, 143-214.7, and 143-215.3(a)(1).

(5)   A process for establishing the liability of a qualified professional who prepares a permit application for a stormwater management system that fails to comply with the Minimum Design Criteria. (2013-82, s. 2.)

§ 143-214.8. Ecosystem Enhancement Program: established.

The Ecosystem Enhancement Program is established within the Department of Environment and Natural Resources. The Ecosystem Enhancement Program shall be developed by the Department as a nonregulatory statewide ecosystem enhancement program for the acquisition, maintenance, restoration, enhancement, and creation of wetland and riparian resources that contribute to the protection and improvement of water quality, flood prevention, fisheries, wildlife habitat, and recreational opportunities. The Ecosystem Enhancement Program shall consist of the following components:

(1)   Restoration and perpetual maintenance of wetlands.

(2)   Development of restoration plans.

(3)   Landowner contact and land acquisition.

(4)   Evaluation of site plans and engineering studies.

(5)   Oversight of construction and monitoring of restoration sites.

(6)   Land ownership and management.

(7)   Mapping, site identification, and assessment of wetlands functions.

(8) Oversight of private wetland mitigation banks to facilitate the components of the Ecosystem Enhancement Program. (1996, 2nd Ex. Sess., c. 18, s. 27.4(a); 1997-443, s. 11A.119(a); 2005-386, s. 3.1.)

§ 143-214.9. Ecosystem Enhancement Program: purposes.

The purposes of the program are as follows:

(1) To restore wetlands functions and values across the State to replace critical functions lost through historic wetlands conversion and through current and future permitted impacts. It is not the policy of the State to destroy upland habitats unless it would further the purposes of the Wetlands Restoration Program.

(2) To provide a consistent and simplified approach to address mitigation requirements associated with permits or authorizations issued by the United States Army Corps of Engineers under 33 U.S.C. § 1344.

(3) To streamline the wetlands permitting process, minimize delays in permit decisions, and decrease the burden of permit applicants of planning and performing compensatory mitigation for wetlands losses.

(4) To increase the ecological effectiveness of compensatory mitigation.

(5) To achieve a net increase in wetland acres, functions, and values in each major river basin.

(6) To foster a comprehensive approach to environmental protection. (1996, 2nd Ex. Sess., c. 18, s. 27.4(a); 2005-386, s. 3.2.)

§ 143-214.10. Ecosystem Enhancement Program: development and implementation of basinwide restoration plans.

Develop Basinwide Restoration Plans. - The Department shall develop basinwide plans for wetlands and riparian area restoration with the goal of protecting and enhancing water quality, flood prevention, fisheries, wildlife habitat, and recreational opportunities within each of the 17 major river basins in the State. The Department shall develop and implement a basinwide restoration plan for each of the 17 river basins in the State in accordance with the basinwide schedule currently established by the Division of Water Resources. (1996, 2nd Ex. Sess., c. 18, s. 27.4(a); 2005-386, s. 3.3; 2013-413, s. 57(j).)

§ 143-214.11. Ecosystem Enhancement Program: compensatory mitigation.

(a) Definitions. - The following definitions apply to this section:

(1) Compensatory mitigation. - The restoration, creation, enhancement, or preservation of jurisdictional waters required as a condition of a permit issued by the Department or by the United States Army Corps of Engineers.

(1a) Compensatory mitigation bank. - A private compensatory mitigation bank or an existing local compensatory mitigation bank.

(1b) Existing local compensatory mitigation bank. - A mitigation bank operated by a unit of local government that is a party to a mitigation banking instrument executed on or before July 1, 2011, notwithstanding subsequent amendments to such instrument executed after July 1, 2011.

(2) Government entity. - The State and its agencies and subdivisions, or the federal government. "Government entity" does not include a unit of local government unless the unit of local government was a party to a mitigation banking instrument executed on or before July 1, 2011, notwithstanding subsequent amendments to such instrument executed after July 1, 2011.

(3) Hydrologic area. - An eight-digit Cataloging Unit designated by the United States Geological Survey.

(4) Jurisdictional waters. - Wetlands, streams, or other waters of the State or of the United States.

(4a) Mitigation banking instrument. - The legal document for the establishment, operation, and use of a mitigation bank.

(4b) Private compensatory mitigation bank. - A site created by a private compensatory mitigation provider and approved for mitigation credit by State and federal regulatory authorities through execution of a mitigation banking instrument. No site owned by a government entity or unit of local government shall be considered a "private compensatory mitigation bank."

(5) Unit of local government. - A "local government," "public authority," or "special district" as defined in G.S. 159-7.

(b) Department to Coordinate Compensatory Mitigation. - All compensatory mitigation required by permits or authorizations issued by the Department or by the United States Army Corps of Engineers shall be coordinated by the Department consistent with the basinwide restoration plans and rules developed by the Environmental Management Commission. All compensatory mitigation, whether performed by the Department or by permit applicants, shall be consistent with the basinwide restoration plans. All compensatory mitigation shall be consistent with rules adopted by the Commission for wetland and stream mitigation and for protection and maintenance of riparian buffers.

(c) Compensatory Mitigation Emphasis on Replacing Ecological Function Within Same River Basin. - The emphasis of compensatory mitigation is on replacing functions within the same river basin unless it is demonstrated that restoration of other areas would be more beneficial to the overall purposes of the Ecosystem Enhancement Program.

(d) Compensatory Mitigation Options Available to Government Entities. - A government entity may satisfy compensatory mitigation requirements by the following actions, if those actions are consistent with the basinwide restoration plans and also meet or exceed the requirements of the Department or of the United States Army Corps of Engineers, as applicable:

(1) Payment of a fee established by the Commission into the Ecosystem Restoration Fund established in G.S. 143-214.12.

(2) Donation of land to the Ecosystem Enhancement Program or to other public or private nonprofit conservation organizations as approved by the Department.

(3) Participation in a compensatory mitigation bank that has been approved by the United States Army Corps of Engineers, provided that the Department or the United States Army Corps of Engineers, as applicable, approves the use of such bank for the required compensatory mitigation.

(4) Preparing and implementing a compensatory mitigation plan.

(d1) Compensatory Mitigation Options Available to Applicants Other than Government Entities. - An applicant other than a government entity may satisfy compensatory mitigation requirements by the following actions, if those actions meet or exceed the requirements of the United States Army Corps of Engineers:

(1) Participation in a compensatory mitigation bank that has been approved by the United States Army Corps of Engineers, provided that the Department or the United States Army Corps of Engineers, as applicable, approves the use of such bank for the required compensatory mitigation. This option is only available in a hydrologic area where there is at least one compensatory mitigation bank that has been approved by the United States Army Corps of Engineers.

(2) Payment of a fee established by the Commission into the Ecosystem Restoration Fund established in G.S. 143-214.12. - This option is only available to an applicant who demonstrates that the option under subdivision (1) of this subsection is not available.

(3) Donation of land to the Ecosystem Enhancement Program or to other public or private nonprofit conservation organizations as approved by the Department.

(4) Preparing and implementing a compensatory mitigation plan.

(e) Payment Schedule. - A standardized schedule of compensatory mitigation payment amounts shall be established by the Commission. Compensatory mitigation payments shall be made by applicants to the Ecosystem Restoration Fund established in G.S. 143-214.12. The monetary payment shall be based on the ecological functions and values of wetlands and streams permitted to be lost and on the cost of restoring or creating wetlands and streams capable of performing the same or similar functions, including directly related costs of wetland and stream restoration planning, long-term monitoring, and maintenance of restored areas. Compensatory mitigation payments for wetlands shall be calculated on a per acre basis. Compensatory mitigation payments for streams shall be calculated on a per linear foot basis.

(f) Mitigation Banks. - State agencies and mitigation banks shall demonstrate that adequate, dedicated financial surety exists to provide for the perpetual land management and hydrological maintenance of lands acquired by the State as mitigation banks, or proposed to the State as privately operated and permitted mitigation banks.

(g) Payment for Taxes. - A State agency acquiring land to restore, enhance, preserve, or create wetlands must also pay a sum in lieu of ad valorem taxes lost by the county in accordance with G.S. 146-22.3.

(h) Sale of Mitigation Credits by Existing Local Compensatory Mitigation Bank. - An existing local compensatory mitigation bank shall comply with the requirements of Article 12 of Chapter 160A of the General Statutes applicable to the disposal of property whenever it transfers any mitigation credits to another person.

(i) The Ecosystem Enhancement Program shall exercise its authority to provide for compensatory mitigation under the authority granted by this section to use mitigation procurement programs in the following order of preference:

(1) Full delivery/bank credit purchase program. - The Ecosystem Enhancement Program shall first seek to meet compensatory mitigation procurement requirements through the Program's full delivery program or by the purchase of credits from a private compensatory mitigation bank.

(2) Existing local compensatory mitigation bank credit purchase program. - Any compensatory mitigation procurement requirements that are not fulfillable under subdivision (1) of this subsection shall be procured from an existing local compensatory mitigation bank, provided that the credit purchase is made to mitigate the impacts of a project located within the mitigation bank service area and hydrologic area of the existing local compensatory mitigation bank.

(3) Design/build program. - Any compensatory mitigation procurement requirements that are not fulfillable under subdivision (1) or (2) of this subsection shall be procured under a program in which Ecosystem Enhancement Program contracts with one private entity to lead or implement the design, construction, and postconstruction monitoring of compensatory mitigation at sites obtained by the Ecosystem Enhancement Program. Such a program shall be considered the procurement of compensatory mitigation credits.

(4) Design-bid-build program. - Any compensatory mitigation procurement requirements that are not fulfillable under either subdivision (1) or (2) of this subsection may be procured under the Ecosystem Enhancement Program's design-bid-build program. The Ecosystem Enhancement Program may utilize this program only when procurement under subdivision (1) or (2) of this subsection is not feasible. Any mitigation site design work currently being

performed through contracts awarded under the design-bid-build program shall be allowed to continue as scheduled. Contracts for construction of projects with a design already approved by the Ecosystem Enhancement Program shall be awarded by the Ecosystem Enhancement Program by issuing a Request for Proposal (RFP). Only contractors who have prequalified under procedures established by the Ecosystem Enhancement Program shall be eligible to bid on Ecosystem Enhancement Program construction projects. Construction contracts issued under this subdivision shall be exempt from the requirements of Article 8B of Chapter 143 of the General Statutes.

(j) The regulatory requirements for the establishment, operation, and monitoring of a compensatory mitigation bank or full delivery project shall vest at the time of the execution of the mitigation banking instrument or the award of a full delivery contract. (1996, 2nd Ex. Sess., c. 18, s. 27.4(a); 1997-443, s. 11A.119(a); 2004-188, s. 2; 2005-386, s. 3.4; 2008-152, s. 1; 2009-337, s. 1; 2011-343, s. 1.1; 2012-201, s. 5(a).)

§ 143-214.12. Ecosystem Enhancement Program: Ecosystem Restoration Fund.

(a) Ecosystem Restoration Fund. - The Ecosystem Restoration Fund is established as a nonreverting fund within the Department. The Fund shall be treated as a special trust fund and shall be credited with interest by the State Treasurer pursuant to G.S. 147-69.2 and G.S. 147-69.3. The Ecosystem Restoration Fund shall provide a repository for monetary contributions and donations or dedications of interests in real property to promote projects for the restoration, enhancement, preservation, or creation of wetlands and riparian areas and for payments made in lieu of compensatory mitigation as described in subsection (b) of this section. No funds shall be expended from this Fund for any purpose other than those directly contributing to the acquisition, perpetual maintenance, enhancement, restoration, or creation of wetlands and riparian areas in accordance with the basinwide plan as described in G.S. 143-214.10. The cost of acquisition includes a payment in lieu of ad valorem taxes required under G.S. 146-22.3 when the Department is the State agency making the acquisition.

(a1) The Department may distribute funds from the Ecosystem Restoration Fund directly to a federal or State agency, a local government, or a private, nonprofit conservation organization to acquire, manage, and maintain real property or an interest in real property for the purposes set out in subsection (a) of this section. A recipient of funds under this subsection shall grant a conservation easement in the real property or interest in real property acquired with the funds to the Department in a form that is acceptable to the Department. The Department may convey real property or an interest in real property that has been acquired under the Ecosystem Enhancement Program to a federal or State agency, a local government, or a private, nonprofit conservation organization to acquire, manage, and maintain real property or an interest in real property for the purposes set out in subsection (a) of this section. A grantee of real property or an interest in real property under this subsection shall grant a conservation easement in the real property or interest in real property to the Department in a form that is acceptable to the Department.

(b) Authorized Methods of Payment. - A person subject to a permit or authorization issued by the United States Army Corps of Engineers under 33 U.S.C. § 1344 may contribute to the Ecosystem Enhancement Program in order to comply with conditions to, or terms of, the permit or authorization if participation in the Ecosystem Enhancement Program will meet the mitigation requirements of the United States Army Corps of Engineers. The Department shall, at the discretion of the applicant, accept payment into the Ecosystem Restoration Fund in lieu of other compensatory mitigation requirements of any authorizations issued by the United States Army Corps of Engineers under 33 U.S.C. § 1344 if the contributions will meet the mitigation requirements of the United States Army Corps of Engineers. Payment may be made in the form of monetary contributions according to a fee schedule established by the Environmental Management Commission or in the form of donations of real property provided that the property is approved by the Department as a suitable site consistent with the basinwide wetlands restoration plan.

(c) Accounting of Payments. - The Department shall provide an itemized statement that accounts for each payment into the Fund. The statement shall include the expenses and activities financed by the payment. (1996, 2nd Ex. Sess., c. 18, s. 27.4(a); 1997-496, s. 13; 1999-329, s. 6.1; 2004-188, s. 3; 2005-386, s. 3.5.)

§ 143-214.13. Ecosystem Enhancement Program: reporting requirement.

(a) The Department of Environment and Natural Resources shall report each year by November 1 to the Environmental Review Commission and to the

Joint Legislative Commission on Governmental Operations regarding its progress in implementing the Ecosystem Enhancement Program and its use of the funds in the Ecosystem Restoration Fund. The report shall document statewide wetlands losses and gains and compensatory mitigation performed under G.S. 143-214.8 through G.S. 143-214.12. The report shall also provide an accounting of receipts and disbursements of the Ecosystem Restoration Fund, an analysis of the per-acre cost of wetlands restoration, and a cost comparison on a per-acre basis between the State's Ecosystem Enhancement Program and private mitigation banks. The Department shall also send a copy of its report to the Fiscal Research Division of the General Assembly.

(b) The Department shall maintain an inventory of all property that is held, managed, maintained, enhanced, restored, or used to create wetlands under the Ecosystem Enhancement Program. The inventory shall also list all conservation easements held by the Department. The inventory shall be included in the annual report required under subsection (a) of this section. (1996, 2nd Ex. Sess., c. 18, s. 27.4(a); 1997-443, s. 11A.119(a); 1999-329, s. 6.2; 2005-386, s. 3.6; 2010-142, s. 3.)

§ 143-214.14. Cooperative State-local coalition water quality protection plans.

(a) Definitions. - The following definitions apply in this section:

(1) "Basin" means a river basin as defined in G.S. 143-215.22G or any subbasin or segment thereof.

(2) "Coalition plan" means a water quality protection plan developed by a coalition of local governments for water quality protection of a basin.

(3) "Local government" means a city, county, special district, authority, or other political subdivision of the State.

(4) "Water quality protection" means management of water use, quantity, and quality.

(b) Legislative Findings. - This section establishes a framework to encourage State-local pollutant reduction strategies for basins under the supervision and coordination of the Commission. The General Assembly finds that:

(1) Water quality conditions and sources of water contamination may vary from one basin to another.

(2) Water quality conditions and sources of water contamination may vary within a basin.

(3) Some local governments have demonstrated greater capacity than others to protect and improve water quality conditions.

(4) In some areas of the State artificial alteration of watercourses by surface water impoundments or other means may have a significant effect on water quality.

(5) Imposition of standard basinwide water quality protection requirements and strategies may not equitably address the varying conditions and needs of all areas.

(6) There is a need to develop distinct approaches to address water quality protection in basins in the State, drawing upon the resources of local governments and the State, under the supervision and coordination of the Commission.

(c) Legislative Goals and Policies. - It is the goal of the General Assembly that, to the extent practicable, the State shall adopt water quality protection plans that are developed and implemented in cooperation and coordination with local governments and that the State shall adopt water quality protection requirements that are proportional to the relative contributions of pollution from all sources in terms of both the loading and proximity of those sources. Furthermore, it is the goal of the General Assembly to encourage and support State-local partnerships for improved water quality protection through the provision of technical and financial assistance available through the Clean Water Management Trust Fund, the Ecosystem Enhancement Program, the Ecosystem Restoration Fund, water quality planning and project grant programs, the State's revolving loan and grant programs for water and wastewater facilities, other funding sources, and future appropriations. The Commission shall implement these goals in accordance with the standards, procedures, and requirements set out in this section.

(d) The Commission may, as an alternative method of attaining water quality standards in a basin, approve a coalition plan proposed by a coalition of local governments whose territorial area collectively includes the affected basin in the manner provided by this section. The Commission may approve a coalition plan proposed by a coalition of local governments whose territorial area or water quality protection plan does not include all of an affected basin if the Commission determines that the omission will not adversely affect water quality.

(e)   A coalition of local governments choosing to propose a coalition plan to the Commission shall do so through a nonprofit corporation the coalition of local governments incorporates with the Secretary of State.

(f)   The Commission may approve a coalition plan only if the Commission first determines that:

(1)   The basin under consideration is an appropriate unit for water quality planning.

(2)   The coalition plan meets the requirements of subsection (g) of this section.

(3)   The coalition of local governments has formed a nonprofit corporation pursuant to subsection (e) of this section.

(4)   The coalition plan has been approved by the governing board of each local government that is a member of the coalition of local governments proposing the coalition plan.

(5)   The coalition plan will provide a viable alternative method of attaining equivalent compliance with federal and State water quality standards, classifications, and management practices in the affected basin.

(g)   A coalition plan shall include all of the following:

(1)   An assessment of water quality and related water quantity management in the affected basin.

(2)   A description of the goals and objectives for protection and improvement of water quality and related water quantity management in the affected basin.

(3)   A workplan that describes proposed water quality protection strategies, including point and nonpoint source programs, for achieving the specified goals and objectives; an implementation strategy including specified tasks, timetables

for action, implementation responsibilities of State and local agencies; and sources of funding, where applicable.

(4) A description of the performance indicators and benchmarks that will be used to measure progress in achieving the specified goals and objectives, and an associated monitoring framework.

(5) A timetable for reporting to the Commission on progress in implementing the coalition plan.

(h) A coalition plan shall cover a specified period. The coalition plan may provide for the phasing in of specific strategies, tasks, or mechanisms by specified dates within the period covered by the plan. The Commission may approve one or more successive coalition plan periods. The coalition plan may include strategies that vary among the subareas or jurisdictions of the geographic area covered by the coalition plan.

(i) If a local government chooses to withdraw from a coalition of local governments or fails to implement a coalition plan, the remaining members of a coalition of local governments may prepare and submit a revised coalition plan for approval by the Commission. If the Commission determines that an approved coalition plan no longer provides a viable alternative method of attaining equivalent compliance with federal and State water quality standards, classifications, and management practices, the Commission may suspend or revoke its approval of the coalition plan.

(j) The Commission may approve one or more amendments to a coalition plan proposed by a coalition of local governments through its nonprofit corporation with the approval of the governing board of each local government that is a member of the coalition of local governments that proposed the coalition plan.

(k) With the approval of the Commission, any coalition of local governments with an approved coalition plan may establish and implement a pollutant trading program for specific pollutants between and among point source dischargers and nonpoint pollution sources.

(l) The Commission shall submit an annual progress report on the implementation of this section to the Environmental Review Commission on or before 1 October of each year. (1997-493, s. 1; 2005-386, s. 3.7.)

§§ 143-214.15 through 143-214.19. Reserved for future codification purposes.

§ 143-214.20. Riparian Buffer Protection Program: Alternatives to maintaining riparian buffers; compensatory mitigation fees.

(a) Compensatory Mitigation for Riparian Buffer Loss. - The Commission shall establish a program to provide alternatives for persons who would otherwise be required to maintain riparian buffers and who can demonstrate that they have attempted to avoid and minimize the loss of the riparian buffer and that there is no practical alternative to the loss of the buffer. This program is intended to allow these persons to perform compensatory mitigation in lieu of complying with laws and rules that require that riparian buffers be protected and maintained. All compensatory mitigation for riparian buffer loss shall be consistent with rules adopted by the Commission for protection and maintenance of riparian buffers.

(a1) Compensatory Mitigation Options Available to Government Entities. - A government entity, as defined in G.S. 143-214.11, may satisfy compensatory mitigation requirements by any of the following actions:

(1) Payment of a compensatory mitigation fee into the Riparian Buffer Restoration Fund established in G.S. 143-214.21.

(2) Donation of real property or of an interest in real property to the Department, another State agency, a unit of local government, or a private nonprofit conservation organization if both the donee organization and the donated real property or interest in real property are approved by the Department. The Department may approve a donee organization only if the donee agrees to maintain the real property or interest in real property as a riparian buffer. The Department may approve a donation of real property or an interest in real property only if the real property or interest in real property either:

a. Is a riparian buffer that will provide protection of water quality that is equivalent to or greater than that provided by the riparian buffer that is lost in the same river basin as the riparian buffer that is lost.

b. Will be used to restore, create, enhance, or maintain a riparian buffer that will provide protection of water quality that is equivalent to or greater than that provided by the riparian buffer that is lost in the same river basin as the riparian buffer that is lost.

(3) Restoration or enhancement of an existing riparian buffer that is not otherwise required to be protected, or creation of a new riparian buffer, that will provide protection of water quality that is equivalent to or greater than that provided by the riparian buffer that is lost in the same river basin as the riparian buffer that is lost and that is approved by the Department.

(4) Construction of an alternative measure that reduces nutrient loading as well or better than the riparian buffer that is lost in the same river basin as the riparian buffer that is lost and that is approved by the Department.

(5) Participation in a compensatory mitigation bank if the Department has approved the bank and the Department approves the use of the bank for the required compensatory mitigation.

(a2) Compensatory Mitigation Options Available to Applicants Other than Government Entities. - An applicant other than a government entity, as defined in G.S. 143-214.11, may satisfy compensatory mitigation requirements by any of the following actions:

(1) Participation in a compensatory mitigation bank if the Department has approved the bank and the Department approves the use of the bank for the required compensatory mitigation. This option is only available in a hydrologic area, as defined in G.S. 143-214.11, where there is at least one compensatory mitigation bank that has been approved by the Department.

(2) Payment of a compensatory mitigation fee into the Riparian Buffer Restoration Fund established in G.S. 143-214.21. This option only is available to an applicant who demonstrates that the option under subdivision (1) of this subsection is not available.

(3) Donation of real property or of an interest in real property to the Department, another State agency, a unit of local government, or a private nonprofit conservation organization if both the donee organization and the donated real property or interest in real property are approved by the Department. The Department may approve a donee organization only if the donee agrees to maintain the real property or interest in real property as a riparian buffer. The Department may approve a donation of real property or an interest in real property only if the real property or interest in real property either:

a. Is a riparian buffer that will provide protection of water quality that is equivalent to or greater than that provided by the riparian buffer that is lost in the same river basin as the riparian buffer that is lost.

b. Will be used to restore, create, enhance, or maintain a riparian buffer that will provide protection of water quality that is equivalent to or greater than that provided by the riparian buffer that is lost in the same river basin as the riparian buffer that is lost.

(4) Restoration or enhancement of an existing riparian buffer that is not otherwise required to be protected, or creation of a new riparian buffer, that will provide protection of water quality that is equivalent to or greater than that provided by the riparian buffer that is lost in the same river basin as the riparian buffer that is lost and that is approved by the Department.

(5) Construction of an alternative measure that reduces nutrient loading as well as or better than the riparian buffer that is lost in the same river basin as the riparian buffer that is lost and that is approved by the Department.

(b) Compensatory mitigation is available for loss of a riparian buffer along an intermittent stream, a perennial stream, or a perennial waterbody.

(c) The Commission shall establish a standard schedule of compensatory mitigation fees for payments to the Riparian Buffer Restoration Fund pursuant to this section. The compensatory mitigation fee schedule shall be based on the area of the riparian buffer that is permitted to be lost and the cost to provide equivalent or greater protection of water quality in the same river basin as that provided by the riparian buffer this is lost by:

(1) Restoration or enhancement of existing riparian buffers.

(2) Acquisition of land for and creation of new riparian buffers.

(3) Maintenance and monitoring of restored, enhanced, or created riparian buffers over time.

(4) Construction of alternative measures that reduce nutrient loading.

(d) The Commission may adopt rules to implement this section. (1999-448, s. 1; 2009-337, s. 2.)

§ 143-214.21. Riparian Buffer Protection Program: Riparian Buffer Restoration Fund.

The Riparian Buffer Restoration Fund is established as a nonreverting fund within the Department. The Fund shall be treated as a special trust fund and shall be credited with interest by the State Treasurer pursuant to G.S. 147-69.2 and G.S. 147-69.3. The Riparian Buffer Restoration Fund shall provide a repository for monetary contributions to promote projects for the restoration, enhancement, or creation of riparian buffers or to construct approved alternative measures that reduce nutrient loading as well or better than a riparian buffer that is lost and for compensatory mitigation fees paid to the Department. The Fund shall be administered by the Department. Moneys shall be expended from the Fund only for those purposes directly related to the restoration, acquisition, creation, enhancement, and maintenance of riparian buffers or to construct approved alternative measures that reduce nutrient loading as well or better than a riparian buffer. Compensatory mitigation fees paid into the Fund in connection with the loss of riparian buffers in a river basin and the interest earned on those fees may be used only for projects in that river basin. (1998-221, s. 1.5(b); 1999-448, s. 2; 2005-443, s. 1.)

§ 143-214.22. Riparian Buffer Protection Program: Department may accept donations of real property.

The Department may accept donations of real property and interests in real property if the real property or interest in real property is a riparian buffer or will be used to restore, create, enhance, or maintain a riparian buffer that will provide protection of water quality. (1998-221, s. 1.13; 1999-448, s. 3.)

§ 143-214.23. Riparian Buffer Protection Program: Delegation of riparian buffer protection requirements to local governments.

(a)   The Commission may delegate responsibility for the implementation and enforcement of the State's riparian buffer protection requirements to units of local government that have the power to regulate land use. A delegation under this section shall not affect the jurisdiction of the Commission over State agencies and units of local government. Any unit of local government that has the power to regulate land use may request that responsibility for the implementation and enforcement of the State's riparian buffer protection requirements be delegated to the unit of local government. To this end, units of local government may adopt ordinances and regulations necessary to establish and enforce the State's riparian buffer protection requirements.

(b) Within 90 days after the Commission receives a complete application requesting delegation of responsibility for the implementation and enforcement of the State's riparian buffer protection requirement, the Commission shall review the application and notify the unit of local government that submitted the application whether the application has been approved, approved with modifications, or disapproved. The Commission shall not approve a delegation unless the Commission finds that local implementation and enforcement of the State's riparian buffer protection requirements will equal implementation and enforcement by the State.

(c) If the Commission determines that a unit of local government is failing to implement or enforce the State's riparian buffer protection requirements, the Commission shall notify the unit of local government in writing and shall specify the deficiencies in implementation and enforcement. If the local government has not corrected the deficiencies within 90 days after the unit of local government receives the notification, the Commission shall rescind delegation and shall implement and enforce the State's riparian buffer protection program. If the unit of local government indicates that it is willing and able to resume implementation and enforcement of the State's riparian buffer protection requirements, the unit of local government may reapply for delegation under this section.

(d) The Department shall provide technical assistance to units of local government in the development, implementation, and enforcement of the State's riparian buffer protection requirements.

(e) The Department shall provide a stream identification training program to train individuals to determine the existence of surface water for purposes of rules adopted by the Commission for the protection and maintenance of riparian buffers. The Department may charge a fee to cover the full cost of the training program. No fee shall be charged to an employee of the State who attends the training program in connection with the employee's official duties.

(e1) Units of local government shall not treat the land within a riparian buffer as if the land is the property of the State or any of its subdivisions unless the land or an interest therein has been acquired by the State or its subdivisions by a conveyance or by eminent domain.

(f) The Commission may adopt rules to implement this section. (1999-448, s. 1; 2012-200, s. 8(a).)

§ 143-214.24. Riparian Buffer Protection Program: Coordination with River Basin Associations.

(a) Prior to drafting temporary or permanent rules that require the preservation of riparian buffers in a river basin, the Department shall consult with major stakeholders who may have an interest in the proposed rules, including the board of directors or representatives designated by the board of directors of any river basin association in the affected river basin that meets all of the following criteria:

(1) The association is a nonprofit corporation, as defined by G.S. 55A-1-40.

(2) The association has as its primary purpose the conservation, preservation, and restoration of the environmental and natural resources of the river basin in which it is located.

(3) Membership in the association is open on a nondiscriminatory basis to all citizens in the river basin.

(4) The membership of the board of directors of the association includes at least one representative from each county with a significant portion of its territory in the river basin.

(5) The membership of the association includes significant representation from each of the following categories of persons:

a. Elected local officials.

b. Persons involved in agriculture.

c. Persons involved in residential and commercial land development.

d. Persons involved in forestry.

e. Representatives of community-based organizations.

f. Representatives of organizations that advocate for protection of the environment and conservation of natural resources.

g. Persons with special training and scientific expertise in protection of water who are affiliated with colleges and universities.

h. Private property owners.

i. Persons with a general interest in water quality protection.

(b) The purpose of the consultation required by subsection (a) of this section is to assure that major stakeholders who may have an interest in the proposed rules have an opportunity to inform the Department of their concerns before the Department drafts the rules. (2000-172, s. 5.1.)

§ 143-214.25. Expired.

§ 143-214.25A. Riparian Buffer Protection Program: Surface Water Identification Training and Certification Program.

(a) The Division of Water Resources of the Department shall develop a program to train and certify individuals to determine the presence of surface waters that would require the application of rules adopted by the Commission for the protection of riparian buffers. The Division may train and certify employees of the Division as determined by the Director of the Division of Water Resources; employees of units of local government to whom responsibility for the implementation and enforcement of the riparian buffer protection rules is delegated pursuant to G.S. 143-214.23; and Registered Foresters under Chapter 89B of the General Statutes who are employees of the North Carolina Forest Service of the Department of Agriculture and Consumer Services as determined by the Assistant Commissioner of the North Carolina Forest Service. The Director of the Division of Water Resources may review the determinations made by individuals who are certified pursuant to this section, may override a determination made by an individual certified under this section, and, if the

Director of the Division of Water Resources determines that an individual is failing to make correct determinations, revoke the certification of that individual.

(b) The Division of Water Resources shall develop standard forms for use in making and reporting determinations. Each individual who is certified to make determinations under this section shall prepare a written report of each determination and shall submit the report to the agency that employs the individual. Each agency shall maintain reports of determinations made by its employees, shall forward a copy of each report to the Director of the Division of Water Resources, and shall maintain these reports and all other records related to determinations so that they will be readily accessible to the public.

(c) In implementing the Surface Water Identification Training and Certification Program established by this section, the Division of Water Resources of the Department of Environment and Natural Resources shall give priority to training and certifying the most highly qualified and experienced personnel in each agency. The Division of Water Resources shall evaluate the effectiveness of the Surface Water Identification Training and Certification Program and shall submit an annual report of its findings and recommendations, if any, to the Environmental Review Commission on or before October 1 of each year. (2010-180, s. 4(a), (b); 2011-145, s. 13.25(uu); 2013-155, s. 22; 2013-413, s. 57(k), (cc).)

§ 143-214.26. Nutrient offset credits.

(a) Nutrient offset credits may be purchased to partially offset nutrient loadings to surface waters as required by the Environmental Management Commission. Nutrient offset projects authorized under this section shall be all of the following:

(1) Consistent with rules adopted by the Commission for implementation of nutrient management strategies.

(2) Located within the same hydrologic area, as defined in G.S. 143-214.11, in which the associated nutrient loading takes place.

(b) A government entity, as defined in G.S. 143-214.11, may purchase nutrient offset credits through either:

(1) Participation in a nutrient offset bank that has been approved by the Department if the Department approves the use of the bank for the required nutrient offsets.

(2) Payment of a nutrient offset fee established by the Department into the Riparian Buffer Restoration Fund established in G.S. 143-214.21.

(c) A party other than a government entity, as defined in G.S. 143-214.11, may purchase nutrient offset credits through either:

(1) Participation in a nutrient offset bank that has been approved by the Department if the Department approves the use of the bank for the required nutrient offsets.

(2) Payment of a nutrient offset fee established by the Department into the Riparian Buffer Restoration Fund established in G.S. 143-214.21. This option is only available to an applicant who demonstrates that the option under subdivision (1) of this subsection is not available. (2009-337, s. 4(a)-(c).)

§ 143-215. Effluent standards or limitations.

(a) The Commission is authorized and directed to develop, adopt, modify and revoke effluent standards or limitations and waste treatment management practices as it determines necessary to prohibit, abate, or control water pollution. The effluent standards or limitations and management practices may provide, without limitation, standards or limitations or management practices for any point source or sources; standards, limitations, management practices, or prohibitions for toxic wastes or combinations of toxic wastes discharged from any point source or sources; and pretreatment standards for wastes discharged to any disposal system subject to effluent standards or limitations or management practices.

(b) The effluent standards or limitations developed and adopted by the Commission shall provide limitations upon the effluents discharged from pretreatment facilities and from outlets and point sources to the waters of the State adequate to limit the waste loads upon the waters of the State to the extent necessary to maintain or enhance the chemical, physical, biological and radiological integrity of the waters. The management practices developed and adopted by the Commission shall prescribe practices necessary to be employed in order to prevent or reduce contribution of pollutants to the State's waters.

(c), (d) Repealed by Session Laws 1995, c. 507, s. 27.

(e)   Repealed by Session Laws 1997-458, s. 13.1. (1967, c. 892, s. 1; 1971, c. 1167, s. 5; 1973, c. 821, s. 4; c. 929; c. 1262, s. 23; 1975, c. 583, s. 1; 1979, c. 633, ss. 2-4; 1987, c. 827, ss. 154, 158; 1989, c. 168, s. 48; 1991, c. 403, s. 2; 1991 (Reg. Sess., 1992), c. 890, s. 15; 1995, c. 507, s. 27.8(s); 1995 (Reg. Sess., 1996), c. 626, s. 4; 1997-458, s. 13.1.)

§ 143-215.1. Control of sources of water pollution; permits required.

(a)   Activities for Which Permits Required. - Except as provided in subsection (a6) of this section, no person shall do any of the following things or carry out any of the following activities unless that person has received a permit from the Commission and has complied with all conditions set forth in the permit:

(1)   Make any outlets into the waters of the State.

(2)   Construct or operate any sewer system, treatment works, or disposal system within the State.

(3)   Alter, extend, or change the construction or method of operation of any sewer system, treatment works, or disposal system within the State.

(4)   Increase the quantity of waste discharged through any outlet or processed in any treatment works or disposal system to any extent that would result in any violation of the effluent standards or limitations established for any point source or that would adversely affect the condition of the receiving waters to the extent of violating any applicable standard.

(5)   Change the nature of the waste discharged through any disposal system in any way that would exceed the effluent standards or limitations established for any point source or that would adversely affect the condition of the receiving waters in relation to any applicable standards.

(6) Cause or permit any waste, directly or indirectly, to be discharged to or in any manner intermixed with the waters of the State in violation of the water quality standards applicable to the assigned classifications or in violation of any effluent standards or limitations established for any point source, unless allowed as a condition of any permit, special order or other appropriate instrument issued or entered into by the Commission under the provisions of this Article.

(7) Cause or permit any wastes for which pretreatment is required by pretreatment standards to be discharged, directly or indirectly, from a pretreatment facility to any disposal system or to alter, extend or change the construction or method of operation or increase the quantity or change the nature of the waste discharged from or processed in that facility.

(8) Enter into a contract for the construction and installation of any outlet, sewer system, treatment works, pretreatment facility or disposal system or for the alteration or extension of any such facility.

(9) Dispose of sludge resulting from the operation of a treatment works, including the removal of in-place sewage sludge from one location and its deposit at another location, consistent with the requirement of the Resource Conservation and Recovery Act and regulations promulgated pursuant thereto.

(10) Cause or permit any pollutant to enter into a defined managed area of the State's waters for the maintenance or production of harvestable freshwater, estuarine, or marine plants or animals.

(11) Cause or permit discharges regulated under G.S. 143-214.7 that result in water pollution.

(12) Construct or operate an animal waste management system, as defined in G.S. 143-215.10B, without obtaining a permit under either this Part or Part 1A of this Article.

(a1) In the event that both effluent standards or limitations and classifications and water quality standards are applicable to any point source or sources and to the waters to which they discharge, the more stringent among the standards established by the Commission shall be applicable and controlling.

(a2) No permit shall be granted for the disposal of waste in waters classified as sources of public water supply where the head of the agency that administers the public water supply program pursuant to Article 10 of Chapter 130A of the

General Statutes, after review of the plans and specifications for the proposed disposal facility, determines and advises the Commission that any outlet for the disposal of waste is, or would be, sufficiently close to the intake works or proposed intake works of a public water supply as to have an adverse effect on the public health.

(a3) If the Commission denies an application for a permit, the Commission shall state in writing the reason for the denial and shall also state the Commission's estimate of the changes in the applicant's proposed activities or plans that would be required in order that the applicant may obtain a permit.

(a4) The Department shall regulate wastewater systems under rules adopted by the Commission for Public Health pursuant to Article 11 of Chapter 130A of the General Statutes except as otherwise provided in this subsection. No permit shall be required under this section for a wastewater system regulated under Article 11 of Chapter 130A of the General Statutes. The following wastewater systems shall be regulated by the Department under rules adopted by the Commission:

(1) Wastewater systems designed to discharge effluent to the land surface or surface waters.

(2) Wastewater systems designed for groundwater remediation, groundwater injection, or landfill leachate collection and disposal.

(3) Wastewater systems designed for the complete recycle or reuse of industrial process wastewater.

(a5) For purposes of this subsection, "agricultural products" means horticultural, viticultural, forestry, dairy, livestock, poultry, bee, and any farm products. Notwithstanding subsection (a) of this section, a permit shall not be required for a wastewater management system for the treatment and disposal of wastewater produced from activities related to the processing of agricultural products if all of the following conditions are met:

(1) The activities related to the processing of the agricultural products are carried out by the owner of the agricultural products.

(2) The activities related to the processing of the agricultural products produce no more than 1,000 gallons of wastewater per day.

(3) The wastewater is not generated by an animal waste management system as defined in G.S. 143-215.10B.

(4) The wastewater is disposed of by land application.

(5) No wastewater is discharged to surface waters.

(6) The disposal of the wastewater does not result in any violation of surface water or groundwater standards.

(a6) No permit shall be required to enter into a contract for the construction, installation, or alteration of any treatment works or disposal system or to construct, install, or alter any treatment works or disposal system within the State when the system's or work's principal function is to conduct, treat, equalize, neutralize, stabilize, recycle, or dispose of industrial waste or sewage from an industrial facility and the discharge of the industrial waste or sewage is authorized under a permit issued for the discharge of the industrial waste or sewage into the waters of the State. Notwithstanding the above, the permit issued for the discharge may be modified if required by federal regulation.

(b) Commission's Power as to Permits. -

(1) The Commission shall act on all permits so as to prevent, so far as reasonably possible, considering relevant standards under State and federal laws, any significant increase in pollution of the waters of the State from any new or enlarged sources. No permit shall be denied and no condition shall be attached to the permit, except when the Commission finds such denial or such conditions necessary to effectuate the purposes of this Article.

(2) The Commission shall also act on all permits so as to prevent violation of water quality standards due to the cumulative effects of permit decisions. Cumulative effects are impacts attributable to the collective effects of a number of projects and include the effects of additional projects similar to the requested permit in areas available for development in the vicinity. All permit decisions shall require that the practicable waste treatment and disposal alternative with the least adverse impact on the environment be utilized.

(3) General permits may be issued under rules adopted pursuant to Chapter 150B of the General Statutes. Such rules may provide that minor activities may occur under a general permit issued in accordance with conditions set out in such rules. All persons covered under general permits shall

be subject to all enforcement procedures and remedies applicable under this Article.

(4) The Commission shall have the power:

a. To grant a permit with such conditions attached as the Commission believes necessary to achieve the purposes of this Article.

b. To require that an applicant satisfy the Department that the applicant, or any parent, subsidiary, or other affiliate of the applicant or parent:

1. Is financially qualified to carry out the activity for which the permit is required under subsection (a) of this section; and

2. Has substantially complied with the effluent standards and limitations and waste management treatment practices applicable to any activity in which the applicant has previously engaged, and has been in substantial compliance with other federal and state laws, regulations, and rules for the protection of the environment.

3. As used in this subdivision, the words "affiliate," "parent," and "subsidiary" have the same meaning as in 17 Code of Federal Regulations § 240.12b-2 (April 1, 1990, Edition).

4. For a privately owned treatment works that serves 15 or more service connections or that regularly serves 25 or more individuals, financial qualification may be demonstrated through the use of a letter of credit, insurance, surety, trust agreement, financial test, bond, or a guarantee by corporate parents or third parties who can pass the financial test. No permit shall be issued under this section for a privately owned treatment works that serves 15 or more service connections or that regularly serves 25 or more individuals, until financial qualification is established and the issuance of the permit shall be contingent on the continuance of the financial qualification for the duration of the activity for which the permit was issued.

c. To modify or revoke any permit upon not less than 60 days' written notice to any person affected.

d. To designate certain classes of minor activities for which a general permit may be issued, after considering:

1. The environmental impact of the activities;

2. How often the activities are carried out;

3. The need for individual permit oversight; and

4. The need for public review and comment on individual permits.

e. To designate certain classes of minor activities for which:

1. Performance conditions may be established by rule; and

2. Individual or general permits are not required.

(5) The Commission shall not issue a permit for a new municipal or domestic wastewater treatment works that would discharge to the surface waters of the State or for the expansion of an existing municipal or domestic wastewater treatment works that would discharge to the surface waters of the State unless the applicant for the permit demonstrates to the satisfaction of the Commission that:

a. The applicant has prepared and considered an engineering, environmental, and fiscal analysis of alternatives to the proposed facility.

b. The applicant is in compliance with the applicable requirements of the systemwide municipal and domestic wastewater collection systems permit program adopted by the Commission.

(b1) Repealed by Session Laws 1991, c. 156, s. 1.

(c) Applications for Permits and Renewals for Facilities Discharging to the Surface Waters. -

(1) All applications for permits and for renewal of existing permits for outlets and point sources and for treatment works and disposal systems discharging to the surface waters of the State shall be in writing, and the Commission may prescribe the form of such applications. All applications shall be filed with the Commission at least 180 days in advance of the date on which it is desired to commence the discharge of wastes or the date on which an existing permit expires, as the case may be. The Commission shall act on a permit application as quickly as possible. The Commission may conduct any inquiry or

investigation it considers necessary before acting on an application and may require an applicant to submit plans, specifications, and other information the Commission considers necessary to evaluate the application.

(2) a. The Department shall refer each application for permit, or renewal of an existing permit, for outlets and point sources and treatment works and disposal systems discharging to the surface waters of the State to its staff for written evaluation and proposed determination with regard to issuance or denial of the permit. If the Commission concurs in the proposed determination, it shall give notice of intent to issue or deny the permit, along with any other data that the Commission may determine appropriate, to be given to the appropriate State, interstate and federal agencies, to interested persons, and to the public.

a1. The Commission shall prescribe the form and content of the notice. Public notice shall be given at least 45 days prior to any proposed final action granting or denying the permit. Public notice shall be given by publication of the notice one time in a newspaper having general circulation within the county.

b. Repealed by Session Laws 1987, c. 734.

(3) If any person desires a public hearing on any application for permit or renewal of an existing permit provided for in this subsection, he shall so request in writing to the Commission within 30 days following date of the notice of intent. The Commission shall consider all such requests for hearing, and if the Commission determines that there is a significant public interest in holding such hearing, at least 30 days' notice of such hearing shall be given to all persons to whom notice of intent was sent and to any other person requesting notice. At least 30 days prior to the date of hearing, the Commission shall also cause a copy of the notice thereof to be published at least one time in a newspaper having general circulation in such county. In any county in which there is more than one newspaper having general circulation in that county, the Commission shall cause a copy of such notice to be published in as many newspapers having general circulation in the county as the Commission in its discretion determines may be necessary to assure that such notice is generally available throughout the county. The Commission shall prescribe the form and content of the notices.

The Commission shall prescribe the procedures to be followed in hearings. If the hearing is not conducted by the Commission, detailed minutes of the hearing shall be kept and shall be submitted, along with any other written comments, exhibits or documents presented at the hearing, to the Commission for its consideration prior to final action granting or denying the permit.

(4)   Not later than 60 days following notice of intent or, if a public hearing is held, within 90 days following consideration of the matters and things presented at such hearing, the Commission shall grant or deny any application for issuance of a new permit or for renewal of an existing permit. All permits or renewals issued by the Commission and all decisions denying application for permit or renewal shall be in writing.

(5)   Repealed by Session Laws 2011-398, s. 60(b), effective July 25, 2011, and applicable to permits that are issued on or after July 1, 2011.

(6)   The Commission shall not act upon an application for a new nonmunicipal domestic wastewater discharge facility until it has received a written statement from each city and county government having jurisdiction over any part of the lands on which the proposed facility and its appurtenances are to be located which states whether the city or county has in effect a zoning or subdivision ordinance and, if such an ordinance is in effect, whether the proposed facility is consistent with the ordinance. The Commission shall not approve a permit application for any facility which a city or county has determined to be inconsistent with its zoning or subdivision ordinance unless it determines that the approval of such application has statewide significance and is in the best interest of the State. An applicant for a permit shall request that each city and county government having jurisdiction issue the statement required by this subdivision by mailing by certified mail, return receipt requested, a written request for such statement and a copy of the draft permit application to the clerk of the city or county. If a local government fails to mail the statement required by this subdivision, as evidenced by a postmark, within 15 days after receiving and signing for the certified mail, the Commission may proceed to consider the permit application notwithstanding this subdivision.

(c1)   Any person who is required to obtain an individual wastewater permit under this section for a facility discharging to the surface waters of the State that have been classified as nutrient sensitive waters (NSW) under rules adopted by the Commission shall not discharge more than an average annual mass load of total nitrogen than would result from a discharge of the permitted flow, determined at the time the Commission makes a finding that those waters are experiencing or are subject to excessive growth of microscopic or macroscopic vegetation, having a total nitrogen concentration of five and one-half milligrams of nitrogen per liter (5.5 mg/l). The total nitrogen concentration of 5.5 mg/l for nutrient sensitive waters required by this subsection applies only to:

(1)   Facilities that were placed into operation prior to 1 July 1997 or for which an authorization to construct was issued prior to 1 July 1997 and that have a design capacity to discharge 500,000 gallons per day or more.

(2)   Facilities for which an authorization to construct is issued on or after 1 July 1997.

(c2)   Any person who is required to obtain an individual wastewater permit under this section for a facility discharging to the surface waters of the State that have been classified as nutrient sensitive waters (NSW) under rules adopted by the Commission where phosphorus is designated by the Commission as a nutrient of concern shall not discharge more than an average annual mass load of total phosphorus than would result from a discharge of the permitted flow, determined at the time the Commission makes a finding that those waters are experiencing or are subject to excessive growth of microscopic or macroscopic vegetation, having a total phosphorus concentration of two milligrams of phosphorus per liter (2.0 mg/l). The total phosphorus concentration of 2.0 mg/l for nutrient sensitive waters required by this subsection applies only to:

(1)   Facilities that were placed into operation prior to 1 July 1997 or for which an authorization to construct was issued prior to 1 July 1997 and that have a design capacity to discharge 500,000 gallons per day or more.

(2)   Facilities for which an authorization to construct is issued on or after 1 July 1997.

(c3)   A person to whom subsection (c1) or (c2) of this section applies may meet the limits established under those subsections either individually or on the basis of a cooperative agreement with other persons who hold individual wastewater permits if the cooperative agreement is approved by the Commission. A person to whom subsection (c1) or (c2) of this section applies whose agreement to accept wastewater from another wastewater treatment facility that discharges into the same water body and that results in the elimination of the discharge from that wastewater treatment facility shall be allowed to increase the average annual mass load of total nitrogen and total phosphorus that person discharges by the average annual mass load of total nitrogen and total phosphorus of the wastewater treatment facility that is eliminated. If the wastewater treatment facility that is eliminated has a permitted flow of less than 500,000 gallons per day, the average annual mass load of total nitrogen or phosphorus shall be calculated from the most recent available data. A person to whom this subsection applies shall comply with nitrogen and phosphorus discharge monitoring requirements established by the Commission. This average annual load of nitrogen or phosphorus shall be assigned to the wastewater discharge allocation of the wastewater treatment facility that accepts the wastewater.

(c4) A person to whom subsection (c1) of this section applies may request the Commission to approve a total nitrogen concentration greater than that set out in subsection (c1) of this section at a decreased permitted flow so long as the average annual mass load of total nitrogen is equal to or is less than that required under subsection (c1) of this section. A person to whom subsection (c2) of this section applies may request the Commission to approve a total phosphorus concentration greater than that set out in subsection (c2) of this section at a decreased permitted flow so long as the average annual mass load of total phosphorus is equal to or is less than that required under subsection (c2) of this section. If, after any 12-month period following approval of a greater concentration at a decreased permitted flow, the Commission finds that the greater concentration at a decreased permitted flow does not result in an average annual mass load of total nitrogen or total phosphorus equal to or less than those that would be achieved under subsections (c1) and (c2) of this section, the Commission shall rescind its approval of the greater concentration at a decreased permitted flow and the requirements of subsections (c1) and (c2) of this section shall apply.

(c5) For surface waters to which the limits set out in subsection (c1) or (c2) of this section apply and for which a calibrated nutrient response model that meets the requirements of this subsection has been approved by the Commission, mass load limits for total nitrogen or total phosphorus shall be based on the results of the nutrient response model. A calibrated nutrient response model shall be developed and maintained with current data, be capable of predicting the impact of nitrogen or phosphorus in the surface waters, and incorporated into nutrient management plans by the Commission. The maximum mass load for total nitrogen or total phosphorus established by the Commission shall be substantiated by the model and may require individual discharges to be limited at concentrations that are different than those set out in subsection (c1) or (c2) of this section. A calibrated nutrient response model shall be developed by the Department in conjunction with the affected parties and is subject to approval by the Commission.

(c6) For surface waters that the Commission classifies as nutrient sensitive waters (NSW) on or after 1 July 1997, the Commission shall establish a date by which facilities that were placed into operation prior to the date on which the surface waters are classified NSW or for which an authorization to construct was issued prior to the date on which the surface waters are classified NSW must comply with subsections (c1) and (c2) of this section. The Commission shall establish the compliance schedule at the time of the classification.

(d) Applications and Permits for Sewer Systems, Sewer System Extensions and Pretreatment Facilities, Land Application of Waste, and for Wastewater Treatment Facilities Not Discharging to the Surface Waters of the State. -

(1) All applications for new permits and for renewals of existing permits for sewer systems, sewer system extensions and for disposal systems, and for land application of waste, or treatment works which do not discharge to the surface waters of the State, and all permits or renewals and decisions denying any application for permit or renewal shall be in writing. The Commission shall act on a permit application as quickly as possible. The Commission may conduct any inquiry or investigation it considers necessary before acting on an application and may require an applicant to submit plans, specifications, and other information the Commission considers necessary to evaluate the application. If the Commission fails to act on an application for a permit, including a renewal of a permit, within 90 days after the applicant submits all information required by the Commission, the application is considered to be approved. Permits and renewals issued in approving such facilities pursuant to this subsection shall be effective until the date specified therein or until rescinded unless modified or revoked by the Commission. Prior to acting on a permit application for the land application of bulk residuals resulting from the operation of a wastewater treatment facility, the Commission shall provide notice and an opportunity for comment from the governing board of the county in which the site of the land application of bulk residuals is proposed to be located. Local governmental units to whom pretreatment program authority has been delegated shall establish, maintain, and provide to the public, upon written request, a list of pretreatment applications received.

(2) An applicant for a permit to dispose of petroleum contaminated soil by land application shall give written notice that he intends to apply for such a permit to each city and county government having jurisdiction over any part of the land on which disposal is proposed to occur. The Commission shall not accept such a permit application unless it is accompanied by a copy of the notice and evidence that the notice was sent to each such government by

certified mail, return receipt requested. The Commission may consider, in determining whether to issue the permit, the comments submitted by local governments.

(d1)   Each applicant under subsections (c) or (d) for a permit (or the renewal thereof) for the operation of a treatment works for a private multi-family or single family residential development, in which the owners of individual residential units are required to organize as a lawfully constituted and incorporated homeowners' association of a subdivision, condominium, planned unit development, or townhouse complex, shall be required to enter into an operational agreement with the Commission as a condition of any such permit granted. The agreement shall address, as necessary, construction, operation, maintenance, assurance of financial solvency, transfers of ownership and abandonment of the plant, systems, or works, and shall be modified as necessary to reflect any changed condition at the treatment plant or in the development. Where the Commission finds appropriate, it may require any other private residential subdivision, condominium, planned unit development or townhouse complex which is served by a private treatment works and does not have a lawfully constituted and incorporated homeowners' association, and for which an applicant applies for a permit or the renewal thereof under subsections (c) or (d), to incorporate as a lawfully constituted homeowners' association, and after such incorporation, to enter into an operational agreement with the Commission and the applicant as a condition of any permit granted under subsections (c) or (d). The local government unit or units having jurisdiction over the development shall receive notice of the application within an established comment period and prior to final decision.

(d2)   No permit issued pursuant to subsection (c) of this section shall be issued or renewed for a term exceeding five years. All other permits issued pursuant to this section for which an expiration date is specified shall be issued for a term not to exceed eight years.

(d3)   The Department may transfer a permit issued pursuant to subsection (d) of this section without the consent of the permit holder to a successor-owner of the property on which the permitted activity is occurring or will occur as provided in this subsection:

(1)   The Department may transfer a permit if all of the following conditions are met:

a. The successor-owner of the property submits to the Department a written request for the transfer of the permit.

b. The Department finds all of the following:

1. The permit holder is one of the following:

I. A natural person who is deceased.

II. A partnership, limited liability corporation, corporation, or any other business association that has been dissolved.

III. A person who has been lawfully and finally divested of title to the property on which the permitted activity is occurring or will occur.

IV. A person who has sold the property on which the permitted activity is occurring or will occur.

2. The successor-owner holds title to the property on which the permitted activity is occurring or will occur.

3. The successor-owner is the sole claimant of the right to engage in the permitted activity.

4. There will be no substantial change in the permitted activity.

(2) The permit holder shall comply with all terms and conditions of the permit until such time as the permit is transferred.

(3) The successor-owner shall comply with all terms and conditions of the permit once the permit has been transferred.

(4) Notwithstanding changes to law made after the original issuance of the permit, the Department may not impose new or different terms and conditions in the permit without the prior express consent of the successor-owner.

(e) Administrative Review. - A permit applicant, a permittee, or a third party who is dissatisfied with a decision of the Commission may commence a contested case by filing a petition under G.S. 150B-23 within 30 days after the Commission notifies the applicant or permittee of its decision. If the permit applicant, the permittee, or a third party does not file a petition within the required time, the Commission's decision is final and is not subject to review.

(f) Local Permit Programs for Sewer Extension and Reclaimed Water Utilization. - Municipalities, counties, local boards or commissions, water and sewer authorities, or groups of municipalities and counties may establish and administer within their utility service areas their own general permit programs in lieu of State permit required in G.S. 143-215.1(a)(2), (3), and (8) above, for construction, operation, alteration, extension, change of proposed or existing sewer system, subject to the prior certification of the Commission. For purposes of this subsection, the service area of a municipality shall include only that area within the corporate limits of the municipality and that area outside a municipality in its extraterritorial jurisdiction where sewer service or a reclaimed water utilization system is already being provided by the municipality to the permit applicant or connection to the municipal sewer system or a reclaimed water utilization system is immediately available to the applicant; the service areas of counties and the other entities or groups shall include only those areas where sewer service or a reclaimed water utilization system is already being provided to the applicant by the permitting authority or connection to the permitting authority's system is immediately available. No later than the 180th day after the receipt of a program and statement submitted by any local government, commission, authority, or board the Commission shall certify any local program that does all of the following:

(1) Provides by ordinance or local law for requirements compatible with those imposed by this Part and the rules implementing this Part.

(2) Provides that the Department receives notice and a copy of each application for a permit and that it receives copies of approved permits and plans upon request by the Commission.

(3) Provides that plans and specifications for all construction, extensions, alterations, and changes be prepared by or under the direct supervision of an engineer licensed to practice in this State.

(4) Provides for the adequate enforcement of the program requirements by appropriate administrative and judicial process.

(5) Provides for the adequate administrative organization, engineering staff, financial and other resources necessary to effectively carry out its plan review program.

(6) Provides that the system is capable of interconnection at an appropriate time with an expanding municipal, county, or regional system.

(7) Provides for the adequate arrangement for the continued operation, service, and maintenance of the sewer or a reclaimed water utilization system.

(8) Is approved by the Commission as adequate to meet the requirements of this Part and the rules implementing this Part.

(f1) The Commission may deny, suspend, or revoke certification of a local program upon a finding that a violation of the provisions in subsection (f) of this section has occurred. A denial, suspension, or revocation of a certification of a local program shall be made only after notice and a public hearing. If the failure of a local program to carry out this subsection creates an imminent hazard, the Commission may summarily revoke the certification of the local program. Chapter 150B of the General Statutes does not apply to proceedings under this subsection.

(f2) Notwithstanding any other provision of subsections (f) and (f1) of this section, if the Commission determines that a sewer system, treatment works, or disposal system is operating in violation of the provisions of this Article and that the appropriate local authorities have not acted to enforce those provisions, the Commission may, after written notice to the appropriate local government, take enforcement action in accordance with the provisions of this Article.

(g) Any person who is required to hold a permit under this section shall submit to the Department a written description of his current and projected plans to reduce the discharge of waste and pollutants under such permit by source reduction or recycling. The written description shall accompany the payment of the annual permit fee. The written description shall also accompany any application for a new permit, or for modification of an existing permit, under this section. The written description required by this subsection shall not be considered part of a permit application and shall not serve as the basis for the denial of a permit or permit modification.

(h) Each applicant for a new permit or the modification of an existing permit issued under subsection (c) of this section shall include with the application: (i) the extent to which the new or modified facility is constructed in whole or in part with funds provided or administered by the State or a unit of local government, (ii) the impact of the facility on water quality, and (iii) whether there are cost-effective alternative technologies that will achieve greater protection of water quality. The Commission shall prepare a quarterly summary and analysis of the information provided by applicants pursuant to this subsection. The Commission shall submit the summary and analysis required by this subsection to the Environmental Review Commission (ERC) as a part of each quarterly report that the Commission is required to make to the ERC under G.S. 143B-282(b).

(i) Any person subject to the requirements of this section who is required to obtain an individual permit from the Commission for a disposal system under the authority of G.S. 143-215.1 or Chapter 130A of the General Statutes shall have a compliance boundary as may be established by rule or permit for various categories of disposal systems and beyond which groundwater quality standards may not be exceeded. The location of the compliance boundary shall be established at the property boundary, except as otherwise established by the Commission. Multiple contiguous properties under common ownership and permitted for use as a disposal system shall be treated as a single property with regard to determination of a compliance boundary under this subsection. Nothing in this subsection shall be interpreted to require a revision to an existing compliance boundary previously approved by rule or permit.

(j) When operation of a disposal system permitted under this section results in an exceedance of the groundwater quality standards adopted in accordance with G.S. 143-214.1, the Commission shall require that the exceedances within the compliance boundary be remedied through cleanup, recovery, containment, or other response only when any of the following conditions occur:

(1) A violation of any water quality standard in adjoining classified waters of the State occurs or can be reasonably predicted to occur considering hydrogeological conditions, modeling, or any other available evidence.

(2) An imminent hazard or threat to the environment, public health, or safety exists.

(3) A violation of any standard in groundwater occurring in the bedrock, including limestone aquifers in Coastal Plain sediments, unless it can be demonstrated that the violation will not adversely affect, or have the potential to adversely affect, a water supply well.

(k) Where operation of a disposal system permitted under this section results in exceedances of the groundwater quality standards at or beyond the compliance boundary established under subsection (i) of this section, exceedances shall be remedied through cleanup, recovery, containment, or other response as directed by the Commission. (1951, c. 606; 1955, c. 1131, s. 1; 1959, c. 779, s. 8; 1967, c. 892, s. 1; 1971, c. 1167, s. 6; 1973, c. 476, s. 128; c. 821, s. 5; c. 1262, s. 23; 1975, c. 19, s. 51; c. 583, ss. 2-4; c. 655, ss. 1, 2; 1977, c. 771, s. 4; 1979, c. 633, s. 5; 1985, c. 446, s. 1; c. 697, s. 2; 1985 (Reg. Sess., 1986), c. 1023, ss. 1-5; 1987, c. 461, s. 1; c. 734, s. 1; c. 827, ss. 154, 159; 1989, c. 51, s. 2; c. 168, s. 29; c. 453, ss. 1, 2; c. 494, s. 1; c. 727, ss. 160, 161; 1989 (Reg. Sess., 1990), c. 1004, s. 17; c. 1024, s. 33; c. 1037, s. 1; 1991, c. 156, s. 1; c. 498, s. 1; 1991 (Reg. Sess., 1992), c. 944, s. 12; 1995 (Reg. Sess., 1996), c. 626, s. 2; 1997-458, ss. 6.1, 9.1, 11.2; 1997-496, s. 3; 1998-212, s. 14.9H(b), (d); 1999-329, s. 10.1; 2004-195, s. 1.5; 2006-250, s. 5; 2007-182, s. 2; 2011-41, s. 1; 2011-394, s. 9; 2011-398, s. 60(b), (c); 2012-194, s. 33; 2012-200, s. 9(a); 2013-121, s. 2; 2013-340, s. 1; 2013-413, ss. 46(a), 53.)

§ 143-215.1A. Closed-loop groundwater remediation systems allowed.

(a) The phrase "closed-loop groundwater remediation system" means a system and attendant processes for cleaning up contaminated groundwater by pumping groundwater, treating the groundwater to reduce the concentration of or remove contaminants, and reintroducing the treated water beneath the surface so that the treated groundwater will be recaptured by the system.

(b) The Secretary may issue a permit for the siting, construction, and operation of a closed-loop groundwater remediation system. Permits shall be issued in accordance with G.S. 143-215.1 and applicable rules of the Commission. A permit issued under this section constitutes prior permission under G.S. 87-88.

(c) A permit for a closed-loop groundwater remediation system shall specify the location at which groundwater is to be reintroduced and shall specify design, construction, operation, and closure requirements for the closed-loop groundwater remediation system necessary to ensure that the treated groundwater will be captured by the contaminant and removal system that extracts the groundwater for treatment. The Secretary may impose any additional permit conditions or limitations necessary to:

(1) Achieve efficient, effective groundwater remediation.

(2) Minimize the possibility of spills or other releases from the closed-loop groundwater remediation system.

(3) Specify or limit the distance between the point at which contaminated groundwater is extracted and the point at which treated groundwater is reintroduced.

(4) Specify the minimum or maximum gradients between the point at which contaminated groundwater is extracted and the point at which treated groundwater is reintroduced.

(5) Specify or limit the chemical, physical, or biological treatment processes that may be used.

(6) Protect the environment or public health.

(d) The Commission may adopt rules to implement this section. (1991 (Reg. Sess., 1992), c. 786, s. 3.)

§ 143-215.1B. Extension of date for compliance with nitrogen and phosphorus discharge limits.

(a) The Commission may extend a compliance date established under G.S. 143-215.1(c6) only in accordance with the requirements of this section and only upon the request of a person who holds a permit under G.S. 143-215.1 that authorizes a discharge into surface waters to which the limits set out in subsections (c1) or (c2) of G.S. 143-215.1 apply. The Commission shall act on a request for an extension of a compliance date within 120 days after the Commission receives the request. The Commission shall not extend a compliance date if the Commission concludes, on the basis of the scientific data available to the Commission at the time of the request, that the extension will result in a violation of the antidegradation policy set out in 40 Code of Federal Regulations § 131.12 (1 July 1997 Edition). The Commission shall not extend a compliance date unless the Commission finds that the permit holder needs additional time to develop a calibrated nutrient response model that meets the requirements of this section. If the Commission requires an individual discharge to be limited to a maximum mass load or concentration that is different from those set out in subsections (c1) or (c2) of G.S. 143-215.1, the maximum mass load or concentration shall be substantiated by the model.

(b) The Commission shall determine the extended compliance date by adding to the date on which the Commission grants the extension: (i) two years for the collection of data needed to prepare a calibrated nutrient response model; (ii) a maximum of one year to prepare the calibrated nutrient response model; (iii) the amount of time, if any, that is required for the Commission to develop a nutrient management strategy and to adopt rules or to modify discharge permits to establish maximum mass loads or concentration limits based on the calibrated nutrient response model; and (iv) a maximum of three years to plan, design, finance, and construct a facility that will comply with those maximum mass loads and concentration limits. If the Commission finds that additional time is needed to complete the construction of a facility, the Commission may further extend an extended compliance date by a maximum of two additional years.

(c) Notwithstanding the provisions of G.S. 150B-21.1(a), the Commission may adopt temporary rules to establish maximum mass loads or concentration limits pursuant to this section or as may otherwise be necessary to implement this section.

(d) A permit holder who is granted an extended compliance date under this section shall:

(1) Develop a calibrated nutrient response model in conjunction with other affected parties and in accordance with a timetable for the development of the model that has been approved by the Commission. The model shall be based on current data, capable of predicting the impact of nitrogen and phosphorus in the surface waters, capable of being incorporated into any nutrient management plan developed by the Commission, and approved by the Commission.

(2) Evaluate and optimize the operation of all facilities operated by the permit holder that are permitted under G.S. 143-215.1(c) and that discharge into the nutrient sensitive waters (NSW) for which the compliance date is extended pursuant to this section in order to reduce nutrient loading.

(3) Evaluate methods to reduce the total mass load of waste that is discharged from all facilities operated by the permit holder that are permitted under G.S. 143-215.1(c) and that discharge into the nutrient sensitive waters (NSW) for which the compliance date is extended pursuant to this section and determine whether these methods are cost-effective.

(4) Evaluate methods to reduce the discharge of treated effluent from all facilities operated by the permit holder that are permitted under G.S. 143-215.1(c) and that discharge into the nutrient sensitive waters (NSW) for which the compliance date is extended pursuant to this section; including land application of treated effluent, the use of restored or created wetlands that are not located in a 100-year floodplain to polish treated effluent, and other methods to reuse treated effluent; and determine whether these methods are cost-effective.

(5) Report to the Commission on progress in the development of the calibrated nutrient response model, on efforts to optimize the operation of facilities, on the evaluation of methods of reducing the total mass load of waste, and on the evaluation of methods to reduce the discharge of treated effluent. The Commission shall establish a schedule for reports that requires the permit holder to report on at least a semiannual basis.

(e) The Commission may revoke an extension granted under this section and impose the limits set out in subsections (c1) and (c2) of G.S. 143-215.1 if the Commission determines that a permit holder who has obtained an extension under this section has, at any time during the period of the extension:

(1) Failed to comply with the requirements of subsection (d) of this section; or

(2) Violated any conditions or limitations of any permit issued under G.S. 143-215.1 or special order issued under G.S. 143-215.2 if the violation is the result of conduct by the permit holder that results in a significant violation of water quality standards. (1998-212, s. 14.9H(c); 2004-195, s. 1.6.)

§ 143-215.1C. Report to wastewater system customers on system performance; publication of notice of discharge of untreated wastewater and waste.

(a) Report to Wastewater System Customers. - The owner or operator of any wastewater collection or treatment works, the operation of which is primarily to collect or treat municipal or domestic wastewater and for which a permit is issued under this Part and having an average annual flow greater than 200,000 gallons per day, shall provide to the users or customers of the collection system or treatment works and to the Department an annual report that summarizes the performance of the collection system or treatment works and the extent to which the collection system or treatment works has violated the permit or federal or State laws, regulations, or rules related to the protection of water quality. The report shall be prepared on either a calendar or fiscal year basis and shall be provided no later than 60 days after the end of the calendar or fiscal year.

(b) Publication of Notice of Discharge of Untreated Wastewater. - The owner or operator of any wastewater collection or treatment works, the operation of which is primarily to collect or treat municipal or domestic wastewater and for which a permit is issued under this Part shall:

(1) In the event of a discharge of 1,000 gallons or more of untreated wastewater to the surface waters of the State, issue a press release to all print and electronic news media that provide general coverage in the county where the discharge occurred setting out the details of the discharge. The owner or operator shall issue the press release within 48 hours after the owner or operator has determined that the discharge has reached the surface waters of the State. The owner or operator shall retain a copy of the press release and a list of the news media to which it was distributed for at least one year after the discharge and shall provide a copy of the press release and the list of the news media to which it was distributed to any person upon request.

(2) In the event of a discharge of 15,000 gallons or more of untreated wastewater to the surface waters of the State, publish a notice of the discharge in a newspaper having general circulation in the county in which the discharge occurs and in each county downstream from the point of discharge that is significantly affected by the discharge. The Secretary shall determine, at the Secretary's sole discretion, which counties are significantly affected by the discharge and shall approve the form and content of the notice and the newspapers in which the notice is to be published. The notice shall be captioned "NOTICE OF DISCHARGE OF UNTREATED SEWAGE". The owner or operator shall publish the notice within 10 days after the Secretary has determined the counties that are significantly affected by the discharge and approved the form and content of the notice and the newspapers in which the notice is to be published. The owner or operator shall file a copy of the notice and proof of publication with the Department within 30 days after the notice is published. Publication of a notice of discharge under this subdivision is in addition to the requirement to issue a press release under subdivision (1) of this subsection.

(c) Publication of Notice of Discharge of Untreated Waste. - The owner or operator of any wastewater collection or treatment works, other than a wastewater collection or treatment works the operation of which is primarily to collect or treat municipal or domestic wastewater, for which a permit is issued under this Part shall:

(1) In the event of a discharge of 1,000 gallons or more of untreated waste to the surface waters of the State, issue a press release to all print and electronic news media that provide general coverage in the county where the discharge occurred setting out the details of the discharge. The owner or operator shall issue the press release within 48 hours after the owner or operator has determined that the discharge has reached the surface waters of the State. The owner or operator shall retain a copy of the press release and a list of the news media to which it was distributed for at least one year after the discharge and shall provide a copy of the press release and the list of the news media to which it was distributed to any person upon request.

(2) In the event of a discharge of 15,000 gallons or more of untreated waste to the surface waters of the State, publish a notice of the discharge in a newspaper having general circulation in the county in which the discharge occurs and in each county downstream from the point of discharge that is significantly affected by the discharge. The Secretary shall determine, at the Secretary's sole discretion, which counties are significantly affected by the discharge and shall approve the form and content of the notice and the newspapers in which the notice is to be published. The notice shall be captioned "NOTICE OF DISCHARGE OF UNTREATED WASTE". The owner or operator shall publish the notice within 10 days after the Secretary has determined the counties that are significantly affected by the discharge and approved the form and content of the notice and the newspapers in which the notice is to be published. The owner or operator shall file a copy of the notice and proof of publication with the Department within 30 days after the notice is published. Publication of a notice of discharge under this subdivision is in addition to the requirement to issue a press release under subdivision (1) of this subsection. (1999-329, s. 8.1; 1999-456, s. 68; 2010-180, s. 5.)

§ 143-215.2. Special orders.

(a) Issuance. - The Commission may, after the effective date of classifications, standards and limitations adopted pursuant to G.S. 143-214.1 or G.S. 143-215, or a water supply watershed management requirement adopted pursuant to G.S. 143-214.5, issue, and from time to time modify or revoke, a special order, or other appropriate instrument, to any person whom it finds responsible for causing or contributing to any pollution of the waters of the State within the area for which standards have been established. The order or instrument may direct the person to take, or refrain from taking an action, or to achieve a result, within a period of time specified by the special order, as the Commission deems necessary and feasible in order to alleviate or eliminate the pollution. The Commission is authorized to enter into consent special orders, assurances of voluntary compliance or other similar documents by agreement with the person responsible for pollution of the water, subject to the provisions of subsection (a1) of this section regarding proposed orders, and the consent order, when entered into by the Commission after public review, shall have the same force and effect as a special order of the Commission issued pursuant to hearing.

(a1) Public Notice and Review of Consent Orders.

(1) The Commission shall give notice of a proposed consent order to the proper State, interstate, and federal agencies, to interested persons, and to the public. The Commission may also provide any other data it considers appropriate to those notified. The Commission shall prescribe the form and content of the notice. The notice shall be given at least 45 days prior to any final action regarding the consent order. Public notice shall be given by publication of the notice one time in a newspaper having general circulation within the county in which the pollution originates.

(2) Any person who desires a public meeting on any proposed consent order may request one in writing to the Commission within 30 days following date of the notice of the proposed consent order. The Commission shall consider all such requests for meetings. If the Commission determines that there is significant public interest in holding a meeting, the Commission shall schedule a meeting and shall give notice of such meeting at least 30 days in advance to all persons to whom notice of the proposed consent order was given and to any other person requesting notice. At least 30 days prior to the date of meeting, the Commission shall also have a copy of the notice of the meeting published at least one time in a newspaper having general circulation within the county in which the pollution originates. The Commission shall prescribe the form and content of notices under this subsection.

(3) The Commission shall prescribe the procedures to be followed in such meetings. If the meeting is not conducted by the Commission, detailed minutes of the meeting shall be kept and shall be submitted, along with any other written

comment, exhibits or other documents presented at the meeting, to the Commission for its consideration prior to final action granting or denying the consent order.

(4) The Commission shall take final action on a proposed consent not later than 60 days following notice of the proposed consent order or, if a public meeting is held, within 90 days following such meeting.

(b) Procedure to Contest Certain Orders. - A special order that is issued without the consent of the person affected may be contested by that person by filing a petition for a contested case under G.S. 150B-23 within 30 days after the order is issued. If the person affected does not file a petition within the required time, the order is final and is not subject to review.

(c) Repealed by Session Laws 1987, c. 827, s. 160.

(d) Effect of Compliance. - Any person who installs a treatment works for the purpose of alleviating or eliminating water pollution in compliance with the terms of, or as a result of the conditions specified in, a permit issued pursuant to G.S. 143-215.1, or a special order, consent special order, assurance of voluntary compliance or similar document issued pursuant to this section, or a final decision of the Commission or a court rendered pursuant to either of said sections, shall not be required to take or refrain from any further action nor be required to achieve any further results under the terms of this or any other State law relating to the control of water pollution, for a period to be fixed by the Commission or court as it shall deem fair and reasonable in the light of all the circumstances after the date when such special order, consent special order, assurance of voluntary compliance, other document, or decision, or the conditions of such permit become finally effective, if:

(1) The treatment works result in the elimination or alleviation of water pollution to the extent required by such permit, special order, consent special order, assurance of voluntary compliance or other document, or decision and complies with any other terms thereof; and

(2) Such person complies with the terms and conditions of such permit, special order, consent special order, assurance of voluntary compliance, other document, or decision within the time limit, if any, specified therein or as the same may be extended, and thereafter remains in compliance. (1951, c. 606; 1955, c. 1131, s. 2; 1967, c. 892, s. 1; 1973, c. 698, s. 3; c. 1262, s. 23; 1975, c.

19, s. 52; 1979, c. 889; 1987, c. 827, ss. 154, 160; 1989, c. 426, s. 3; c. 766, s. 1; 1995 (Reg. Sess., 1996), c. 626, s. 3.)

§ 143-215.3. General powers of Commission and Department; auxiliary powers.

(a)   Additional Powers. - In addition to the specific powers prescribed elsewhere in this Article, and for the purpose of carrying out its duties, the Commission shall have the power:

(1)   To make rules implementing Articles 21, 21A, 21B, or 38 of this Chapter.

(1a)   To adopt fee schedules and collect fees for the following:

a.   Processing of applications for permits or registrations issued under Article 21, other than Parts 1 and 1A, Articles 21A, 21B, and 38 of this Chapter;

b.   Administering permits or registrations issued under Article 21, other than Parts 1 and 1A, Articles 21A, 21B, and 38 of this Chapter including monitoring compliance with the terms of those permits; and

c.   Reviewing, processing, and publicizing applications for construction grant awards under the Federal Water Pollution Control Act.

No fee may be charged under this provision, however, to a farmer who submits an application that pertains to his farming operations.

(1b)   The fee to be charged pursuant to G.S. 143-215.3(a)(1a) for processing an application for a permit under G.S. 143-215.108 and G.S. 143-215.109 of Article 21B of this Chapter may not exceed five hundred dollars ($500.00). The fee to be charged pursuant to G.S. 143-215.3(a)(1a) for processing a registration under Part 2A of this Article or Article 38 of this Chapter may not exceed fifty dollars ($50.00) for any single registration. An additional fee of twenty percent (20%) of the registration processing fee may be assessed for a late registration under Article 38 of this Chapter. The fee for administering and compliance monitoring under Article 21, other than Parts 1 and 1A, and G.S. 143-215.108 and G.S. 143-215.109 of Article 21B shall be charged on an annual basis for each year of the permit term and may not exceed one thousand five hundred dollars ($1,500) per year. Fees for processing all permits under

Article 21A and all other sections of Article 21B shall not exceed one hundred dollars ($100.00) for any single permit. The total payment for fees that are set by the Commission under this subsection for all permits for any single facility shall not exceed seven thousand five hundred dollars ($7,500) per year, which amount shall include all application fees and fees for administration and compliance monitoring. A single facility is defined to be any contiguous area under one ownership and in which permitted activities occur. For all permits issued under these Articles where a fee schedule is not specified in the statutes, the Commission, or other commission specified by statute shall adopt a fee schedule in a rule following the procedures established by the Administrative Procedure Act. Fee schedules shall be established to reflect the size of the emission or discharge, the potential impact on the environment, the staff costs involved, relative costs of the issuance of new permits and the reissuance of existing permits, and shall include adequate safeguards to prevent unusual fee assessments which would result in serious economic burden on an individual applicant. A system shall be considered to allow consolidated annual payments for persons with multiple permits. In its rulemaking to establish fee schedules, the Commission is also directed to consider a method of rewarding facilities which achieve full compliance with administrative and self-monitoring reporting requirements, and to consider, in those cases where the cost of renewal or amendment of a permit is less than for the original permit, a lower fee for the renewal or amendment.

(1c)   Moneys collected pursuant to G.S. 143-215.3(a)(1a) shall be used to:

a.   Eliminate, insofar as possible, backlogs of permit applications awaiting agency action;

b.   Improve the quality of permits issued;

c.   Improve the rate of compliance of permitted activities with environmental standards; and

d.   Decrease the length of the processing period for permit applications.

(1d)   The Commission may adopt and implement a graduated fee schedule sufficient to cover all direct and indirect costs required for the State to develop and administer a permit program which meets the requirements of Title V. The provisions of subdivision (1b) of this subsection do not apply to the adoption of a fee schedule under this subdivision. In adopting and implementing a fee schedule, the Commission shall require that the owner or operator of all air contaminant sources subject to the requirement to obtain a permit under Title V to pay an annual fee, or the equivalent over some other period, sufficient to cover costs as provided in section 502(b)(3)(A) of Title V. The fee schedule shall be adopted according to the procedures set out in Chapter 150B of the General Statutes.

a. The total amount of fees collected under the fee schedule adopted pursuant to this subdivision shall conform to the requirements of section 502(b)(3)(B) of Title V. No fee shall be collected for more than 4,000 tons per year of any individual regulated pollutant, as defined in section 502(b)(3)(B)(ii) of Title V, emitted by any source. Fees collected pursuant to this subdivision shall be credited to the Title V Account.

b. The Commission may reduce any permit fee required under this section to take into account the financial resources of small business stationary sources as defined under Title V and regulations promulgated by the United States Environmental Protection Agency.

c. When funds in the Title V Account exceed the total amount necessary to cover the cost of the Title V program for the next fiscal year, the Secretary shall reduce the amount billed for the next fiscal year so that the excess funds are used to supplement the cost of administering the Title V permit program in that fiscal year.

(1e) The Commission shall collect the application, annual, and project fees for processing and administering permits, certificates of coverage under general permits, and certifications issued under Parts 1 and 1A of this Article and for compliance monitoring under Parts 1 and 1A of this Article as provided in G.S. 143-215.3D and G.S. 143-215.10G.

(2) To direct that such investigation be conducted as it may reasonably deem necessary to carry out its duties as prescribed by this Article or Article 21A or Article 21B of this Chapter, and for this purpose to enter at reasonable times upon any property, public or private, for the purpose of investigating the condition of any waters and the discharge therein of any sewage, industrial waste, or other waste or for the purpose of investigating the condition of the air, air pollution, air contaminant sources, emissions, or the installation and operation of any air-cleaning devices, and to require written statements or the filing of reports under oath, with respect to pertinent questions relating to the operation of any air-cleaning device, sewer system, disposal system, or treatment works. In the case of effluent or emission data, any records, reports,

or information obtained under this Article or Article 21A or Article 21B of this Chapter shall be related to any applicable effluent or emission limitations or toxic, pretreatment, or new source performance standards. No person shall refuse entry or access to any authorized representative of the Commission or Department who requests entry for purposes of inspection, and who presents appropriate credentials, nor shall any person obstruct, hamper or interfere with any such representative while in the process of carrying out his official duties.

(3)   To conduct public hearings and to delegate the power to conduct public hearings in accordance with the procedures prescribed by this Article or by Article 21B of this Chapter.

(4)   To delegate such of the powers of the Commission as the Commission deems necessary to one or more of its members, to the Secretary or any other qualified employee of the Department. The Commission shall not delegate to persons other than its own members and the designated employees of the Department the power to conduct hearings with respect to the classification of waters, the assignment of classifications, air quality standards, air contaminant source classifications, emission control standards, or the issuance of any special order except in the case of an emergency under subdivision (12) of this subsection for the abatement of existing water or air pollution. Any employee of the Department to whom a delegation of power is made to conduct a hearing shall report the hearing with its evidence and record to the Commission.

(5)   To institute such actions in the superior court of any county in which a violation of this Article, Article 21B of this Chapter, or the rules of the Commission has occurred, or, in the discretion of the Commission, in the superior court of the county in which any defendant resides, or has his or its principal place of business, as the Commission may deem necessary for the enforcement of any of the provisions of this Article, Article 21B of this Chapter, or of any official action of the Commission, including proceedings to enforce subpoenas or for the punishment of contempt of the Commission.

(6)   To agree upon or enter into any settlements or compromises of any actions and to prosecute any appeals or other proceedings.

(7)   To direct the investigation of any killing of fish and wildlife which, in the opinion of the Commission, is of sufficient magnitude to justify investigation and is known or believed to have resulted from the pollution of the waters or air as defined in this Article, and whenever any person, whether or not he shall have been issued a certificate of approval, permit or other document of approval

authorized by this or any other State law, has negligently, or carelessly or unlawfully, or willfully and unlawfully, caused pollution of the waters or air as defined in this Article, in such quantity, concentration or manner that fish or wildlife are killed as the result thereof, the Commission, may recover, in the name of the State, damages from such person. The measure of damages shall be the amount determined by the Department and the North Carolina Wildlife Resources Commission, whichever has jurisdiction over the fish and wildlife destroyed to be the replacement cost thereof plus the cost of all reasonable and necessary investigations made or caused to be made by the State in connection therewith. Upon receipt of the estimate of damages caused, the Department shall notify the persons responsible for the destruction of the fish or wildlife in question and may effect such settlement as the Commission may deem proper and reasonable, and if no settlement is reached within a reasonable time, the Commission shall bring a civil action to recover such damages in the superior court in the county in which the discharge took place. Upon such action being brought the superior court shall have jurisdiction to hear and determine all issues or questions of law or fact, arising on the pleadings, including issues of liability and the amount of damages. On such hearing, the estimate of the replacement costs of the fish or wildlife destroyed shall be prima facie evidence of the actual replacement costs of such fish or wildlife. In arriving at such estimate, any reasonably accurate method may be used and it shall not be necessary for any agent of the Wildlife Resources Commission or the Department to collect, handle or weigh numerous specimens of dead fish or wildlife.

      The State of North Carolina shall be deemed the owner of the fish or wildlife killed and all actions for recovery shall be brought by the Commission on behalf of the State as the owner of the fish or wildlife. The fact that the person or persons alleged to be responsible for the pollution which killed the fish or wildlife holds or has held a certificate of approval, permit or other document of approval authorized by this Article or any other law of the State shall not bar any such action. The proceeds of any recovery, less the cost of investigation, shall be used to replace, insofar as and as promptly as possible, the fish and wildlife killed, or in cases where replacement is not practicable, the proceeds shall be used in whatever manner the responsible agency deems proper for improving the fish and wildlife habitat in question. Any such funds received are hereby appropriated for these designated purposes. Nothing in this paragraph shall be construed in any way to limit or prevent any other action which is now authorized by this Article.

(8) After issuance of an appropriate order, to withhold the granting of any permit or permits pursuant to G.S. 143-215.1 or G.S. 143-215.108 for the construction or operation of any new or additional disposal system or systems or air-cleaning device or devices in any area of the State. Such order may be issued only upon determination by the Commission, after public hearing, that the permitting of any new or additional source or sources of water or air pollution will result in a generalized condition of water or air pollution within the area contrary to the public interest, detrimental to the public health, safety, and welfare, and contrary to the policy and intent declared in this Article or Article 21B of this Chapter. The Commission may make reasonable distinctions among the various sources of water and air pollution and may direct that its order shall apply only to those sources which it determines will result in a generalized condition of water or air pollution.

The determination of the Commission shall be supported by detailed findings of fact and conclusions set forth in the order and based upon competent evidence of record. The order shall describe the geographical area of the State affected thereby with particularity and shall prohibit the issuance of permits pending a determination by the Commission that the generalized condition of water or air pollution has ceased.

Notice of hearing shall be given in accordance with the provisions of G.S. 150B-21.2.

A person aggrieved by an order of the Commission under this subdivision may seek judicial review of the order under Article 4 of Chapter 150B of the General Statutes without first commencing a contested case. An order may not be stayed while it is being reviewed.

(9) If an investigation conducted pursuant to this Article or Article 21B of this Chapter reveals a violation of any rules, standards, or limitations adopted by the Commission pursuant to this Article or Article 21B of this Chapter, or a violation of any terms or conditions of any permit issued pursuant to G.S. 143-215.1 or 143-215.108, or special order or other document issued pursuant to G.S. 143-215.2 or G.S. 143-215.110, the Commission may assess the reasonable costs of any investigation, inspection or monitoring survey which revealed the violation against the person responsible therefor. If the violation resulted in an unauthorized discharge to the waters or atmosphere of the State, the Commission may also assess the person responsible for the violation for any actual and necessary costs incurred by the State in removing, correcting or abating any adverse effects upon the water or air resulting from the

unauthorized discharge. If the person responsible for the violation refuses or fails within a reasonable time to pay any sums assessed, the Commission may institute a civil action in the superior court of the county in which the violation occurred or, in the Commission's discretion, in the superior court of the county in which such person resides or has his or its principal place of business, to recover such sums.

(10)   To require a laboratory facility that performs any tests, analyses, measurements, or monitoring required under this Article or Article 21B of this Chapter to be certified annually by the Department, to establish standards that a laboratory facility and its employees must meet and maintain in order for the laboratory facility to be certified, and to charge a laboratory facility a fee for certification. Fees collected under this subdivision shall be credited to the Water and Air Account and used to administer this subdivision. These fees shall be applied to the cost of certifying commercial, industrial, and municipal laboratory facilities.

(11)   Repealed by Session Laws 1983, c. 296, s. 6.

(12)   To declare an emergency when it finds that a generalized condition of water or air pollution which is causing imminent danger to the health or safety of the public. Regardless of any other provisions of law, if the Department finds that such a condition of water or air pollution exists and that it creates an emergency requiring immediate action to protect the public health and safety or to protect fish and wildlife, the Secretary of the Department with the concurrence of the Governor, shall order persons causing or contributing to the water or air pollution in question to reduce or discontinue immediately the emission of air contaminants or the discharge of wastes. Immediately after the issuance of such order, the chairman of the Commission shall fix a place and time for a hearing before the Commission to be held within 24 hours after issuance of such order, and within 24 hours after the commencement of such hearing, and without adjournment thereof, the Commission shall either affirm, modify or set aside the order.

In the absence of a generalized condition of air or water pollution of the type referred to above, if the Secretary finds that the emissions from one or more air contaminant sources or the discharge of wastes from one or more sources of water pollution is causing imminent danger to human health and safety or to fish and wildlife, he may with the concurrence of the Governor order the person or persons responsible for the operation or operations in question to immediately reduce or discontinue the emissions of air contaminants or the discharge of wastes or to take such other measures as are, in his judgment, necessary, without regard to any other provisions of this Article or Article 21B of this Chapter. In such event, the requirements for hearing and affirmance, modification or setting aside of such orders set forth in the preceding paragraph of this subdivision shall apply.

(13) Repealed by Session Laws 1983, c. 296, s. 6.

(14) To certify and approve, by appropriate delegations and conditions in permits required by G.S. 143-215.1, requests by publicly owned treatment works to implement, administer and enforce a pretreatment program for the control of pollutants which pass through or interfere with treatment processes in such treatment works; and to require such programs to be developed where necessary to comply with the Federal Water Pollution Control Act and the Resource Conservation and Recovery Act, including the addition of conditions and compliance schedules in permits required by G.S. 143-215.1. Pretreatment programs submitted by publicly owned treatment works shall include, at a minimum, the adoption of pretreatment standards, a permit or equally effective system for the control of pollutants contributed to the treatment works, and the ability to effectively enforce compliance with the program.

(15) To adopt rules for the prevention of pollution from underground tanks containing petroleum, petroleum products, or hazardous substances. Rules adopted under this section may incorporate standards and restrictions which exceed and are more comprehensive than comparable federal regulations.

(16) To adopt rules limiting the manufacture, storage, sale, distribution or use of cleaning agents containing phosphorus pursuant to G.S. 143-214.4(e), and to adopt rules limiting the manufacture, storage, sale, distribution or use of cleaning agents containing nitrilotriacetic acid.

(17) To adopt rules to implement Part 2A of Article 21A of Chapter 143.

(b) Research Functions. - The Department shall have the power to conduct scientific experiments, research, and investigations to discover economical and practical corrective methods for air pollution and waste disposal problems. To this end, the Department may cooperate with any public or private agency or agencies in the conduct of such experiments, research, and investigations, and may, when funds permit, establish research studies in any North Carolina educational institution, with the consent of such institution. In addition, the Department shall have the power to cooperate and enter into contracts with technical divisions of State agencies, institutions and with municipalities, industries, and other persons in the execution of such surveys, studies, and research as it may deem necessary in fulfilling its functions under this Article or Article 21B of this Chapter. All State departments shall advise with and cooperate with the Department on matters of mutual interest.

(c)   Relation with the Federal Government. - The Commission as official water and air pollution control agency for the State is delegated to act in local administration of all matters covered by any existing federal statutes and future legislation by Congress relating to water and air quality control. In order for the State of North Carolina to effectively participate in programs administered by federal agencies for the regulation and abatement of water and air pollution, the Department is authorized to accept and administer funds provided by federal agencies for water and air pollution programs and to enter into contracts with federal agencies regarding the use of such funds.

(d)   Relations with Other States. - The Commission or the Department may, with the approval of the Governor, consult with qualified representatives of adjoining states relative to the establishment of regulations for the protection of waters and air of mutual interest, but the approval of the General Assembly shall be required to make any regulations binding.

(e)   Variances. - Any person subject to the provisions of G.S. 143-215.1 or 143-215.108 may apply to the Commission for a variance from rules, standards, or limitations established pursuant to G.S. 143-214.1, 143-215, or 143-215.107. The Commission may grant such variance, for fixed or indefinite periods after public hearing on due notice, or where it is found that circumstances so require, for a period not to exceed 90 days without prior hearing and notice. Prior to granting a variance hereunder, the Commission shall find that:

(1)   The discharge of waste or the emission of air contaminants occurring or proposed to occur do not endanger human health or safety; and

(2)   Compliance with the rules, standards, or limitations from which variance is sought cannot be achieved by application of best available technology found to be economically reasonable at the time of application for such variances, and would produce serious hardship without equal or greater benefits to the public, provided that such variances shall be consistent with the provisions of the Federal Water Pollution Control Act as amended or the Clean Air Act as amended; and provided further, that any person who would otherwise be entitled to a variance or modification under the Federal Water Pollution Control

Act as amended or the Clean Air Act as amended shall also be entitled to the same variance from or modification in rules, standards, or limitations established pursuant to G.S. 143-214.1, 143-215, and 143-215.107, respectively.

(f) Notification of Completed Remedial Action. - The definitions set out in G.S. 130A-310.31(b) apply to this subsection. Any person may submit a written request to the Department for a determination that groundwater has been remediated to meet the standards and classifications established under this Part. A request for a determination that groundwater has been remediated to meet the standards and classifications established under this Part shall be accompanied by the fee required by G.S. 130A-310.39(a)(2). If the Department determines that groundwater has been remediated to established standards and classifications, the Department shall issue a written notification that no further remediation of the groundwater will be required. The notification shall state that no further remediation of the groundwater will be required unless the Department later determines, based on new information or information not previously provided to the Department, that the groundwater has not been remediated to established standards and classifications or that the Department was provided with false or incomplete information. Under any of those circumstances, the Department may withdraw the notification and require responsible parties to remediate the groundwater to established standards and classifications. (1951, c. 606; 1957, c. 1267, s. 3; 1959, c. 779, s. 8; 1963, c. 1086; 1967, c. 892, s. 1; 1969, c. 538; 1971, c. 1167, ss. 7, 8; 1973, c. 698, ss. 1-7, 9, 17; c. 712, s. 1; c. 1262, ss. 23, 86; c. 1331, s. 3; 1975, c. 583, ss. 5, 6; c. 655, s. 3; 1977, c. 771, s. 4; 1979, c. 633, ss. 6-8; 1979, 2nd Sess., c. 1158, ss. 1, 3, 4; 1983, c. 296, ss. 5-8; 1985, c. 551, s. 2; 1987, c. 111, s. 2; c. 767, s. 1; c. 827, ss. 1, 154, 161, 266; 1987 (Reg. Sess., 1988), c. 1035, s. 2; 1989, c. 500, s. 122; c. 652, s. 1; 1991, c. 552, ss. 2, 11; c. 712, s. 2; 1991 (Reg. Sess., 1992), c. 890, s. 16; c. 1039, ss. 14, 20.1; 1993, c. 344, s. 2; c. 400, ss. 1(c), 2, 3, 15; c. 496, s. 4; 1993 (Reg. Sess., 1994), c. 694, s. 1; 1995, c. 484, s. 5; 1997-357, s. 6; 1997-496, s. 4; 1998-212, s. 29A.11(b).)

§ 143-215.3A. Water and Air Quality Account; use of application and permit fees; Title V Account; I & M Air Pollution Control Account; reports.

(a) The Water and Air Quality Account is established as an account within the Department. Revenue in the Account shall be applied to the costs of administering the programs for which the fees were collected. Revenue credited to the Account pursuant to G.S. 105-449.43, G.S. 105-449.125, and G.S. 105-

449.136 shall be used to administer the air quality program. Any funds credited to the Account from fees collected for laboratory facility certifications under G.S. 143-215.3(a)(10) that are not expended at the end of each fiscal year for the purposes for which these fees may be used under G.S. 143-215.3(a)(10) shall revert. Any other funds credited to the Account that are not expended at the end of each fiscal year shall not revert. Except for the following fees, all application fees and permit administration fees collected by the State for permits issued under Articles 21, 21A, 21B, and 38 of this Chapter shall be credited to the Account:

(1) Fees collected under Part 2 of Article 21A and credited to the Oil or Other Hazardous Substances Pollution Protection Fund.

(2) Fees credited to the Title V Account.

(3) Repealed by Session Laws 2005-454, s. 7, effective January 1, 2006.

(4) Fees collected under G.S. 143-215.28A.

(5) Fees collected under G.S. 143-215.94C shall be credited to the Commercial Leaking Petroleum Underground Storage Tank Cleanup Fund.

(a1) The total monies collected per year from fees for permits under G.S. 143-215.3(a)(1a), after deducting those monies collected under G.S. 143-215.3(a)(1d), shall not exceed thirty percent (30%) of the total budgets from all sources of environmental permitting and compliance programs within the Department. This subsection shall not be construed to relieve any person of the obligation to pay a fee established under this Article or Articles 21A, 21B, or 38 of this Chapter.

(b) The Title V Account is established as a nonreverting account within the Department. Revenue in the Account shall be used for developing and implementing a permit program that meets the requirements of Title V. The Title V Account shall consist of fees collected pursuant to G.S. 143-215.3(a)(1d) and G.S. 143-215.106A. Fees collected under G.S. 143-215.3(a)(1d) shall be used only to cover the direct and indirect costs required to develop and administer the Title V permit program, and fees collected under G.S. 143-215.106A shall be used only for the eligible expenses of the Title V program. Expenses of the ombudsman for the Small Business Stationary Source Technical and Environmental Compliance Assistance Program, support staff, equipment, legal services provided by the Attorney General, and contracts with consultants and program expenses listed in section 502(b)(3)(A) of Title V shall be included among Title V program expenses.

(b1) The I & M Air Pollution Control Account is established as a nonreverting account within the Department. Fees transferred to the Division of Air Quality of the Department pursuant to G.S. 20-183.7(c) shall be credited to the I & M Air Pollution Control Account and shall be applied to the costs of developing and implementing an air pollution control program for mobile sources.

(c) The Department shall report to the Environmental Review Commission and the Fiscal Research Division on the cost of the State's environmental permitting programs contained within the Department on or before 1 November of each year. In addition, the Department shall report to the Environmental Review Commission and the Fiscal Research Division on the cost of the Title V Program on or before 1 November of each year. The reports shall include, but are not limited to, fees set and established under this Article, fees collected under this Article, revenues received from other sources for environmental permitting and compliance programs, changes made in the fee schedule since the last report, anticipated revenues from all other sources, interest earned and any other information requested by the General Assembly. (1987, c. 767, s. 2; 1989, c. 500, s. 121; c. 727, s. 218(104); 1989 (Reg. Sess., 1990), c. 976, s. 2; 1991, c. 552, s. 3; 1991 (Reg. Sess., 1992), c. 1039, s. 12; 1993, c. 400, s. 14; 1995, c. 390, s. 28; 1995 (Reg. Sess., 1996), c. 743, s. 13; 1998-212, s. 29A.11(c); 2001-452, s. 2.4; 2001-474, s. 27; 2005-386, s. 8.1; 2005-454, s. 7; 2008-198, s. 11.2; 2011-145, s. 13.7; 2011-266, ss. 1.35(b), 3.3(b).)

§ 143-215.3B: Repealed by Session Laws, 2005-454, s. 8, effective January 1, 2006.

§ 143-215.3C. Confidential information protected.

(a) Information obtained under this Article or Article 21A or 21B of this Chapter shall be available to the public except that, upon a showing satisfactory to the Commission by any person that information to which the Commission has access, if made public, would divulge methods or processes entitled to protection as trade secrets pursuant to G.S. 132-1.2, the Commission shall consider the information confidential.

(b) Effluent data, as defined in 40 Code of Federal Regulations § 2.302 (1 July 1993 Edition) and emission data, as defined in 40 Code of Federal Regulations § 2.301 (1 July 1993 Edition) is not entitled to confidential treatment under this section.

(c) Confidential information may be disclosed to any officer, employee, or authorized representative of any federal or state agency if disclosure is necessary to carry out a proper function of the Department or other agency or when relevant in any proceeding under this Article or Article 21A or Article 21B of this Chapter.

(d) The Commission shall provide for adequate notice to any person who submits information of any decision that the information is not entitled to confidential treatment and of any decision to release information that the person who submits the information contends is entitled to confidential treatment. Any person who requests information and any person who submits information who is dissatisfied with a decision of the Commission to withhold or release information may request a declaratory ruling from the Commission under G.S. 150B-4 within 10 days after the Commission notifies the person of its decision. The information may not be released by the Commission until the Commission issues a declaratory ruling or, if judicial review of the final agency decision is sought by any party, the information may not be released by the Commission until a final judicial determination has been made. (1993 (Reg. Sess., 1994), c. 694, s. 2.)

§ 143-215.3D. Fee schedule for water quality permits.

(a) Annual fees for discharge and nondischarge permits under G.S. 143-215.1. -

(1) Major Individual NPDES Permits. - The annual fee for an individual permit for a point source discharge of 1,000,000 or more gallons per day, a publicly owned treatment works (POTW) that administers a POTW pretreatment program, as defined in 40 Code of Federal Regulations § 403.3 (1 July 1996 Edition), or an industrial waste treatment works that has a high toxic pollutant potential is three thousand four hundred forty dollars ($3,440).

(2) Minor Individual NPDES Permits. - The annual fee for an individual permit for a point source discharge other than a point source discharge to which

subdivision (1) of this subsection applies is eight hundred sixty dollars ($860.00).

(3) Single-Family Residence. - The annual fee for a certificate of coverage under a general permit for a point source discharge or an individual nondischarge permit from a single-family residence is sixty dollars ($60.00).

(4) Stormwater and Wastewater Discharge General Permits. - The annual fee for a certificate of coverage under a general permit for a point source discharge of stormwater or wastewater is one hundred dollars ($100.00).

(5) Recycle Systems. - The annual fee for an individual permit for a recycle system nondischarge permit is three hundred sixty dollars ($360.00).

(6) Major Nondischarge Permits. - The annual fee for an individual permit for a nondischarge of 10,000 or more gallons per day or requiring 300 or more acres of land is one thousand three hundred ten dollars ($1,310).

(7) Minor Nondischarge Permits. - The annual fee for an individual permit for a nondischarge of less than 10,000 gallons per day or requiring less than 300 acres of land is eight hundred ten dollars ($810.00).

(8) Animal Waste Management Systems. - The annual fee for animal waste management systems is as set out in G.S. 143-215.10G.

(b) Application fee for new discharge and nondischarge permits. - An application for a new permit of the type set out in subsection (a) of this section shall be accompanied by an initial application fee equal to the annual fee for that permit. If a permit is issued, the application fee shall be applied as the annual fee for the first year that the permit is in effect. If the application is denied, the application fee shall not be refunded.

(c) Application and annual fees for consent special orders. -

(1) Major Consent Special Orders. - If the Commission enters into a consent special order, assurance of voluntary compliance, or similar document pursuant to G.S. 143-215.2 for an activity subject to an annual fee under subdivision (1) or (6) of subsection (a) of this section, the initial project fee is four hundred dollars ($400.00) and the annual fee is five hundred dollars ($500.00). These fees are in addition to the annual fee due under subsection (a) of this section.

(2) Minor Consent Special Orders. - If the Commission enters into a consent special order, assurance of voluntary compliance, or similar document pursuant to G.S. 143-215.2 for an activity subject to an annual fee under subdivision (2) or (7) of subsection (a) of this section, the initial project fee is four hundred dollars ($400.00) and the annual fee is two hundred fifty dollars ($250.00). These fees are in addition to the annual fee due under subsection (a) of this section.

(d) Fee for major permit modifications. - An application for a major modification of a permit of the type set out in subsection (a) of this section shall be accompanied by an application fee equal to thirty percent (30%) of the annual fee applicable to that permit. A major modification of a permit is any modification that would allow an increase in the volume or pollutant load of the discharge or nondischarge or that would result in a significant relocation of the point of discharge, as determined by the Commission. This fee is in addition to the fees due under subsections (a) and (c) of this section. If the application is denied, the application fee shall not be refunded.

(e) Other fees under this Article. -

(1) Sewer System Extension Permits. - The application fee for a permit for the construction of a new sewer system or for the extension of an existing sewer system is four hundred eighty dollars ($480.00).

(2) State Stormwater Permits. - The application fee for a permit regulating stormwater runoff under G.S. 143-214.7 and G.S. 143-215.1 is five hundred five dollars ($505.00).

(3) Major Water Quality Certifications. - The fee for a water quality certification involving one acre or more of wetland fill or 150 feet or more of stream impact is five hundred seventy dollars ($570.00).

(4) Minor Water Quality Certifications. - The fee for a water quality certification involving less than one acre of wetland fill or less than 150 feet of stream impact is two hundred forty dollars ($240.00).

(5) Permit for Land Application of Petroleum Contaminated Soils. - The fee for a permit to apply petroleum contaminated soil to land is four hundred eighty dollars ($480.00).

(6) Fee Nonrefundable. - If an application for a permit or a certification described in this subsection is denied, the application or certification fee shall not be refunded.

(7) Limit Water Quality Certification Fee Required for CAMA Permit. - An applicant for a permit under Article 7 of Chapter 113A of the General Statutes for which a water quality certification is required shall pay a fee established by the Secretary. The Secretary shall not establish a fee that exceeds the greater of the fee for a permit under Article 7 of Chapter 113A of the General Statutes or the fee for a water quality certification under subdivision (3) or (4) of this subsection.

(f) Local Government Fee Authority Not Impaired. - This section shall not be construed to limit any authority that a unit of local government may have pursuant to any other provision of law to assess or collect a fee for the review of an application for a permit, the review of a mitigation plan, or the inspection of a site or a facility under any local program that is approved by the Commission under this Article. (1998-212, s. 29A.11(a); 1999-413, s. 6; 2006-250, s. 4; 2007-323, s. 30.3(a).)

§ 143-215.4. Mailing list for rules; procedures for public input; form of order or decision; seal; official notice.

(a) Mailing List. - When the Commission proposes or adopts a rule establishing water quality classifications and standards under G.S. 143-214.1 or establishing effluent standards or waste treatment management practices under G.S. 143-215, it shall send notice of the action to each person who has requested to be notified of these matters. The Department shall maintain a mailing list for this purpose on which it shall record the name and address of each person who has made a written request to be on the list and the date on which the request was made. In making a request to be put on the list, a person may request to be added to the list for a specified period or indefinitely.

(b) Procedures for Public Input. -

(1) The Commission may, on its own motion or when required by federal law, request public comments on or hold public hearings on matters within the scope of its authority under this Article or Articles 21A or 21B of this Chapter. To request public comments on a matter, the Commission shall notify appropriate

agencies of the opportunity to submit written comments to the Commission on the matter and shall publish a notice in a newspaper having general circulation in the affected area, stating the matter under consideration by the Commission and informing the public of its opportunity to submit written comments to the Commission on the matter. A public comment period shall extend for at least 30 days after the notice is published.

(2) To hold a public hearing on a matter, the Commission shall notify, by personal service or certified mail, persons directly affected by the matter under consideration and shall publish a notice in a newspaper having general circulation in the affected area, stating the matter under consideration by the Commission and the time, date, and place of a public hearing to be held on the matter. A public hearing shall be held no sooner than 20 days after the notice is published. The proceedings at a public hearing held under this subsection shall be recorded. Upon payment of a fee established by the Commission, any person may obtain a copy of the record of the public hearing. After a public hearing, the Commission shall accept written comments for the time period prescribed by the Commission.

(3) This subsection does not apply to rule-making proceedings, contested case hearings, or the issuance of permits required under Title V. The Commission shall establish procedures for public hearings, public notice, and public comment respecting permits required by Title V as provided by G.S. 143-215.111(4).

(4) The Commission may hold a public meeting on any matter within its scope of authority. The Commission may hold a public meeting in addition to any public hearing that is required under any provision of law, but a public meeting may not be substituted for any required public hearing. Except as may be otherwise provided by law, the Commission may determine the procedures for any public meeting it holds.

(c) Decisions and Orders. - An order or decision of the Commission shall state the Commission's findings of fact and conclusions of law and shall state the statute or rule on which the order or decision is based.

(d) Seal/Official Notice. - The Department shall have the authority to adopt a seal which shall be judicially noticed by the courts of the State. Any document, proceeding, order, decree, special order, rule, rule of procedure or any other official act or records of the Commission or its minutes may be certified by the secretary of the department under his hand and the seal of the Department and when so certified shall be received in evidence in all actions or proceedings in the courts of the State without further proof of the identity of the same if such records are competent, relevant and material in any such action or proceeding. The Commission shall have the right to take official notice of all studies, reports, statistical data or any other official reports or records of the federal government or of any sister state and all such records, reports and data may be placed in evidence by the Commission or by any other person or interested party where material, relevant and competent. (1951, c. 606; 1967, c. 892, s. 1; 1973, c. 698, s. 10; c. 1262, s. 23; 1977, c. 374, s. 1; c. 771, s. 4; 1983, c. 296, s. 9; 1987, c. 827, ss. 154, 162, 169; 1993, c. 400, s. 4; 1995, c. 504, s. 10; 1997-496, s. 5.)

§ 143-215.5. Judicial review.

(a) Article 4 of Chapter 150B of the General Statutes governs judicial review of a final agency decision or order of the Secretary or of the Commission under this Article and Articles 21A and 21B of this Chapter. If a case that concerns an action of the Secretary or of the Commission under this Article or Article 21A or 21B of this Chapter is appealed from the superior court to the Appellate Division of the General Court of Justice, no bond shall be required of the Secretary or of the Commission.

(b) A person aggrieved, as defined in G.S. 150B-2, other than the applicant or permittee, who seeks judicial review of a final agency decision on an application for a permit required under Title V shall file a petition for judicial review under G.S. 150B-45 within 30 days after public notice of the final agency decision is given as provided in rules adopted by the Commission pursuant to G.S. 143-215.4(b)(3). A permit applicant, permittee, or other person aggrieved who seeks judicial review of a failure of the Commission to act within the time specified in rules adopted pursuant to G.S. 143-215.108(d)(2) on an application for a permit required by Title V or G.S. 143-215.108 shall file a petition for judicial review under G.S. 150B-45 within 30 days after the expiration of the time specified for action on the application. (1951, c. 606; 1967, c. 892, s. 1; 1973, c. 108, s. 88; c. 698, s. 11; c. 1262, s. 23; 1983, c. 296, s. 4; 1987, c. 827, ss. 154, 163; 1991 (Reg. Sess., 1992), c. 1028, s. 3; 1993, c. 400, s. 5.)

§ 143-215.6: Recodified as §§ 143-215.6A through 143-215.6C.

(a)   Recodified as G.S. 143-215.6A by Session Laws 1989 (Regular Session, 1990), c. 1045, s. 1.

(b)   Recodified as G.S. 143-215.6B by Session Laws 1989 (Regular Session, 1990), c. 1045, s. 2.

(c)   Recodified as G.S. 143-215.6C by Session Laws 1989 (Regular Session, 1990), c. 1045, s. 3.

§ 143-215.6A. Enforcement procedures: civil penalties.

(a)   A civil penalty of not more than twenty-five thousand dollars ($25,000) may be assessed by the Secretary against any person who:

(1)   Violates any classification, standard, limitation, or management practice established pursuant to G.S. 143-214.1, 143-214.2, or 143-215.

(2)   Is required but fails to apply for or to secure a permit required by G.S. 143-215.1, or who violates or fails to act in accordance with the terms, conditions, or requirements of such permit or any other permit or certification issued pursuant to authority conferred by this Part, including pretreatment permits issued by local governments and laboratory certifications.

(3)   Violates or fails to act in accordance with the terms, conditions, or requirements of any special order or other appropriate document issued pursuant to G.S. 143-215.2.

(4)   Fails to file, submit, or make available, as the case may be, any documents, data, or reports required by this Article or G.S. 143-355(k) relating to water use information.

(5)   Refuses access to the Commission or its duly designated representative to any premises for the purpose of conducting a lawful inspection provided for in this Article.

(6)   Violates a rule of the Commission implementing this Part, Part 2A of this Article, or G.S. 143-355(k).

(7) Violates or fails to act in accordance with the statewide minimum water supply watershed management requirements adopted pursuant to G.S. 143-214.5, whether enforced by the Commission or a local government.

(8) Violates the offenses set out in G.S. 143-215.6B.

(9) Is required, but fails, to apply for or to secure a certificate required by G.S. 143-215.22L, or who violates or fails to act in accordance with the terms, conditions, or requirements of the certificate.

(10) Violates subsections (c1) through (c5) of G.S. 143-215.1 or a rule adopted pursuant to subsections (c1) through (c5) of G.S. 143-215.1.

(11) Violates or fails to act in accordance with G.S. 143-214.7(d1).

(a1) For purposes of this section, the term "Part" includes Part 1A of this Article.

(b) If any action or failure to act for which a penalty may be assessed under this section is continuous, the Secretary may assess a penalty not to exceed twenty-five thousand dollars ($25,000) per day for so long as the violation continues, unless otherwise stipulated.

(b1) The Secretary may assess a civil penalty of more than ten thousand dollars ($10,000) or, in the case of a continuing violation, more than ten thousand dollars ($10,000) per day, against a violator only if a civil penalty has been imposed against the violator within the five years preceding the violation. The Secretary may assess a civil penalty of more than ten thousand dollars ($10,000) or, in the case of a continuing violation, more than ten thousand dollars ($10,000) per day for so long as the violation continues, for a violation of subdivision (4) of subsection (a) of this section only if the Secretary determines that the violation is intentional.

(c) In determining the amount of the penalty the Secretary shall consider the factors set out in G.S. 143B-282.1(b). The procedures set out in G.S. 143B-282.1 shall apply to civil penalty assessments that are presented to the Commission for final agency decision.

(d) The Secretary shall notify any person assessed a civil penalty of the assessment and the specific reasons therefor by registered or certified mail, or by any means authorized by G.S. 1A-1, Rule 4. Contested case petitions shall be filed within 30 days of receipt of the notice of assessment.

(e) Consistent with G.S. 143B-282.1, a civil penalty of not more than ten thousand dollars ($10,000) per month may be assessed by the Commission against any local government that fails to adopt a local water supply watershed protection program as required by G.S. 143-214.5, or willfully fails to administer or enforce the provisions of its program in substantial compliance with the minimum statewide water supply watershed management requirements. No such penalty shall be imposed against a local government until the Commission has assumed the responsibility for administering and enforcing the local water supply watershed protection program. Civil penalties shall be imposed pursuant to a uniform schedule adopted by the Commission. The schedule of civil penalties shall be based on acreage and other relevant cost factors and shall be designed to recoup the costs of administration and enforcement.

(f) Requests for remission of civil penalties shall be filed with the Secretary. Remission requests shall not be considered unless made within 30 days of receipt of the notice of assessment. Remission requests must be accompanied by a waiver of the right to a contested case hearing pursuant to Chapter 150B and a stipulation of the facts on which the assessment was based. Consistent with the limitations in G.S. 143B-282.1(c) and (d), remission requests may be resolved by the Secretary and the violator. If the Secretary and the violator are unable to resolve the request, the Secretary shall deliver remission requests and his recommended action to the Committee on Civil Penalty Remissions of the Environmental Management Commission appointed pursuant to G.S. 143B-282.1(c).

(g) If any civil penalty has not been paid within 30 days after notice of assessment has been served on the violator, the Secretary shall request the Attorney General to institute a civil action in the Superior Court of any county in which the violator resides or has his or its principal place of business to recover the amount of the assessment, unless the violator contests the assessment as provided in subsection (d) of this section, or requests remission of the assessment in whole or in part as provided in subsection (f) of this section. If any civil penalty has not been paid within 30 days after the final agency decision or court order has been served on the violator, the Secretary shall request the Attorney General to institute a civil action in the Superior Court of any county in which the violator resides or has his or its principal place of business to recover the amount of the assessment. Such civil actions must be filed within three years of the date the final agency decision or court order was served on the violator.

(h)   Repealed by Session Laws 1995 (Regular Session, 1996), c. 743, s. 14.

(h1)   The clear proceeds of civil penalties assessed by the Secretary or the Commission pursuant to this section shall be remitted to the Civil Penalty and Forfeiture Fund in accordance with G.S. 115C-457.2.

(i)   As used in this subsection, "municipality" refers to any unit of local government which operates a wastewater treatment plant. As used in this subsection, "unit of local government" has the same meaning as in G.S. 130A-290. The provisions of this subsection shall apply whenever a municipality that operates a wastewater treatment plant with an influent bypass diversion structure and with a permitted discharge of 10 million gallons per day or more into any of the surface waters of the State that have been classified as nutrient sensitive waters (NSW) under rules adopted by the Commission is subject to a court order which specifies (i) a schedule of activities with respect to the treatment of wastewater by the municipality; (ii) deadlines for the completion of scheduled activities; and (iii) stipulated penalties for failure to meet such deadlines. A municipality as specified herein that violates any provision of such order for which a penalty is stipulated shall pay the full amount of such penalty as provided in the order unless such penalty is modified, remitted, or reduced by the court.

(j)   Local governments certified and approved by the Commission to administer and enforce pretreatment programs pursuant to G.S. 143-215.3(a)(14), stormwater programs pursuant to G.S. 143-214.7, or riparian buffer protection programs pursuant to G.S. 143-214.23 may assess civil penalties for violations of their respective programs in accordance with the powers conferred upon the Commission and the Secretary in this section, except that actions for collection of unpaid civil penalties shall be referred to the attorney representing the assessing local government. The total of the civil penalty assessed by a local government and the civil penalty assessed by the Secretary for any violation may not exceed the maximum civil penalty for such violation under this section.

(k)   A person who has been assessed a civil penalty by a local government as provided by subsection (j) of this section may request a review of the assessment by filing a request for review with the local government within 30 days of the date the notice of assessment is received. If a local ordinance provides for a local administrative hearing, the hearing shall afford minimum due process including an unbiased hearing official. The local government shall make a final decision on the request for review within 90 days of the date the request for review is filed. The final decision on a request for review shall be subject to review by the superior court pursuant to Article 27 of Chapter 1 of the General Statutes. If the local ordinance does not provide for a local administrative hearing, a person who has been assessed a civil penalty by a local government as provided by subsection (j) of this section may contest the assessment by filing a civil action in superior court within 60 days of the date the notice of assessment is received. (1951, c. 606; 1967, c. 892, s. 1; 1973, c. 698, s. 12; c. 712, s. 2; c. 1262, s. 23; c. 1331, s. 3; 1975, c. 583, s. 7; c. 842, ss. 6, 7; 1977, c. 771, s. 4; 1979, c. 633, ss. 9-11; 1981, c. 514, s. 1; c. 585, s. 13; 1987, c. 271; c. 827, ss. 154, 164; 1989, c. 426, s. 4; 1989 (Reg. Sess., 1990), c. 951, s. 1; c. 1036, s. 3; c. 1045, s. 1; c. 1075, s. 6; 1991, c. 579, s. 2; c. 725, s. 3; 1993, c. 348, s. 2; 1995 (Reg. Sess., 1996), c. 743, s. 14; 1997-458, s. 6.2; 1998-215, s. 63; 1999-329, ss. 5.1, 5.3, 5.5, 5.7; 2004-124, s. 6.29(b); 2006-250, s. 6; 2007-484, s. 43.7C; 2007-518, s. 5; 2007-536, s. 3.)

§ 143-215.6B. Enforcement procedures: criminal penalties.

(a)   For purposes of this section, the term "person" shall mean, in addition to the definition contained in G.S. 143-212, any responsible corporate or public officer or employee; provided, however, that where a vote of the people is required to effectuate the intent and purpose of this Article by a county, city, town, or other political subdivision of the State, and the vote on the referendum is against the means or machinery for carrying said intent and purpose into effect, then, and only then, this section shall not apply to elected officials or to any responsible appointed officials or employees of such county, city, town, or political subdivision.

(a1)   For purposes of this section, the term "Part" includes Part 1A of this Article.

(b)   No proceeding shall be brought or continued under this section for or on account of a violation by any person who has previously been convicted of a federal violation based upon the same set of facts.

(c)   In proving the defendant's possession of actual knowledge, circumstantial evidence may be used, including evidence that the defendant took affirmative steps to shield himself from relevant information. Consistent with the principles of common law, the subjective mental state of defendants may be inferred from their conduct.

(d)   For the purposes of the felony provisions of this section, a person's state of mind shall not be found "knowingly and willfully" or "knowingly" if the conduct that is the subject of the prosecution is the result of any of the following occurrences or circumstances:

(1)   A natural disaster or other act of God which could not have been prevented or avoided by the exercise of due care or foresight.

(2)   An act of third parties other than agents, employees, contractors, or subcontractors of the defendant.

(3)   An act done in reliance on the written advice or emergency on-site direction of an employee of the Department. In emergencies, oral advice may be relied upon if written confirmation is delivered to the employee as soon as practicable after receiving and relying on the advice.

(4)   An act causing no significant harm to the environment or risk to the public health, safety, or welfare and done in compliance with other conflicting environmental requirements or other constraints imposed in writing by environmental agencies or officials after written notice is delivered to all relevant agencies that the conflict exists and will cause a violation of the identified standard.

(5)   Violations of permit limitations causing no significant harm to the environment or risk to the public health, safety, or welfare for which no enforcement action or civil penalty could have been imposed under any written civil enforcement guidelines in use by the Department at the time, including but not limited to, guidelines for the pretreatment permit civil penalties. This subdivision shall not be construed to require the Department to develop or use written civil enforcement guidelines.

(6)   Occasional, inadvertent, short-term violations of permit limitations causing no significant harm to the environment or risk to the public health, safety, or welfare. If the violation occurs within 30 days of a prior violation or lasts for more than 24 hours, it is not an occasional, short-term violation.

(e) All general defenses, affirmative defenses, and bars to prosecution that may apply with respect to other criminal offenses under State criminal offenses may apply to prosecutions brought under this section or other criminal statutes that refer to this section and shall be determined by the courts of this State according to the principles of common law as they may be applied in the light of reason and experience. Concepts of justification and excuse applicable under this section may be developed in the light of reason and experience.

(f) Any person who negligently violates any: (i) classification, standard, or limitation established in rules adopted by the Commission pursuant to G.S. 143-214.1, 143-214.2, or 143-215; (ii) term, condition, or requirement of a permit issued pursuant to this Part, including permits issued pursuant to G.S. 143-215.1, pretreatment permits issued by local governments, and laboratory certifications; (iii) term, condition, or requirement of a special order or other appropriate document issued pursuant to G.S. 143-215.2; or (iv) rule of the Commission implementing this Part; and any person who negligently fails to apply for or to secure a permit required by G.S. 143-215.1 shall be guilty of a Class 2 misdemeanor which may include a fine not to exceed fifteen thousand dollars ($15,000) per day of violation, provided that such fine shall not exceed a cumulative total of two hundred thousand dollars ($200,000) for each period of 30 days during which a violation continues.

(g) Any person who knowingly and willfully violates any (i) classification, standard, or limitation established in rules adopted by the Commission pursuant to G.S. 143-214.1, 143-214.2, or 143-215; (ii) term, condition, or requirement of a permit issued pursuant to this Part, including permits issued pursuant to G.S. 143-215.1, pretreatment permits issued by local governments, and laboratory certifications; or (iii) term, condition, or requirement of a special order or other appropriate document issued pursuant to G.S. 143-215.2; and any person who knowingly and willfully fails to apply for or to secure a permit required by G.S. 143-215.1 shall be guilty of a Class I felony, which may include a fine not to exceed one hundred thousand dollars ($100,000) per day of violation, provided that this fine shall not exceed a cumulative total of five hundred thousand dollars ($500,000) for each period of 30 days during which a violation continues. For the purposes of this subsection, the phrase "knowingly and willfully" shall mean intentionally and consciously as the courts of this State, according to the principles of common law interpret the phrase in the light of reason and experience.

(h) (1) Any person who knowingly violates any: (i) classification, standard, or limitation established in rules adopted by the Commission pursuant to G.S. 143-214.1, 143-214.2, 143-215; (ii) term, condition, or requirement of a permit issued pursuant to this Part, including permits issued pursuant to G.S. 143-215.1, pretreatment permits issued by local governments, and laboratory certifications; or (iii) term, condition, or requirement of a special order or other appropriate document issued pursuant to G.S. 143-215.2; and any person who knowingly fails to apply for or to secure a permit required by G.S. 143-215.1 and who knows at that time that he thereby places another person in imminent danger of death or serious bodily injury shall be guilty of a Class C felony, which may include a fine not to exceed two hundred fifty thousand dollars ($250,000) per day of violation, provided that this fine shall not exceed a cumulative total of one million dollars ($1,000,000) for each period of 30 days during which a violation continues.

(2)   For the purposes of this subsection, a person's state of mind is knowing with respect to:

a.   His conduct, if he is aware of the nature of his conduct;

b.   An existing circumstance, if he is aware or believes that the circumstance exists; or

c.   A result of his conduct, if he is aware or believes that his conduct is substantially certain to cause danger of death or serious bodily injury.

(3)   Under this subsection, in determining whether a defendant who is a natural person knew that his conduct placed another person in imminent danger of death or serious bodily injury:

a.   The person is responsible only for actual awareness or actual belief that he possessed; and

b.   Knowledge possessed by a person other than the defendant but not by the defendant himself may not be attributed to the defendant.

(4)   It is an affirmative defense to a prosecution under this subsection that the conduct charged was conduct consented to by the person endangered and that the danger and conduct charged were reasonably foreseeable hazards of an occupation, a business, or a profession; or of medical treatment or medical or scientific experimentation conducted by professionally approved methods and such other person had been made aware of the risks involved prior to giving

consent. The defendant may establish an affirmative defense under this subdivision by a preponderance of the evidence.

(i) Any person who knowingly makes any false statement, representation, or certification in any application, record, report, plan, or other document filed or required to be maintained under this Article or a rule implementing this Article; or who knowingly makes a false statement of a material fact in a rulemaking proceeding or contested case under this Article; or who falsifies, tampers with, or knowingly renders inaccurate any recording or monitoring device or method required to be operated or maintained under this Article or rules of the Commission implementing this Article shall be guilty of a Class 2 misdemeanor which may include a fine not to exceed ten thousand dollars ($10,000).

(j) Repealed by Session Laws 1993, c. 539, s. 1315.

(k) The Secretary shall refer to the State Bureau of Investigation for review any discharge of waste by any person or facility in any manner that violates this Article or rules adopted pursuant to this Article that involves the possible commission of a felony. Upon receipt of a referral under this section, the State Bureau of Investigation may conduct an investigation and, if appropriate, refer the matter to the district attorney in whose jurisdiction any criminal offense has occurred. This subsection shall not be construed to limit the authority of the Secretary to refer any matter to the State Bureau of Investigation for review. (1951, c. 606; 1967, c. 892, s. 1; 1973, c. 698, s. 12; c. 712, s. 2; c. 1262, s. 23; c. 1331, s. 3; 1975, c. 583, s. 7; c. 842, ss. 6, 7; 1977, c. 771, s. 4; 1979, c. 633, ss. 9-11; 1981, c. 514, s. 1; c. 585, s. 13; 1987, c. 271; c. 827, ss. 154, 164; 1989, c. 426, s. 4; 1989 (Reg. Sess., 1990), c. 1004, s. 48; c. 1045, s. 2; 1991, c. 725, s. 4; 1993, c. 539, ss. 1018, 1019, 1313-1315; 1994, Ex. Sess., c. 24, s. 14(c); 1997-458, s. 11.1; 2007-536, s. 4.)

§ 143-215.6C. Enforcement procedures; injunctive relief.

Whenever the Department has reasonable cause to believe that any person has violated or is threatening to violate any of the provisions of this Part, any of the terms of any permit issued pursuant to this Part, or a rule implementing this Part, the Department may, either before or after the institution of any other action or proceeding authorized by this Part, request the Attorney General to institute a civil action in the name of the State upon the relation of the Department for injunctive relief to restrain the violation or threatened violation and for such other and further relief in the premises as the court shall deem proper. The Attorney General may institute such action in the superior court of the county in which the violation occurred or may occur or, in his discretion, in the superior court of the county in which the person responsible for the violation or threatened violation resides or has his or its principal place of business. Upon a determination by the court that the alleged violation of the provisions of this Part or the regulations of the Commission has occurred or is threatened, the court shall grant the relief necessary to prevent or abate the violation or threatened violation. Neither the institution of the action nor any of the proceedings thereon shall relieve any party to such proceedings from any penalty prescribed for violation of this Part. For purposes of this section references to "this Part" include Part 1A of this Article and G.S. 143-355(k) relating to water use information. (1951, c. 606; 1967, c. 892, s. 1; 1973, c. 698, s. 12; c. 712, s. 2; c. 1262, s. 23; c. 1331, s. 3; 1975, c. 583, s. 7; c. 842, ss. 6, 7; 1977, c. 771, s. 4; 1979, c. 633, ss. 9-11; 1981, c. 514, s. 1; c. 585, s. 13; 1987, c. 217; c. 827, ss. 154, 164; 1989, c. 426, s. 4; 1989 (Reg. Sess., 1990), c. 1045, s. 3; 2007-536, s. 5.)

§ 143-215.6D. Additional requirements applicable to certain municipal wastewater treatment facilities.

(a) As used in this section, "municipal" and "municipality" refer to any unit of local government which operates a wastewater treatment plant. As used in this section, "unit of local government" has the same meaning as in G.S. 130A-290.

(b) A municipality that operates a wastewater treatment plant with an influent bypass diversion structure and with a permitted discharge of five million gallons per day or more into any of the surface waters of the State shall maintain a notification list of units of local government which have requested to be on such list. Any unit of local government with territorial jurisdiction over or adjacent to any part of the surface waters of the State located within 100 miles downstream from the point of discharge from a municipal wastewater treatment plant to which this section applies as measured along the path of the stream, and any unit of local government which withdraws water from such surface waters to supply water to the public, may request the municipality operating the wastewater treatment plant to include the names of appropriate officials of the unit of local government on the notification list required by this subsection. The municipality operating such municipal wastewater treatment plant shall give notice of each instance when untreated or partially treated wastewater is diverted so as to bypass the wastewater treatment plant to each person on the notification list at least 24 hours before any such instance which is planned or anticipated and within 24 hours after any such instance which is unplanned or unanticipated. (1989 (Reg. Sess., 1990), c. 951, s. 2, c. 1075, s. 6.)

§ 143-215.6E. Violation Points System applicable to swine farms.

(a) The Commission shall develop a Violation Points System applicable to permits for animal waste management systems for swine farms. This system shall operate in addition to the provisions of G.S. 143-215.6A. This system shall not alter the authority of the Commission to revoke a permit for an animal waste management system for a swine farm. The Violation Points System shall provide that:

(1) Violations that involve the greatest harm to the natural resources of the State, the groundwater or surface water quantity or quality, public health, or the environment shall receive the most points and shall be considered significant violations.

(2) Violations that are committed willfully or intentionally shall be considered significant violations.

(3) The number of points received shall be directly related to the degree of negligence or willfulness.

(4) The commission of three significant violations, or the commission of lesser violations that result in a predetermined cumulative number of points, within a limited period of time of not less than five years shall result in the mandatory revocation of a permit.

(5) The commission of one willful violation that results in serious harm may result in the revocation of a permit.

(b) In developing the Violation Points System under this section, the Commission shall determine the:

(1) Number of points that lesser violations must cumulatively total to result in the revocation of a permit.

(2) Limited period of time during which the commission of three significant violations, or the commission of a greater number of lesser violations, will result in the revocation of the operator's permit. This limited period of time shall not be less than five years.

(3) Duration of the permit revocation.

(4) Conditions under which the person whose permit is revoked may reapply for another permit for an animal waste management system for a swine farm.

(c) In developing the Violation Points System under this section, the Commission shall provide for an appeals process. (1997-458, s. 10.1.)

§ 143-215.7. Effect on laws applicable to public water supplies and the sanitary disposal of sewage.

This Article shall not be construed as amending, repealing, or in any manner abridging or interfering with the provisions of Article 10 of Chapter 130A of the General Statutes relating to the control of public water supplies; nor shall the provisions of this Article be construed as being applicable to or in anywise affecting the authority of the Department to control the sanitary disposal of sewage as provided in Article 11 of Chapter 130A of the General Statutes, or as affecting the powers, duties and authority of local health departments or as affecting the charter powers, or other lawful authority of municipal corporations, to pass ordinances in regard to sewage disposal. (1951, c. 606; 1957, c. 1357, s. 11; 1967, c. 892, s. 1; 1973, c. 476, s. 128; 1987, c. 827, s. 165; 1989, c. 727, s. 162; 1997-502, s. 9.)

§ 143-215.8. Repealed by Session Laws 1973, c. 698, s. 13.

§ 143-215.8A. Planning.

(a) Policy, Purpose and Intent. - The Commission and Department shall undertake a continuing planning process to develop and adopt plans and programs to assure that the policy, purpose and intent declared in this Article are carried out with regard to establishing and enforcing standards of water purity designed to protect human health, to prevent injury to plant and animal life, to prevent damage to public and private property, to enhance the quality of the environment, to insure the continued enjoyment of the natural attractions of the State, to encourage the expansion of employment opportunities, to provide a permanent foundation for healthy industrial development, and to insure the beneficial use of the water resources of the State.

(b) Goals. - The goals of the continuing planning process shall be the enhancement of the quality of life and protection of the environment through development by the Commission of water quality plans and programs utilizing the resources of the State on a priority basis to attain, maintain, and enhance water quality standards and water purity throughout the State.

(c) Statewide and Regional Planning. - The planning process may be conducted on a statewide or regional basis, as the Commission shall determine appropriate. If the Commission elects to proceed on a regional basis, it shall delineate the boundaries of each region by preparation of appropriate maps; by description referring to geographical features, established landmarks or political boundaries; or such other manner that the extent and limits of each region shall be easily ascertainable. The Commission shall consult officials and agencies of localities and regions in the development of plans affecting those areas.

(d) Local Planning Organizations. - The Commission shall submit to the Governor or his designee any plans, projections, data, comments or recommendations that he may request. If the Governor determines that the goals of this section will be more expeditiously and efficiently achieved, he may designate a representative organization, capable of carrying out a planning process for any region of the State or area therein, to develop plans, consistent with the State's water quality management plans, for the control or abatement of water pollution within such region or area. The Commission shall consult with, advise, and assist any organization so designated in the preparation of its plans and shall submit to the Governor the Commission's comments and recommendations regarding such plans. All such organizations shall submit plans developed by them to the Governor for review, and no plan shall be effective until concurred in and approved by him.

(e) Interstate Planning Regions. - The Governor may consult and cooperate with the governor of any adjoining state in establishing an interstate planning region or area and in designating a representative organization, capable of carrying out a planning process for the region or area, to develop plans, consistent with the State's water quality management plans, for the control or abatement of water pollution within such region or area, if he determines that such region or area has common water quality control problems for which an interstate plan would be most effective.

(f) Repealed by Session Laws 1987, c. 827, s. 166. (1973, c. 698, s. 13; c. 1262, s. 23; 1977, c. 771, s. 4; 1987, c. 827, ss. 154, 166.)

§ 143-215.8B. Basinwide water quality management plans.

(a) The Commission shall develop and implement a basinwide water quality management plan for each of the 17 major river basins in the State. In developing and implementing each plan, the Commission shall consider the cumulative impacts of all of the following:

(1) All activities across a river basin and all point sources and nonpoint sources of pollutants, including municipal wastewater facilities, industrial wastewater systems, septic tank systems, stormwater management systems, golf courses, farms that use fertilizers and pesticides for crops, public and commercial lawns and gardens, atmospheric deposition, and animal operations.

(2) All transfers into and from a river basin that are required to be registered under G.S. 143-215.22H.

(b) Each basinwide water quality management plan shall:

(1) Provide that all point sources and nonpoint sources of pollutants jointly share the responsibility of reducing the pollutants in the State's waters in a fair, reasonable, and proportionate manner, using computer modeling and the best science and technology reasonably available and considering future anticipated population growth and economic development.

(2) If any of the waters located within the river basin are designated as nutrient sensitive waters, then the basinwide water quality management plan shall establish a goal to reduce the average annual mass load of nutrients that are delivered to surface waters within the river basin from point and nonpoint sources. The Commission shall establish a nutrient reduction goal for the nutrient or nutrients of concern that will result in improvements to water quality

such that the designated uses of the water, as provided in the classification of the water under G.S. 143-214.1(d), are not impaired. The plan shall require incremental progress toward achieving the goal. In developing the plan, the Commission shall determine and allow appropriate credit toward achieving the goal for reductions of water pollution by point and nonpoint sources through voluntary measures.

(c) The Commission shall review and revise its 17 basinwide water quality management plans at least every 10 years to reflect changes in water quality, improvements in modeling methods, improvements in wastewater treatment technology, and advances in scientific knowledge and, as need to support designated uses of water, modifications to management strategies.

(d) The Commission and the Department shall each report on or before 1 October of each year on an annual basis to the Environmental Review Commission on the progress in developing and implementing basinwide water quality management plans and on increasing public involvement and public education in connection with basinwide water quality management planning. The report to the Environmental Review Commission by the Department shall include a written statement as to all concentrations of heavy metals and other pollutants in the surface waters of the State that are identified in the course of preparing or revising the basinwide water quality management plans.

(e) A basinwide water quality management plan is not a rule and Article 2A of Chapter 150B of the General Statutes does not apply to the development of basinwide water quality management plans. Any water quality standard or classification and any requirement or limitation of general applicability that implements a basinwide water quality management plan is a rule and must be adopted as provided in Article 2A of Chapter 150B of the General Statutes. (1997-458, s. 8.2; 1998-168, s. 2; 2012-200, s. 9(b).)

§ 143-215.8C: Repealed by Session Laws 2005-386, s. 2.1, effective December 1, 2005.

§ 143-215.8D. North Carolina Water Quality Workgroup; Rivernet.

(a) The Department of Environment and Natural Resources and North Carolina State University shall jointly establish the North Carolina Water Quality Workgroup. The Workgroup shall work collaboratively with the appropriate divisions of the Department of Environment and Natural Resources and North Carolina State University, the Environmental Management Commission, and the Environmental Review Commission to identify the scientific and State agency databases that can be used to formulate public policy regarding the State's water quality, evaluate those databases to determine the information gaps in those databases, and establish the priorities for obtaining the information lacking in those databases. The Workgroup shall have the following duties:

(1) To address specifically the ongoing need of evaluation, synthesis, and presentation of current scientific knowledge that can be used to formulate public policy on water quality issues.

(2) To identify knowledge gaps in the current understanding of water quality problems and fill these gaps with appropriate research projects.

(3) To maintain a web-based water quality data distribution site.

(4) To organize and evaluate existing scientific and State agency water quality databases.

(5) To prioritize recognized knowledge gaps in water quality issues for immediate funding.

(b) The North Carolina Water Quality Workgroup shall be composed of no more than 15 members. Those members shall be jointly appointed by the Chancellor of North Carolina State University and the Secretary of Environment and Natural Resources. Any person appointed as a member of the Workgroup shall be knowledgeable in one of the following areas:

(1) Water Quality Assessment, Water Quality Monitoring, and Water Quality Permitting.

(2) Nutrient Management.

(3) Water Pollution Control.

(4) Waste Management.

(5)   Groundwater Resources.

(6)   Stream Hydrology.

(7)   Aquatic Biology.

(8)   Environmental Education and Web-Based Data Dissemination.

(c)   North Carolina State University shall provide meeting facilities for the North Carolina Water Quality Workgroup as requested by the Chair.

(d)   The members of the North Carolina Water Quality Workgroup shall elect a Chair. The Chair shall call meetings of the Workgroup and set the meeting agenda.

(e)   The Chair of the North Carolina Water Quality Workgroup shall report each year by January 30 to the Environmental Review Commission, to the Cochairs of the House of Representatives and Senate Appropriations Subcommittees on Natural and Economic Resources, and to the Chancellor of North Carolina State University or the Chancellor's designee on the previous year's activities, findings, and recommendations of the North Carolina Water Quality Workgroup.

(f)   The North Carolina Water Quality Workgroup shall develop a water quality monitoring system to be known as Rivernet that effectively uses the combined resources of North Carolina State University and State agencies. The Rivernet system shall be designed to implement advances in monitoring technology and information management systems with web-based data dissemination in the waters that are impaired based on the criteria of the State's basinwide water quality management plans. Water quality and nutrient parameters shall be continuously monitored at each station, and the data shall be sent back to a centralized computer server.

The Rivernet system shall be coordinated with related data collection and monitoring activities of the Department of Environment and Natural Resources, the Water Resources Research Institute, the North Carolina Water Quality Workgroup, and other research efforts pursued by academic institutions or State government entities. If the North Carolina Water Quality Workgroup chooses to employ a technology for which there are testing procedure guidelines promulgated by the United States Environmental Protection Agency, the American Public Health Association, the American Water Works Association, or the Water Environment Federation then the testing procedures shall comply with the appropriate guidelines. If the North Carolina Water Quality Workgroup chooses to employ a technology for which there are no testing procedure guidelines promulgated by any of the groups cited in this subsection, then the North Carolina Water Quality Workgroup may establish testing procedure guidelines.

The Rivernet system shall also have the capabilities to trigger alarms and notify the appropriate member of the Workgroup when monitoring stations exceed defined limits indicating a spill or a significant water quality or nutrient measurement event, which then can be comprehensively analyzed. (2001-424, s. 19.5; 2004-195, ss. 3.3, 3.4.)

§ 143-215.9. Restrictions on authority of the Commission.

Nothing in this Article shall be construed to:

(1) Grant to the Commission any jurisdiction or authority with respect to air contamination existing solely within commercial and industrial plants, works or shops;

(2) Affect the relations between employers and employees with respect or arising out of conditions of air contamination or air pollution;

(3) Supersede or limit the applicability of any law, rules and regulations or ordinances relating to industrial health or safety. (1967, c. 892, s. 1; 1973, c. 1262, s. 23; 1987, c. 827, s. 154.)

§ 143-215.9A. Reports.

(a) The Department shall report to the Environmental Review Commission and the Fiscal Research Division on or before 1 October of each year on the status of facilities discharging into surface waters during the previous fiscal year. The report shall include:

(1) The names and locations of all persons permitted under G.S. 143-215.1(c).

(2) The number of compliance inspections of persons permitted under G.S. 143-215.1(c) that the Department has conducted since the last report.

(3) The number of violations found during each inspection, including the date on which the violation occurred and the nature of the violation; the status of enforcement actions taken and pending; and the penalties imposed, collected, and in the process of being negotiated for each violation.

(4) Any other information that the Department determines to be appropriate or that is requested by the Environmental Review Commission or the Fiscal Research Division.

(b) The information to be included in the report pursuant to subsection (a) of this section shall be itemized by each regional office of the Department, with totals for the State indicated.

(c) Repealed by Session Laws 2002-148, s. 5. (1998-221, s. 4.1; 2002-148, s. 5.)

§ 143-215.9B. Systemwide municipal and domestic wastewater collection system permit program report.

The Environmental Management Commission shall develop and implement a permit program for municipal and domestic wastewater collection systems on a systemwide basis. The collection system permit program shall provide for performance standards, minimum design and construction requirements, a capital improvement plan, operation and maintenance requirements, and minimum reporting requirements. In order to ensure an orderly and cost-effective phase-in of the collection system permit program, the Commission shall implement the permit program over a five-year period beginning 1 July 2000. The Commission shall issue permits for approximately twenty percent (20%) of municipal and domestic wastewater collection systems that are in operation on 1 July 2000 during each of the five calendar years beginning 1 July 2000 and shall give priority to those collection systems serving the largest populations, those under a moratorium imposed by the Commission under G.S. 143-215.67, and those for which the Department of Environment and Natural Resources has issued a notice of violation for the discharge of untreated wastewater. The Commission shall report on its progress in developing and implementing the collection system permit program required by this section as a part of each quarterly report the Environmental Management Commission makes to the Environmental Review Commission pursuant to G.S. 143B-282(b). (2001-452, s. 2.6.)

§ 143-215.9C. Use of certain types of culverts allowed.

(a) The Division of Water Resources in the Department of Environment and Natural Resources shall allow the use of structures known as three-sided, open-bottom, or bottomless culverts. A culvert authorized under this section shall be designed, constructed, and installed so that it satisfies all of the following requirements:

(1) Adheres to professional engineering standards and sound engineering practices.

(2) To the extent practicable, minimizes the erosive velocity of water.

(3) Has an inside that is greater than or equal to 1.2 times the bankfull width of the spanned waterbody. For purposes of this subdivision, "bankfull width" means the width of the stream where over-bank flow begins during a flood event.

(b) The Division shall allow the use of culverts authorized under this section throughout the State and may not limit their use to locations where they must be tied into bedrock. Culverts authorized under this section may only be used on private property and may not be transferred to, or operated or maintained by, the Department of Transportation. (2009-478, s. 1; 2013-413, s. 57(l).)

§ 143-215.10: Repealed by Session Laws 1973, c. 1262, s. 23.

Part 1A. Animal Waste Management Systems.

§ 143-215.10A. Legislative findings and intent.

The General Assembly finds that animal operations provide significant economic and other benefits to this State. The growth of animal operations in recent years has increased the importance of good animal waste management practices to protect water quality. It is critical that the State balance growth with prudent environmental safeguards. It is the intention of the State to promote a cooperative and coordinated approach to animal waste management among the agencies of the State with a primary emphasis on technical assistance to farmers. To this end, the General Assembly intends to establish a permitting program for animal waste management systems that will protect water quality and promote innovative systems and practices while minimizing the regulatory burden. Technical assistance will be provided by the Division of Soil and Water Conservation of the Department of Agriculture and Consumer Services. Inspection and enforcement will be provided by the Division of Water Resources. (1995 (Reg. Sess., 1996), c. 626, s. 1; 1996, 2nd Ex. Sess., c. 18, s. 27.34(a); 2002-176, s. 1.2; 2011-145, ss. 13.22(a), 13.22A(p); 2013-413, s. 57(m).)

§ 143-215.10B. Definitions.

As used in this Part:

(1) "Animal operation" means any agricultural feedlot activity involving 250 or more swine, 100 or more confined cattle, 75 or more horses, 1,000 or more sheep, or 30,000 or more confined poultry with a liquid animal waste management system, or any agricultural feedlot activity with a liquid animal waste management system that discharges to the surface waters of the State. A public livestock market regulated under Article 35 of Chapter 106 of the General Statutes is an animal operation for purposes of this Part.

(2) "Animal waste" means livestock or poultry excreta or a mixture of excreta with feed, bedding, litter, or other materials from an animal operation.

(3) "Animal waste management system" means a combination of structures and nonstructural practices serving a feedlot that provide for the collection, treatment, storage, or land application of animal waste.

(4) "Division" means the Division of Water Resources of the Department.

(5) "Feedlot" means a lot or building or combination of lots and buildings intended for the confined feeding, breeding, raising, or holding of animals and either specifically designed as a confinement area in which animal waste may accumulate or where the concentration of animals is such that an established vegetative cover cannot be maintained. A building or lot is not a feedlot unless animals are confined for 45 or more days, which may or may not be consecutive, in a 12-month period. Pastures shall not be considered feedlots for purposes of this Part.

(6) "Technical specialist" means an individual designated by the Soil and Water Conservation Commission, pursuant to rules adopted by that Commission, to certify animal waste management plans. (1995 (Reg. Sess., 1996), c. 626, s. 1; 1996, 2nd Ex. Sess., c. 18, s. 27.34(b); 2001-326, s. 1; 2004-176, s. 1; 2013-413, s. 57(n).)

§ 143-215.10C. Applications and permits.

(a) No person shall construct or operate an animal waste management system for an animal operation or operate an animal waste management system for a dry litter poultry facility that is required to be permitted under 40 Code of Federal Regulations § 122, as amended at 73 Federal Register 70418 (November 20, 2008), without first obtaining an individual permit or a general permit under this Article. The Commission shall develop a system of individual and general permits for animal operations and dry litter poultry facilities based on species, number of animals, and other relevant factors. It is the intent of the General Assembly that most animal waste management systems be permitted under a general permit. The Commission, in its discretion, may require that an animal waste management system be permitted under an individual permit if the Commission determines that an individual permit is necessary to protect water quality, public health, or the environment. The owner or operator of an animal operation shall submit an application for a permit at least 180 days prior to construction of a new animal waste management system or expansion of an existing animal waste management system and shall obtain the permit prior to commencement of the construction or expansion. The owner or operator of a dry litter poultry facility that is required to be permitted under 40 Code of Federal Regulations § 122, as amended at 73 Federal Register 70418 (November 20, 2008), shall submit an application for a permit at least 180 days prior to operation of a new animal waste management system.

(a1) An owner or operator of an animal waste management system for an animal operation or a dry litter poultry facility that is required to be permitted under 40 Code of Federal Regulations § 122, as amended at 73 Federal Register 70418 (November 20, 2008), shall apply for an individual National Pollutant Discharge Elimination System (NPDES) permit or a general NPDES permit under this Article and may not discharge into waters of the State except in compliance with an NPDES permit.

(b) An animal waste management system that is not required to be permitted under 40 Code of Federal Regulations § 122, as amended at 73 Federal Register 70418 (November 20, 2008), shall be designed, constructed, and operated so that the animal operation served by the animal waste management system does not cause pollution in the waters of the State except as may result because of rainfall from a storm event more severe than the 25-year, 24-hour storm.

(b1) An existing animal waste management system that is required to be permitted under 40 Code of Federal Regulations § 122, as amended at 73 Federal Register 70418 (November 20, 2008), shall be designed, constructed, maintained, and operated in accordance with 40 Code of Federal Regulations § 412, as amended at 73 Federal Register 70418 (November 20, 2008), so that the animal operation served by the animal waste management system does not cause pollution in waters of the State except as may result because of rainfall from a storm event more severe than the 25-year, 24-hour storm. A new animal operation or dry litter poultry facility that is required to be permitted under 40 Code of Federal Regulations § 412.46, as amended at 73 Federal Register 70418 (November 20, 2008), shall be designed, constructed, maintained, and operated so that there is no discharge of pollutants to waters of the State.

(c) The Commission shall act on a permit application as quickly as possible and may conduct any inquiry or investigation it considers necessary before acting on an application.

(d) All applications for permits or for renewal of an existing permit shall be in writing, and the Commission may prescribe the form of the applications. All applications shall include an animal waste management system plan approved by a technical specialist. The Commission may require an applicant to submit additional information the Commission considers necessary to evaluate the application. Permits and renewals issued pursuant to this section shall be effective until the date specified therein or until rescinded unless modified or revoked by the Commission.

(e)   An animal waste management plan for an animal operation shall include all of the following components:

(1)   A checklist of potential odor sources and a choice of site-specific, cost-effective remedial best management practices to minimize those sources.

(2)   A checklist of potential insect sources and a choice of site-specific, cost-effective best management practices to minimize insect problems.

(3)   Provisions that set forth acceptable methods of disposing of mortalities.

(4)   Provisions regarding best management practices for riparian buffers or equivalent controls, particularly along perennial streams.

(5)   Provisions regarding the use of emergency spillways and site-specific emergency management plans that set forth operating procedures to follow during emergencies in order to minimize the risk of environmental damage.

(6)   Provisions regarding periodic testing of waste products used as nutrient sources as close to the time of application as practical and at least within 60 days of the date of application and periodic testing, at least once every three years, of soils at crop sites where the waste products are applied. Nitrogen shall be a rate-determining element. Phosphorus shall be evaluated according to the nutrient management standard approved by the Soil and Water Conservation Commission of the Department of Agriculture and Consumer Services and the Natural Resources Conservation Service of the United States Department of Agriculture for facilities that are required to be permitted under 40 Code of Federal Regulations § 122, as amended at 73 Federal Register 70418 (November 20, 2008). If the evaluation demonstrates the need to limit the application of phosphorus in order to comply with the nutrient management standard, then phosphorus shall be a rate-determining element. Zinc and copper levels in the soils shall be monitored, and alternative crop sites shall be used when these metals approach excess levels.

(7)   Provisions regarding waste utilization plans that assure a balance between nitrogen application rates and nitrogen crop requirements, that assure that lime is applied to maintain pH in the optimum range for crop production, and that include corrective action, including revisions to the waste utilization plan based on data of crop yields and crops analysis, that will be taken if this balance is not achieved as determined by testing conducted pursuant to subdivision (6) of this subsection.

(8) Provisions regarding the completion and maintenance of records on forms developed by the Department, which records shall include information addressed in subdivisions (6) and (7) of this subsection, including the dates and rates that waste products are applied to soils at crop sites, and shall be made available upon request by the Department.

(f) Any owner or operator of a dry litter poultry facility that is not required to be permitted under 40 Code of Federal Regulations § 122, as amended at 73 Federal Register 70418 (November 20, 2008), but that involves 30,000 or more birds shall develop an animal waste management plan that complies with the testing and record-keeping requirements under subdivisions (6) through (8) of subsection (e) of this section. Any operator of this type of animal waste management system shall retain records required under this section and by the Department on-site for three years.

(f1) An animal waste management plan for a dry litter poultry facility required to be permitted under 40 Code of Federal Regulations § 122, as amended at 73 Federal Register 70418 (November 20, 2008), shall include the components set out in subdivisions (3), (6), (7), and (8) of subsection (e) of this section, and to the extent required by 40 Code of Federal Regulations § 122, as amended at 73 Federal Register 70418 (November 20, 2008), for land application discharges, subdivision (4) of subsection (e) of this section.

(g) The Commission shall encourage the development of alternative and innovative animal waste management technologies. The Commission shall provide sufficient flexibility in the regulatory process to allow for the timely evaluation of alternative and innovative animal waste management technologies and shall encourage operators of animal waste management systems to participate in the evaluation of these technologies. The Commission shall provide sufficient flexibility in the regulatory process to allow for the prompt implementation of alternative and innovative animal waste management technologies that are demonstrated to provide improved protection to public health and the environment.

(h) The owner or operator of an animal waste management system shall:

(1) In the event of a discharge of 1,000 gallons or more of animal waste to the surface waters of the State, issue a press release to all print and electronic news media that provide general coverage in the county where the discharge occurred setting out the details of the discharge. The owner or operator shall issue the press release within 48 hours after the owner or operator has

determined that the discharge has reached the surface waters of the State. The owner or operator shall retain a copy of the press release and a list of the news media to which it was distributed for at least one year after the discharge and shall provide a copy of the press release and the list of the news media to which it was distributed to any person upon request.

(2) In the event of a discharge of 15,000 gallons or more of animal waste to the surface waters of the State, publish a notice of the discharge in a newspaper having general circulation in the county in which the discharge occurs and in each county downstream from the point of discharge that is significantly affected by the discharge. The Secretary shall determine, at the Secretary's sole discretion, which counties are significantly affected by the discharge and shall approve the form and content of the notice and the newspapers in which the notice is to be published. The notice shall be captioned "NOTICE OF DISCHARGE OF ANIMAL WASTE". The owner or operator shall publish the notice within 10 days after the Secretary has determined the counties that are significantly affected by the discharge and approved the form and content of the notice and the newspapers in which the notice is to be published. The owner or operator shall file a copy of the notice and proof of publication with the Department within 30 days after the notice is published. Publication of a notice of discharge under this subdivision is in addition to the requirement to issue a press release under subdivision (1) of this subsection.

(i) A person who obtains an individual permit under G.S. 143-215.1 for an animal waste management system that serves a public livestock market shall not be required to obtain a permit under this Part and is not subject to the requirements of this Part. (1995 (Reg. Sess., 1996), c. 626, s. 1; 1997-458, s. 9.2; 1999-329, s. 8.2; 1999-456, s. 68; 2001-254, ss. 3, 4; 2001-326, s. 2; 2004-176, s. 2; 2009-92, s. 1; 2011-145, s. 13.22A(q); 2013-228, s. 1.)

§ 143-215.10D. Operations review.

(a) The Division, in cooperation with the Division of Soil and Water Conservation of the Department of Agriculture and Consumer Services, shall develop a reporting procedure for use by technical specialists who conduct operations reviews of animal operations. The reporting procedure shall be consistent with the Division's inspection procedure of animal operations and with this Part. The report shall include any corrective action recommended by the technical specialist to assist the owner or operator of the animal operation in complying with all permit requirements. The report shall be submitted to the Division within 10 days following the operations review unless the technical specialist observes a violation described in G.S. 143-215.10E. If the technical specialist finds a violation described in G.S. 143-215.10E, the report shall be filed with the Division immediately.

(b) An animal operation may request an operations review. The operations review shall be conducted by a technical specialist employed by the Division of Soil and Water Conservation of the Department of Agriculture and Consumer Services, a local Soil and Water Conservation District, or the federal Natural Resources Conservation Services working under the direction of the Division of Soil and Water Conservation.

(c) Operations reviews shall not be performed by technical specialists with a financial interest in any animal operation. (1995 (Reg. Sess., 1996), c. 626, s. 1; 2011-145, ss. 13.22(b), 13.22A(r); 2011-391, s. 30; 2012-194, s. 42(a).)

§ 143-215.10E. Violations requiring immediate notification.

(a) Any employee of a State agency or unit of local government lawfully on the premises and engaged in activities relating to the animal operation who observes any of the following violations shall immediately notify the owner or operator of the animal operation and the Division:

(1) Any direct discharge of animal waste into the waters of the State.

(2) Any deterioration or leak in a lagoon system that poses an immediate threat to the environment.

(3) Failure to maintain adequate storage capacity in a lagoon that poses an immediate threat to public health or the environment.

(4) Overspraying animal waste either in excess of the limits set out in the animal waste management plan or where runoff enters waters of the State.

(5) Any discharge that bypasses a lagoon system.

(b) Any employee of a federal agency lawfully on the premises and engaged in activities relating to the animal operation who observes any of the above violations is encouraged to immediately notify the Division. (1995 (Reg. Sess., 1996), c. 626, s. 1.)

§ 143-215.10F. Inspections.

(a) Except as provided in subsection (b) of this section, the Division shall conduct inspections of all animal operations that are subject to a permit under G.S. 143-215.10C at least once a year to determine whether the system is causing a violation of water quality standards and whether the system is in compliance with its animal waste management plan or any other condition of the permit.

(b) As an alternative to the inspection program set forth in subsection (a) of this section, the Division of Soil and Water Conservation of the Department of Agriculture and Consumer Services shall conduct inspections of all animal operations that are subject to a permit under G.S. 143-215.10C at least once a year to determine whether the system is causing a violation of water quality standards and whether the system is in compliance with its animal waste management plan or any other condition of the permit. The alternative inspection program shall be located in up to four counties selected using the criteria set forth in Section 15.4(a) of S.L. 1997-443, as amended, as it existed prior to its expiration. The Department of Agriculture and Consumer Services shall establish procedures whereby resources within the local Soil and Water Conservation Districts serving the counties are used for quick response to complaints and reported problems previously referred only to the Division of Water Resources. (1995 (Reg. Sess., 1996), c. 626, s. 1; 2013-131, s. 1; 2013-413, s. 57(gg).)

§ 143-215.10G. Fees for animal waste management systems.

(a) The Department shall charge an annual permit fee to an animal operation that is subject to a permit under G.S. 143-215.10C for an animal waste management system according to the following schedule:

(1) For a system with a design capacity of 38,500 or more and less than 100,000 pounds steady state live weight, sixty dollars ($60.00).

(2) For a system with a design capacity of 100,000 or more and less than 800,000 pounds steady state live weight, one hundred eighty dollars ($180.00).

(3) For a system with a design capacity of 800,000 pounds or more steady state live weight, three hundred sixty dollars ($360.00).

(a1) The Department shall charge an annual permit fee to a dry litter poultry facility that is subject to a permit under G.S. 143-215.10C for an animal waste management system according to the following schedule:

(1) For a system with a permitted capacity of less than 25,000 laying chickens, less than 37,500 nonlaying chickens, or less than 16,500 turkeys, sixty dollars ($60.00).

(2) For a system with a permitted capacity of 25,000 or more but less than 200,000 laying chickens, 37,500 or more but less than 290,000 nonlaying chickens, 16,500 or more but less than 133,000 turkeys, one hundred eighty dollars ($180.00).

(3) For a system with a permitted capacity of more than 200,000 laying chickens, more than 290,000 nonlaying chickens, or more than 133,000 turkeys, three hundred sixty dollars ($360.00).

(b) An application for a new permit under this section shall be accompanied by an initial application fee equal to the annual fee for that permit. If a permit is issued, the application fee shall be applied as the annual fee for the first year that the permit is in effect. If the application is denied, the application fee shall not be refunded.

(c) Fees collected under this section shall be credited to the Water and Air Quality Account. The Department shall use fees collected pursuant to this section to cover the costs of administering this Part. (1995 (Reg. Sess., 1996), c. 626, s. 1; 1997-496, s. 14; 1998-212, s. 29A.11(d); 2004-176, s. 3; 2007-323, s. 30.3(b).)

§ 143-215.10H. Swine integrator registration.

(a) Definitions. - As used in this section:

(1) "Grower" means a person who holds a permit for an animal waste management system under this Part or Part 1 of this Article for a swine farm, or who operates a swine farm that is subject to an operations review conducted pursuant to G.S. 143-215.10D or an inspection conducted pursuant to G.S. 143-215.10F.

(2) "Swine farm" has the same meaning as in G.S. 106-802.

(3) "Swine operation integrator" or "integrator" means a person, other than a grower, who provides 250 or more animals to a swine farm and who either has an ownership interest in the animals or otherwise establishes management and production standards for the permit holder for the maintenance, care, and raising of the animals. An ownership interest includes a right or option to purchase the animals.

(b) Registration Required. - As part of an operations review conducted pursuant to G.S. 143-215.10D or an inspection conducted pursuant to G.S. 143-215.10F, the Department shall require a grower to register any swine operation integrator with which the grower has a contractual relationship to raise swine. The registration shall be in writing and shall include only:

(1) The name of the owner of the swine farm.

(2) The mailing address of the owner of the swine farm.

(3) The physical location of the swine farm.

(4) The swine farm facility number.

(5) A description of the animal waste management system for the swine farm.

(6) The name and address of the grower, if different from the owner of the swine farm.

(7) The name and mailing address of the integrator.

(c) Notice of Termination or New Relationship. - If the swine operation integrator removes all animals from a swine farm or terminates the integrator's relationship with the swine farm, the grower shall notify the Department of the termination or removal within 30 days. If the grower terminates the grower's relationship with the integrator or enters into a relationship with a different integrator, the grower shall notify the Department of the termination or new relationship within 30 days.

(d) Disclosure of Violations. - The Department shall notify a swine operation integrator of all notices of deficiencies and violations of laws and rules governing the animal waste management system at any swine farm for which the integrator has been registered with the Department. A notice of deficiency or violation of any law or rule governing an animal waste management system is a public record within the meaning of G.S. 132-1 and is subject to disclosure as provided in Chapter 132 of the General Statutes. (1998-188, s. 1.)

§ 143-215.10I. Performance standards for animal waste management systems that serve swine farms; lagoon and sprayfield systems prohibited.

(a) As used in this section:

(1) "Anaerobic lagoon" means a lagoon that treats waste by converting it into carbon dioxide, methane, ammonia, and other gaseous compounds; organic acids; and cell tissue through an anaerobic process.

(2) "Anaerobic process" means a biological treatment process that occurs in the absence of dissolved oxygen.

(3) "Lagoon" has the same meaning as in G.S. 106-802.

(4) "Swine farm" has the same meaning as in G.S. 106-802.

(b) The Commission shall not issue or modify a permit to authorize the construction, operation, or expansion of an animal waste management system that serves a swine farm that employs an anaerobic lagoon as the primary method of treatment and land application of waste by means of a sprayfield as the primary method of waste disposal. The Commission may issue a permit for the construction, operation, or expansion of an animal waste management system that serves a swine farm under this Article only if the Commission determines that the animal waste management system will meet or exceed all of the following performance standards:

(1) Eliminate the discharge of animal waste to surface water and groundwater through direct discharge, seepage, or runoff.

(2) Substantially eliminate atmospheric emission of ammonia.

(3) Substantially eliminate the emission of odor that is detectable beyond the boundaries of the parcel or tract of land on which the swine farm is located.

(4) Substantially eliminate the release of disease-transmitting vectors and airborne pathogens.

(5) Substantially eliminate nutrient and heavy metal contamination of soil and groundwater. (2007-523, s. 1(a).)

§ 143-215.10J. Reserved for future codification purposes.

§ 143-215.10K. Reserved for future codification purposes.

§ 143-215.10L. Reserved for future codification purposes.

§ 143-215.10M. Reports.

(a) The Department shall report to the Environmental Review Commission and the Fiscal Research Division on or before 1 October of each year as required by this section. Each report shall include:

(1) The number of permits for animal waste management systems, itemized by type of animal subject to such permits, issued since the last report.

(2) The number of operations reviews of animal waste management systems that the Division of Soil and Water Conservation of the Department of Agriculture and Consumer Services has conducted since the last report.

(3) The number of operations reviews of animal waste management systems conducted by agencies other than the Division of Soil and Water Conservation of the Department of Agriculture and Consumer Services that have been conducted since the last report.

(4)   The number of reinspections associated with operations reviews conducted by the Division of Soil and Water Conservation of the Department of Agriculture and Consumer Services since the last report.

(5)   The number of reinspections associated with operations reviews conducted by agencies other than the Division of Soil and Water Conservation of the Department of Agriculture and Consumer Services since the last report.

(6)   The number of compliance inspections of animal waste management systems that the Division of Water Resources has conducted since the last report.

(7)   The number of follow-up inspections associated with compliance inspections conducted by the Division of Water Resources since the last report.

(8)   The average length of time for each category of reviews and inspections under subdivisions (2) through (7) of this subsection.

(9)   The number of violations found during each category of review and inspection under subdivisions (2) through (7) of this subsection, the status of enforcement actions taken and pending, and the penalties imposed, collected, and in the process of being negotiated for each such violation.

(10)   Any other information that the Department determines to be appropriate or that is requested by the Environmental Review Commission or the Fiscal Research Division.

(b)   The information to be included in the reports pursuant to subsection (a) of this section shall be itemized by each regional office of the Department, with totals for the State indicated.

(c)   Repealed by Session Laws 2002-148, s. 6 effective October 9, 2002. (1998-221, s. 4.2; 2002-148, s. 6; 2011-145, s. 13.22A(s); 2013-413, s. 57(o).)

Part 2. Regulation of Use of Water Resources.

§ 143-215.11. Short title.

This Part shall be known and may be cited as the Water Use Act of 1967. (1967, c. 933, s. 1.)

§ 143-215.12. Declaration of purpose.

It is hereby declared that the general welfare and public interest require that the water resources of the State be put to beneficial use to the fullest extent to which they are capable, subject to reasonable regulation in order to conserve these resources and to provide and maintain conditions which are conducive to the development and use of water resources. (1967, c. 933, s. 2.)

§ 143-215.13. Declaration of capacity use areas.

(a)   The Environmental Management Commission may declare and delineate from time to time, and may modify, capacity use areas of the State where it finds that the use of groundwater or surface water or both require coordination and limited regulation for protection of the interests and rights of residents or property owners of such areas or of the public interest.

(b)   Within the meaning of this Part "a capacity use area" is one where the Commission finds that the aggregate uses of groundwater or surface water, or both, in or affecting said area (i) have developed or threatened to develop to a degree which requires coordination and regulation, or (ii) exceed or threaten to exceed, or otherwise threaten or impair, the renewal or replenishment of such waters or any part of them.

(c)   The Commission may declare and delineate capacity use areas in accordance with the following procedures:

(1)   Whenever the Commission believes that a capacity use situation exists or may be emerging in any area of the State, it may direct the Department to investigate and report to the Commission thereon.

(2)   In conducting its investigation the Department shall consult with all interested persons, groups and agencies; may retain consultants; and shall consider all factors relevant to the conservation and use of water in the area, including established or pending water classifications under Part 1 of this Article

and the criteria for such classifications. Following its investigation the Department shall render a written report to the Commission. This report shall indicate whether the water use problems of the area involve surface waters, groundwaters or both and shall identify the Department's suggested boundaries for any capacity use area that may be proposed. It shall present such alternatives as the Department deems appropriate, including actions by any agency or person which might preclude the need for additional regulation at that time, and measures which might be employed limited to surface water or groundwater.

(3)   If the Commission finds, following its review of the departmental report (or thereafter following its evaluation of measures taken falling short of regulation) that a capacity use area should be declared, it may adopt a rule declaring said capacity use area. A rule declaring an area to be a capacity use area shall delineate the boundaries of the area.

(4)   to (6) Repealed by Session Laws 1981, c. 585, s. 3.

(7)   Repealed by Session Laws 1987, c. 827, s. 167.

(d)   The Commission may conduct a public hearing pursuant to the provisions of this subsection in any area of the State, whether or not a capacity use area has been declared, when it has reason to believe that the withdrawal of water from or the discharge of water pollutants to the waters in such area is having an unreasonably adverse effect upon such waters. If the Commission determines that withdrawals of water from or discharge of water pollutants to the waters within such area has resulted or probably will result in a generalized condition of water depletion or water pollution within the area to the extent that the availability or fitness for use of such water has been impaired for existing or proposed uses and that injury to the public health, safety or welfare will result if increased or additional withdrawals or discharges occur, the Commission may issue a rule:

(1)   Prohibiting any person withdrawing waters in excess of 100,000 gallons per day from increasing the amount of the withdrawal above such limit as may be established in the rule.

(2)   Prohibiting any person from constructing, installing or operating any new well or withdrawal facilities having a capacity in excess of a rate established in the rule; but such prohibition shall not extend to any new well or facility having a capacity of less than 10,000 gallons per day.

(3) Prohibiting any person discharging water pollutants to the waters from increasing the rate of discharge in excess of the rate established in the rule.

(4) Prohibiting any person from constructing, installing or operating any facility that will or may result in the discharge of water pollutants to the waters in excess of the rate established in the rule.

(5) Prohibiting any agency or political subdivision of the State from issuing any permit or similar document for the construction, installation, or operation of any new or existing facilities for withdrawing water from or discharging water pollutants to the waters in such area in excess of the rates established in the rule.

The determination of the Commission shall be based upon the record of the public hearing and other information considered by the Commission in the rule-making proceeding. The rule shall describe the geographical area of the State affected thereby with particularity and shall provide that the prohibitions set forth therein shall continue pending a determination by the Commission that the generalized condition of water depletion or water pollution within the area has ceased.

Upon issuance of any rule by the Commission pursuant to this subsection, a certified copy of such rule shall be mailed by registered or certified mail to the governing body of every county, city, town, and affected political subdivision lying, in whole or in part, within the area and to every affected or interested State and federal agency. A certified copy of the rule shall be posted at the courthouse in every county lying, in whole or in part, within the area, and a notice setting forth the substantive provisions and effective date of the rule shall be published once a week for two successive weeks in a newspaper or newspapers having general circulation within the area. After publication of notice is completed, any person violating any provision of such rule after the effective date thereof shall be subject to the penalties and proceedings set forth in G.S. 143-215.17. (1967, c. 933, s. 3; 1973, c. 698, s. 14; c. 1262, s. 23; 1977, c. 771, s. 4; 1981, c. 585, ss. 1-4; 1987, c. 827, ss. 154, 167.)

§ 143-215.14. Rules within capacity use areas; scope and procedures.

(a) Following the declaration of a capacity use area by the Commission, it shall prepare proposed rules to be applied in said area, containing such of the following provisions as the Commission finds appropriate concerning the use of surface waters or groundwaters or both:

(1) Provisions requiring water users within the area to submit reports not more frequently than at 30-day intervals concerning quantity of water used or withdrawn, sources of water and the nature of the use thereof.

(2) With respect to surface waters, groundwaters, or both: provisions concerning the timing of withdrawals; provisions to protect against or abate salt water encroachment; provisions to protect against or abate unreasonable adverse effects on other water users within the area, including but not limited to adverse effects on public use.

(3) With respect to groundwaters: provisions concerning well-spacing controls; and provisions establishing a range of prescribed pumping levels (elevations below which water may not be pumped) or maximum pumping rates, or both, in wells or for the aquifer or for any part thereof based on the capacities and characteristics of the aquifer.

(4) Such other provisions not inconsistent with this Part as the Commission finds necessary to implement the purposes of this Part.

(b) In adopting rules for a capacity use area, the Commission shall consider the factors listed in G.S. 143-215.15(h). (1967, c. 933, s. 4; 1973, c. 1262, s. 23; 1981, c. 585, s. 5; 1987, c. 827, ss. 154, 168.)

§ 143-215.15. Permits for water use within capacity use areas - Procedures.

(a) In areas declared by the Commission to be capacity use areas no person shall (after the expiration of such period, not in excess of six months, as the Commission may designate) withdraw, obtain, or utilize surface waters or groundwaters or both, as the case may be, in excess of 100,000 gallons per day for any purpose unless such person shall first obtain a permit therefor from the Commission.

(b) When sufficient evidence is provided by the applicant that the water withdrawn or used from a stream or the ground is not consumptively used, a permit therefor shall be issued by the Commission without a hearing and without the conditions provided in subsection (c) of this section. Applications for such permits shall set forth such facts as the Commission shall deem necessary to enable it to establish and maintain adequate records of all water uses within the capacity use area.

(c) In all cases in which sufficient evidence of a nonconsumptive use is not presented the Department shall notify each person required by this Part to secure a permit of the Commission's proposed action concerning such permit, and shall transmit with such notice a copy of any permit it proposes to issue to such persons, which permit will become final unless a request for a hearing is made within 15 days from the date of service of such notice. If sufficient evidence of a nonconsumptive use is not presented, the Commission may: (i) grant such permit with conditions as the Commission deems necessary to implement the rules adopted pursuant to G.S. 143-215.14; (ii) grant any temporary permit for such period of time as the Commission shall specify where conditions make such temporary permit essential, even though the action allowed by such permit may not be consistent with the Commission's rules applicable to such capacity use area; (iii) modify or revoke any permit upon not less than 60 days' written notice to any person affected; and (iv) deny such permit if the application therefor or the effect of the water use proposed or described therein upon the water resources of the area is found to be contrary to public interest. Before issuing a permit under this subsection, the Commission shall notify the permit applicant of its proposed action by sending the permit applicant a copy of the permit the Commission proposes to issue. Unless the permit applicant contests the proposed permit, the proposed permit shall become effective on the date set in the proposed permit. A water user who is dissatisifed with a decision of the Commission concerning that user's or another user's permit application or permit may commence a contested case under G.S. 150B-23.

(d) The Commission shall give notice of receipt of an application for a permit under this Part to all other holders of permits and applicants for permits under this Part within the same capacity use area, and to all other persons who have requested to be notified of permit applications. Notice of receipt of an application shall be given within 10 days of the receipt of the application by the Commission. The Commission shall also give notice of its proposed action on any permit application under this Part to all permit holders or permit applicants within the same capacity use area at least 18 days prior to the effective date of the proposed action. Notices of receipt of applications for permits and notice of proposed action on permits shall be by first-class mail and shall be effective upon depositing the notice, postage prepaid, in the United States mail.

(e) Repealed by Session Laws 1981, c. 585, s. 8.

(f) (1) Recodified as G.S. 143-215.4(d) by Session Laws 1987, c. 827, s. 169.

(2), (3) Repealed by Session Laws 1987, c. 827, s. 169.

(g) Repealed by Session Laws 1987, c. 827, s. 169.

(h) In determining whether to issue, modify, revoke, or deny a permit under this section, the Commission shall consider:

(1) The number of persons using an aquifer or stream and the object, extent and necessity of their respective withdrawals or uses;

(2) The nature and size of the stream or aquifer;

(3) The physical and chemical nature of any impairment of the aquifer or stream, adversely affecting its availability or fitness for other water uses (including public use);

(4) The probable severity and duration of such impairment under foreseeable conditions;

(5) The injury to public health, safety or welfare which would result if such impairment were not prevented or abated;

(6) The kinds of businesses or activities to which the various uses are related;

(7) The importance and necessity of the uses claimed by permit applicants (under this section), or of the water uses of the area (under G.S. 143-215.14) and the extent of any injury or detriment caused or expected to be caused to other water uses (including public use);

(8) Diversion from or reduction of flows in other watercourses or aquifers; and

(9) Any other relevant factors. (1967, c. 933, s. 5; 1973, c. 108, s. 89; c. 698, s. 15; c. 1262, s. 23; 1977, c. 771, s. 4; 1981, c. 585, ss. 6-10; 1987, c. 827, ss. 154, 169.)

§ 143-215.16. Permits for water use within capacity use areas - duration, transfer, reporting, measurement, present use, fees and penalties.

(a) No permit under G.S. 143-215.15 shall be issued for a longer period than the longest of the following: (i) 10 years, or (ii) the duration of the existence of a capacity use area, or (iii) the period found by the Commission to be necessary for reasonable amortization of the applicant's water-withdrawal and water-using facilities. Permits may be renewed following their expiration upon compliance with the provisions of G.S. 143-215.15.

(b) Permits shall not be transferred except with the approval of the Commission.

(c) Every person in a capacity use area who is required by this Part to secure a permit shall file with the Commission in the manner prescribed by the Commission a certified statement of quantities of water used and withdrawn, sources of water, and the nature of the use thereof not more frequently than 30-day intervals. Such statements shall be filed on forms furnished by the Department within 90 days after the adoption of an order by the Commission declaring a capacity use area. Water users in a capacity use area not required to secure a permit shall comply with procedures established to protect and manage the water resources of the area. Such procedures shall be adapted to the specific needs of the area, shall be within the provisions of this and other North Carolina water resource acts, and shall be adopted after public hearing in the area. The requirements embodied in the two preceding sentences shall not apply to individual domestic water use.

(d) If any person who is required to secure a permit under this Part is unable to furnish accurate information concerning amounts of water being withdrawn or used, or if there is evidence that his certified statement is false or inaccurate or that he is withdrawing or using a larger quantity of water or under different conditions than has been authorized by the Commission, the Commission shall have the authority to require such person to install water meters, or some other more economical means for measuring water use acceptable to the Commission. In determining the amount of water being withdrawn or used by a permit holder or applicant the Commission may use the rated capacity of his pumps, the rated capacity of his cooling system, data furnished by the applicant, or the standards or methods employed by the United States Geological Survey in determining such quantities or by any other accepted method.

(e) In any case where a permit applicant can prove to the Commission's satisfaction that the applicant was withdrawing or using water prior to the date of declaration of a capacity use area, the Commission shall take into consideration the extent to which such prior use or withdrawal was reasonably necessary in the judgment of the Commission to meet its needs, and shall grant a permit which shall meet those reasonable needs. Provided, however, that the granting of such permit shall not have unreasonably adverse effects upon other water uses in the area, including public use, and including potential as well as present use.

(f) The Commission shall also take into consideration in the granting of any permit the prior investments of any person in lands, and plans for the usage of water in connection with such lands which plans have been submitted to the Commission within a reasonable time after June 27, 1967. Provided, however, that the granting of such permit shall not have unreasonably adverse effects upon other water uses in the area, including public use, and including potential as well as present use.

(g) It is the intention of the General Assembly that if the provisions of subsection (e) or subsection (f) of this section are held invalid as a grant of an exclusive or separate emolument or privilege, within the meaning of Article I, Sec. 7 of the North Carolina Constitution, the remainder of this Part shall be given effect without the invalid provision or provisions.

(h) Pending the issuance or denial of a permit pursuant to subsection (e) or (f) of this section, the applicant may continue the same withdrawal or use which existed prior to the date of declaration of the capacity use area. (1967, c. 933, s. 6; 1973, c. 1262, s. 23; 1977, c. 771, s. 4; 1987, c. 827, s. 154.)

§ 143-215.17. Enforcement procedures.

(a) Criminal Penalties. - Any person who shall be adjudged to have violated any provision of this Part shall be guilty of a Class 3 misdemeanor and shall only be liable to a penalty of not less than one hundred dollars ($100.00) nor more than one thousand dollars ($1,000) for each violation. In addition, if any person is adjudged to have committed such violation willfully, the court may determine that each day during which such violation continued constitutes a separate violation subject to the foregoing penalty.

(b) Civil Penalties. -

(1) The Secretary may assess a civil penalty of not less than one hundred dollars ($100.00) nor more than one thousand dollars ($1,000) against any person who violates any provisions of, or any order issued pursuant to this Part, or who violates a rule of the Commission implementing this Part.

(2) If any action or failure to act for which a penalty may be assessed under this Part is willful, the Secretary may assess a penalty not to exceed one thousand dollars ($1,000) per day for each day of violation.

(3) In determining the amount of the penalty the Secretary shall consider the factors set out in G.S. 143B-282.1(b). The procedures set out in G.S. 143B-282.1 shall apply to civil penalty assessments that are presented to the Commission for final agency decision.

(4) The Secretary shall notify any person assessed a civil penalty of the assessment and the specific reasons therefor by registered or certified mail, or by any means authorized by G.S. 1A-1, Rule 4. Contested case petitions shall be filed within 30 days of receipt of the notice of assessment.

(5) Requests for remission of civil penalties shall be filed with the Secretary. Remission requests shall not be considered unless made within 30 days of receipt of the notice of assessment. Remission requests must be accompanied by a waiver of the right to a contested case hearing pursuant to Chapter 150B and a stipulation of the facts on which the assessment was based. Consistent with the limitations in G.S. 143B-282.1(c) and (d), remission requests may be resolved by the Secretary and the violator. If the Secretary and the violator are unable to resolve the request, the Secretary shall deliver remission requests and his recommended action to the Committee on Civil Penalty Remissions of the Environmental Management Commission appointed pursuant to G.S. 143B-282.1(c).

(6) If any civil penalty has not been paid within 30 days after notice of assessment has been served on the violator, the Secretary shall request the Attorney General to institute a civil action in the Superior Court of any county in which the violator resides or has his or its principal place of business to recover the amount of the assessment, unless the violator contests the assessment as provided in subdivision (4) of this subsection, or requests remission of the assessment in whole or in part as provided in subdivision (5) of this subsection. If any civil penalty has not been paid within 30 days after the final agency

decision or court order has been served on the violator, the Secretary shall request the Attorney General to institute a civil action in the Superior Court of any county in which the violator resides or has his or its principal place of business to recover the amount of the assessment.

(7) Repealed by Session Laws 1995 (Regular Session, 1996), c. 743, s. 15.

(8) The clear proceeds of civil penalties assessed pursuant to this subsection shall be remitted to the Civil Penalty and Forfeiture Fund in accordance with G.S. 115C-457.2.

(c) Injunctive Relief. - Upon violation of any of the provisions of this Part, a rule implementing this Part, or an order issued under this Part, the Secretary may, either before or after the institution of proceedings for the collection of the penalty imposed by this Part for such violations, request the Attorney General to institute a civil action in the superior court of the county or counties where the violation occurred in the name of the State upon the relation of the Department for injunctive relief to restrain the violation or require corrective action, and for such other or further relief in the premises as said court shall deem proper. Neither the institution of the action nor any of the proceedings thereon shall relieve any party to such proceedings from the penalty prescribed by this Part for any violation of same. (1967, c. 933, s. 7; 1973, c. 698, s. 16; c. 1262, s. 23; 1975, c. 842, s. 2; 1977, c. 771, s. 4; 1981, c. 585, s. 11; 1987, c. 827, ss. 154, 170; 1989 (Reg. Sess., 1990), c. 1036, s. 4; 1993, c. 539, s. 1020; 1994, Ex. Sess., c. 24, s. 14(c); 1995 (Reg. Sess., 1996), c. 743, s. 15; 1998-215, s. 64; 2009-134, s. 1.)

§ 143-215.18. Map or description of boundaries of capacity use areas.

(a) The Commission in designating and the Department in recommending the boundaries of any capacity use area may define such boundaries by showing them on a map or drawings, by a written description, or by any combination thereof, to be designated appropriately and filed permanently with the Department. Alterations in these lines shall be indicated by appropriate entries upon or additions to such map or description. Such entries shall be made under the direction of the Secretary of Environment and Natural Resources. Photographic, typed or other copies of such map or description, certified by the Secretary of Environment and Natural Resources, shall be admitted in evidence in all courts and shall have the same force and effect as would the original map or description. If the boundaries are changed pursuant to other provisions of this Part, the Department may provide for the redrawing of any such map. A redrawn map shall supersede for all purposes the earlier map or all maps which it is designated to replace.

(b) The Department shall file with the Secretary of State a certified copy of the map, drawings, description or combination thereof, showing the boundaries of any capacity use area designated by the Commission; and a certified copy of any redrawn or altered map or drawing, and of any amendments or additions to written descriptions, showing alterations to said boundaries. (1967, c. 933, s. 8; 1973, c. 1262, s. 23; c. 1331, s. 3; 1977, c. 771, s. 4; 1987, c. 827, ss. 154, 171; 1989, c. 727, s. 218(107); 1997-443, s. 11A.119(a).)

§ 143-215.19. Administrative inspection; reports.

(a) When necessary for enforcement of this Part, and when authorized by rules of the Commission, employees of the Commission may inspect any property, public or private, to investigate:

(1) The condition, withdrawal or use of any waters;

(2) Water sources; or

(3) The installation or operation of any well or surface water withdrawal or use facility.

(b) The Commission's rules must state appropriate standards for determining when property may be inspected under subsection (a).

(c) Entry to inspect property may be made without the possessor's consent only if the employee seeking to inspect has a valid administrative inspection warrant issued pursuant to G.S. 15-27.2.

(d) The Commission may also require the owner or possessor of any property to file written statements or submit reports under oath concerning the installation or operation of any well or surface water withdrawal or use facility.

(e) The Commission shall accompany any request or demand for information under this section with a notice that any trade secrets or confidential information concerning business activities is entitled to confidentiality as provided in this subsection. Upon a contention by any person that records, reports or information or any particular part thereof to which the Commission has access under this section, if made public would divulge methods or processes entitled to protection as trade secrets or would divulge confidential information concerning business activities, the Commission shall consider the material referred to as confidential, except that it may be made available in a separate file marked "Confidential Business Information" to employees of the department concerned with carrying out the provisions of this Part for that purpose only. The disclosure or use of such information in any administrative or judicial proceeding shall be governed by the rules of evidence, but the affected business shall be notified by the Commission at least seven days prior to any such proposed disclosure or use of information, and the Commission will not oppose a motion by any affected business to intervene as a party to the judicial or administrative proceeding. (1967, c. 933, s. 9; 1973, c. 1262, s. 23; 1981, c. 585, s. 12; 1987, c. 827, ss. 154, 172.)

§ 143-215.20. Repealed by Session Laws 1987, c. 827, s. 173.

§ 143-215.21. Definitions.

Unless the context otherwise requires, the following terms as used in this Part are defined as follows:

(1), (2) Repealed by Session Laws 1987, c. 827, s. 174.

(3) "Consumptive use" means any use of water withdrawn from a stream or the ground other than a "nonconsumptive use," as defined in this Part.

(4) Repealed by Session Laws 1987, c. 827, s. 174.

(5) "Nonconsumptive use" means (i) the use of water withdrawn from a stream in such a manner that it is returned to the stream without substantial diminution in quantity at or near the point from which it was taken; or, if the user owns both sides of the stream at the point of withdrawal, the water is returned to the stream upstream of the next property below the point of diversion on either side of the stream; (ii) the use of water withdrawn from a groundwater system or

aquifer in such a manner that it is returned to the groundwater system or aquifer from which it was withdrawn without substantial diminution in quantity or substantial impairment in quality at or near the point from which it was withdrawn; (iii) provided, however, that (in determining whether a use of groundwater is nonconsumptive) the Commission may take into consideration whether any material injury or detriment to other water users of the area by reason of reduction of water pressure in the aquifer or system has not been adequately compensated by the permit applicant who caused or substantially contributed to such injury or detriment.

(6), (7) Repealed by Session Laws 1987, c. 827, s. 174. (1967, c. 933, s. 11; 1973, c. 1262, s. 23; 1977, c. 771, s. 4; 1987, c. 827, ss. 154, 174.)

§ 143-215.22. Law of riparian rights not changed.

Nothing contained in this Part shall change or modify existing common or statutory law with respect to the relative rights of riparian owners concerning the use of surface water in this State. (1967, c. 933, s. 12.)

§ 143-215.22A. Water withdrawal policy; remedies.

(a) It is against the public policy of North Carolina to withdraw water from any major river or reservoir if both of the following factors are present: (i) the withdrawal will cause the natural flow of water in the river or a portion of the reservoir to be reversed; and (ii) substantial portions of the water are not returned to the river system after use. For purposes of this section, a withdrawal will cause natural flow to be reversed if as a result of the withdrawal, the rate of flow in the river or discrete portion of the reservoir is 15 cubic feet per second or more, moving in a generally opposite direction than prior to the withdrawal, over a distance of more than one mile. To correct for periodic effects, including tidal influences and reservoir fluctuations, flow speed and direction shall be calculated by using annual average flow data to determine pre-withdrawal flows, and projected annual average flow assuming the maximum practical rate of withdrawal, to determine post-withdrawal flows.

(b) This section shall not be construed to create an independent cause of action by the State or by any person. This section shall not apply to any project or facility for which a withdrawal of water began prior to the date this section is effective. (1991, c. 567, c. 712, ss. 5, 6.)

§ 143-215.22B. Roanoke River Basin water rights.

The State reserves and allocates to itself, as protector of the public interest, all rights in the water located in those portions of Kerr Lake and Lake Gaston that are in the State. (1995, c. 504, s. 1.)

§§ 143-215.22C through 143-215.22F. Reserved for future codification purposes.

Part 2A. Registration of Water Withdrawals and Transfers; Regulation of Surface Water Transfers.

§ 143-215.22G. Definitions.

In addition to the definitions set forth in G.S. 143-212 and G.S. 143-213, the following definitions apply to this Part.

(1) "Mainstem" means that portion of a river having the same name as a river basin defined in subdivision (1b) of this section. "Mainstem" does not include named or unnamed tributaries.

(1a) "Public water system" means any unit of local government or large community water system subject to the requirements of G.S. 143-355(l).

(1b) "River basin" means any of the following river basins designated on the map entitled "Major River Basins and Sub-basins in North Carolina" and filed in the Office of the Secretary of State on 16 April 1991. The term "river basin" includes any portion of the river basin that extends into another state. Any area outside North Carolina that is not included in one of the river basins listed in this subdivision comprises a separate river basin.

| a. | 1-1 | Broad River. |

b.	2-1	Haw River.
c.	2-2	Deep River.
d.	2-3	Cape Fear River.
e.	2-4	South River.
f.	2-5	Northeast Cape Fear River.
g.	2-6	New River.
h.	3-1	Catawba River.
i.	3-2	South Fork Catawba River.
j.	4-1	Chowan River.
k.	4-2	Meherrin River.
l.	5-1	Nolichucky River.
m.	5-2	French Broad River.
n.	5-3	Pigeon River.
o.	6-1	Hiwassee River.
p.	7-1	Little Tennessee River.
q.	7-2	Tuskasegee (Tuckasegee) River.
r.	8-1	Savannah River.
s.	9-1	Lumber River.
t.	9-2	Big Shoe Heel Creek.
u.	9-3	Waccamaw River.
v.	9-4	Shallotte River.

w.	10-1	Neuse River.
x.	10-2	Contentnea Creek.
y.	10-3	Trent River.
z.	11-1	New River.
aa.	12-1	Albemarle Sound.
bb.	13-1	Ocoee River.
cc.	14-1	Roanoke River.
dd.	15-1	Tar River.
ee.	15-2	Fishing Creek.
ff.	15-3	Pamlico River and Sound.
gg.	16-1	Watauga River.
hh.	17-1	White Oak River.
ii.	18-1	Yadkin (Yadkin-Pee Dee) River.
jj.	18-2	South Yadkin River.
kk.	18-3	Uwharrie River.
ll.	18-4	Rocky River.

(2) "Surface water" means any of the waters of the State located on the land surface that are not derived by pumping from groundwater.

(3) "Transfer" means the withdrawal, diversion, or pumping of surface water from one river basin and discharge of all or any part of the water in a river basin different from the origin. However, notwithstanding the basin definitions in G.S. 143-215.22G(1b), the following are not transfers under this Part:

a. The discharge of water upstream from the point where it is withdrawn.

b. The discharge of water downstream from the point where it is withdrawn. (1991, c. 712, s. 1; 1993, c. 348, s. 1; 1997-443, s. 15.48(b); 2013-388, s. 1.)

§ 143-215.22H. Registration of water withdrawals and transfers required.

(a) Any person who withdraws 100,000 gallons per day or more of water from the surface or groundwaters of the State or who transfers 100,000 gallons per day or more of water from one river basin to another shall register the withdrawal or transfer with the Commission. A person registering a water withdrawal or transfer shall provide the Commission with the following information:

(1) The maximum daily amount of the water withdrawal or transfer expressed in thousands of gallons per day.

(1a) The monthly average withdrawal or transfer expressed in thousands of gallons per day.

(2) The location of the points of withdrawal and discharge and the capacity of each facility used to make the withdrawal or transfer.

(3) The monthly average discharge expressed in thousands of gallons per day.

(b) Any person initiating a new water withdrawal or transfer of 100,000 gallons per day or more shall register the withdrawal or transfer with the Commission not later than two months after the initiation of the withdrawal or transfer. The information required under subsection (a) of this section shall be submitted with respect to the new withdrawal or transfer.

(b1) Subsections (a) and (b) of this section shall not apply to a person who withdraws or transfers less than 1,000,000 gallons per day of water for activities directly related or incidental to the production of crops, fruits, vegetables, ornamental and flowering plants, dairy products, livestock, poultry, and other agricultural products, or to the creation or maintenance of waterfowl impoundments.

(b2) Registration of a withdrawal or transfer of water under this section or information that is provided by a water user pursuant to G.S. 106-24 and authorized for release to the Commission by the individual water user may be used as evidence of historic water use in the event that it becomes necessary or desirable to allocate available water resources among specific classes, persons, or individuals who use water resources.

(c) A unit of local government that has completed a local water supply plan that meets the requirements of G.S. 143-355(l) and that has periodically revised and updated its plan as required by the Department has satisfied the requirements of this section and is not required to separately register a water withdrawal or transfer or to update a registration under this section.

(d) Any person who is required to register a water withdrawal or transfer under this section shall update the registration by providing the Commission with a current version of the information required by subsection (a) of this section at five-year intervals following the initial registration. A person who submits information to update a registration of a water withdrawal or transfer is not required to pay an additional registration fee under G.S. 143-215.3(a)(1a) and G.S. 143-215.3(a)(1b), but is subject to the civil penalty established under this section in the event that updated information is not submitted as required by this subsection.

(e) Any person who is required to register a water transfer or withdrawal under this section and fails to do so shall pay, in addition to the registration fee required under G.S. 143-215.3(a)(1a) and G.S. 143-215.3(a)(1b), a civil penalty of one hundred dollars ($100.00). A person who is required to update a registration under this section and fails to do so shall pay a civil penalty of fifty dollars ($50.00). For each willful action or failure to act for which a penalty may be assessed under this subsection, the Commission may consider each day the action or inaction continues after notice is given of the violation as a separate violation. A separate penalty may be assessed for each separate violation. (1991, c. 712, s. 1; 1993, c. 344, s. 1; c. 553, s. 81; 1998-168, s. 3; 2008-143, s. 1; 2008-198, s. 11.6.)

§ 143-215.22I: Repealed by Session Laws 2007-518, s. 2, effective August 31, 2007, and applicable to any petition for a certificate for a transfer of surface water from one river basin to another river basin for which preparation of an environmental assessment or an environmental impact statement has begun on or after August 31, 2007.

§ 143-215.22J: Repealed by Session Laws 2004-195, s. 3.1, effective August 17, 2004.

§ 143-215.22K: Repealed by Session Laws 2004-195, s. 3.1, effective August 17, 2004.

§ 143-215.22L. Regulation of surface water transfers.

(a) Certificate Required. - No person, without first obtaining a certificate from the Commission, may:

(1) Initiate a transfer of 2,000,000 gallons of water or more per day, calculated as a daily average of a calendar month and not to exceed 3,000,000 gallons per day in any one day, from one river basin to another.

(2) Increase the amount of an existing transfer of water from one river basin to another by twenty-five percent (25%) or more above the average daily amount transferred during the year ending 1 July 1993 if the total transfer including the increase is 2,000,000 gallons or more per day.

(3) Increase an existing transfer of water from one river basin to another above the amount approved by the Commission in a certificate issued under G.S. 162A-7 prior to 1 July 1993.

(b) Exception. - Notwithstanding the provisions of subsection (a) of this section, a certificate shall not be required to transfer water from one river basin to another up to the full capacity of a facility to transfer water from one basin to another if the facility was in existence or under construction on 1 July 1993.

(c) Notice of Intent to File a Petition. - An applicant shall prepare a notice of intent to file a petition that includes a nontechnical description of the applicant's request and an identification of the proposed water source. Within 90 days after the applicant files a notice of intent to file a petition, the applicant shall hold at least one public meeting in the source river basin upstream from the proposed point of withdrawal, at least one public meeting in the source river basin downstream from the proposed point of withdrawal, and at least one public meeting in the receiving river basin to provide information to interested parties and the public regarding the nature and extent of the proposed transfer and to receive comment on the scope of the environmental documents. Written notice of the public meetings shall be provided at least 30 days before the public meetings. At the time the applicant gives notice of the public meetings, the applicant shall request comment on the alternatives and issues that should be addressed in the environmental documents required by this section. The applicant shall accept written comment on the scope of the environmental documents for a minimum of 30 days following the last public meeting. Notice of the public meetings and opportunity to comment on the scope of the environmental documents shall be provided as follows:

(1) By publishing notice in the North Carolina Register.

(2) By publishing notice in a newspaper of general circulation in:

a. Each county in this State located in whole or in part of the area of the source river basin upstream from the proposed point of withdrawal.

b. Each city or county located in a state located in whole or in part of the surface drainage basin area of the source river basin that also falls within, in whole or in part, the area denoted by one of the following eight-digit cataloging units as organized by the United States Geological Survey:

03050105 (Broad River: NC and SC);

03050106 (Broad River: SC);

03050107 (Broad River: SC);

03050108 (Broad River: SC);

05050001 (New River: NC and VA);

05050002 (New River: VA and WV);

03050101 (Catawba River: NC and SC);

03050103 (Catawba River: NC and SC);

03050104 (Catawba River: SC);

03010203 (Chowan River: NC and VA);

03010204 (Chowan River: NC and VA);

06010105 (French Broad River: NC and TN);

06010106 (French Broad River: NC and TN);

06010107 (French Broad River: TN);

06010108 (French Broad River: NC and TN);

06020001 (Hiwassee River: AL, GA, TN);

06020002 (Hiwassee River: GA, NC, TN);

06010201 (Little Tennessee River: TN);

06010202 (Little Tennessee River: TN, GA, and NC);

06010204 (Little Tennessee River: NC and TN);

03060101 (Savannah River: NC and SC);

03060102 (Savannah River: GA, NC, and SC);

03060103 (Savannah River: GA and SC);

03060104 (Savannah River: GA);

03060105 (Savannah River: GA);

03040203 (Lumber River: NC and SC);

03040204 (Lumber River: NC and SC);

03040206 (Lumber River: NC and SC);

03040207 (Lumber River: NC and SC);

03010205 (Albemarle Sound: NC and VA);

06020003 (Ocoee River: GA, NC, and TN);

03010101 (Roanoke River: VA);

03010102 (Roanoke River: NC and VA);

03010103 (Roanoke River: NC and VA);

03010104 (Roanoke River: NC and VA);

03010105 (Roanoke River: VA);

03010106 (Roanoke River: NC and VA);

06010102 (Watauga River: TN and VA);

06010103 (Watauga River: NC and TN);

03040101 (Yadkin River: VA and NC);

03040104 (Yadkin River: NC and SC);

03040105 (Yadkin River: NC and SC);

03040201 (Yadkin River: NC and SC);

03040202 (Yadkin River: NC and SC).

c. Each county in this State located in whole or in part of the area of the source river basin downstream from the proposed point of withdrawal.

d. Any area in the State in a river basin for which the source river basin has been identified as a future source of water in a local water supply plan prepared pursuant to G.S. 143-355(l).

e. Each county in the State located in whole or in part of the receiving river basin.

(3) By giving notice by first-class mail or electronic mail to each of the following:

a. The board of commissioners of each county in this State or the governing body of any county or city that is politically independent of a county in any state that is located entirely or partially within the source river basin of the proposed transfer and that also falls within, in whole or in part, the area denoted by one of the eight-digit cataloging units listed in sub-subdivision b. of subdivision (2) of this subsection.

b. The board of commissioners of each county in this State or the governing body of any county or city that is politically independent of a county in any state that is located entirely or partially within the receiving river basin of the proposed transfer and that also falls within, in whole or in part, the area denoted by one of the eight-digit cataloging units listed in sub-subdivision b. of subdivision (2) of this subsection.

c. The governing body of any public water system that withdraws water upstream or downstream from the withdrawal point of the proposed transfer.

d. If any portion of the source or receiving river basins is located in another state, all state water management or use agencies, environmental protection agencies, and the office of the governor in that state upstream or downstream from the withdrawal point of the proposed transfer.

e. All persons who have registered a water withdrawal or transfer from the proposed source river basin under this Part or under similar law in an another state.

f. All persons who hold a certificate for a transfer of water from the proposed source river basin under this Part or under similar law in an another state.

g. All persons who hold a National Pollutant Discharge Elimination System (NPDES) wastewater discharge permit for a discharge of 100,000 gallons per day or more upstream or downstream from the proposed point of withdrawal.

h. To any other person who submits to the applicant a written request to receive all notices relating to the petition.

(d) Environmental Documents. - The definitions set out in G.S. 113A-9 apply to this section. The Department shall conduct a study of the environmental impacts of any proposed transfer of water for which a certificate is required under this section. The study shall meet all of the requirements set forth in G.S. 113A-4 and rules adopted pursuant to G.S. 113A-4. An environmental assessment shall be prepared for any petition for a certificate under this section. The determination of whether an environmental impact statement shall also be required shall be made in accordance with the provisions of Article 1 of Chapter

113A of the General Statutes; except that an environmental impact statement shall be prepared for every proposed transfer of water from one major river basin to another for which a certificate is required under this section. The applicant who petitions the Commission for a certificate under this section shall pay the cost of special studies necessary to comply with Article 1 of Chapter 113A of the General Statutes. An environmental impact statement prepared pursuant to this subsection shall include all of the following:

(1) A comprehensive analysis of the impacts that would occur in the source river basin and the receiving river basin if the petition for a certificate is granted.

(2) An evaluation of alternatives to the proposed interbasin transfer, including water supply sources that do not require an interbasin transfer and use of water conservation measures.

(3) A description of measures to mitigate any adverse impacts that may arise from the proposed interbasin transfer.

(e) Public Hearing on the Draft Environmental Document. - The Commission shall hold a public hearing on the draft environmental document for a proposed interbasin transfer after giving at least 30 days' written notice of the hearing in the Environmental Bulletin and as provided in subdivisions (2) and (3) of subsection (c) of this section. The notice shall indicate where a copy of the environmental document can be reviewed and the procedure to be followed by anyone wishing to submit written comments and questions on the environmental document. The Commission shall prepare a record of all comments and written responses to questions posed in writing. The record shall include complete copies of scientific or technical comments related to the potential impact of the interbasin transfer. The Commission shall accept written comment on the draft environmental document for a minimum of 30 days following the last public hearing. The applicant who petitions the Commission for a certificate under this section shall pay the costs associated with the notice and public hearing on the draft environmental document.

(f) Determination of Adequacy of Environmental Document. - The Commission shall not act on any petition for an interbasin transfer until the Commission has determined that the environmental document is complete and adequate. A decision on the adequacy of the environmental document is subject to review in a contested case on the decision of the Commission to issue or deny a certificate under this section.

(g) Petition. - An applicant for a certificate shall petition the Commission for the certificate. The petition shall be in writing and shall include all of the following:

(1) A general description of the facilities to be used to transfer the water, including current and projected areas to be served by the transfer, current and projected capacities of intakes, and other relevant facilities.

(2) A description of all the proposed consumptive and nonconsumptive uses of the water to be transferred.

(3) A description of the water quality of the source river and receiving river, including information on aquatic habitat for rare, threatened, and endangered species; in-stream flow data for segments of the source and receiving rivers that may be affected by the transfer; and any waters that are impaired pursuant to section 303(d) of the federal Clean Water Act (33 U.S.C. § 1313(d)).

(4) A description of the water conservation measures used by the applicant at the time of the petition and any additional water conservation measures that the applicant will implement if the certificate is granted.

(5) A description of all sources of water within the receiving river basin, including surface water impoundments, groundwater wells, reinjection storage, and purchase of water from another source within the river basin, that is a practicable alternative to the proposed transfer that would meet the applicant's water supply needs. The description of water sources shall include sources available at the time of the petition for a certificate and any planned or potential water sources.

(6) A description of water transfers and withdrawals registered under G.S. 143-215.22H or included in a local water supply plan prepared pursuant to G.S. 143-355(l) from the source river basin, including transfers and withdrawals at the time of the petition for a certificate and any planned or reasonably foreseeable transfers or withdrawals by a public water system with service area located within the source river basin.

(7) A demonstration that the proposed transfer, if added to all other transfers and withdrawals required to be registered under G.S. 143-215.22H or included in any local water supply plan prepared by a public water system with service area located within the source basin pursuant to G.S. 143-355(l) from the source river basin at the time of the petition for a certificate, would not

reduce the amount of water available for use in the source river basin to a degree that would impair existing uses, pursuant to the antidegradation policy set out in 40 Code of Federal Regulation § 131.12 (Antidegradation Policy) (1 July 2006 Edition) and the statewide antidegradation policy adopted pursuant thereto, or existing and planned consumptive and nonconsumptive uses of the water in the source river basin. If the proposed transfer would impact a reservoir within the source river basin, the demonstration must include a finding that the transfer would not result in a water level in the reservoir that is inadequate to support existing uses of the reservoir, including recreational uses.

(8) The applicant's future water supply needs and the present and reasonably foreseeable future water supply needs for public water systems with service area located within the source river basin. The analysis of future water supply needs shall include agricultural, recreational, and industrial uses, and electric power generation. Local water supply plans prepared pursuant to G.S. 143-355(l) for water systems with service area located within the source river basin shall be used to evaluate the projected future water needs in the source river basin that will be met by public water systems.

(9) The applicant's water supply plan prepared pursuant to G.S. 143-355(l). If the applicant's water supply plan is more than two years old at the time of the petition, then the applicant shall include with the petition an updated water supply plan.

(10) Any other information deemed necessary by the Commission for review of the proposed water transfer.

(h) Settlement Discussions. - Upon the request of the applicant, any interested party, or the Department, or upon its own motion, the Commission may appoint a mediation officer. The mediation officer may be a member of the Commission, an employee of the Department, or a neutral third party but shall not be a hearing officer under subsections (e) or (j) of this section. The mediation officer shall make a reasonable effort to initiate settlement discussions between the applicant and all other interested parties. Evidence of statements made and conduct that occurs in a settlement discussion conducted under this subsection, whether attributable to a party, a mediation officer, or other person shall not be subject to discovery and shall be inadmissible in any subsequent proceeding on the petition for a certificate. The Commission may adopt rules to govern the conduct of the mediation process.

(i) Draft Determination. - Within 90 days after the Commission determines that the environmental document prepared in accordance with subsection (d) of this section is adequate or the applicant submits its petition for a certificate, whichever occurs later, the Commission shall issue a draft determination on whether to grant the certificate. The draft determination shall be based on the criteria set out in this section and shall include the conditions and limitations, findings of fact, and conclusions of law that would be required in a final determination. Notice of the draft determination shall be given as provided in subsection (c) of this section.

(j) Public Hearing on the Draft Determination. - Within 60 days of the issuance of the draft determination as provided in subsection (i) of this section, the Commission shall hold public hearings on the draft determination. At least one hearing shall be held in the affected area of the source river basin, and at least one hearing shall be held in the affected area of the receiving river basin. In determining whether more than one public hearing should be held within either the source or receiving river basins, the Commission shall consider the differing or conflicting interests that may exist within the river basins, including the interests of both upstream and downstream parties potentially affected by the proposed transfer. The public hearings shall be conducted by one or more hearing officers appointed by the Chair of the Commission. The hearing officers may be members of the Commission or employees of the Department. The Commission shall give at least 30 days' written notice of the public hearing as provided in subsection (c) of this section. The Commission shall accept written comment on the draft determination for a minimum of 30 days following the last public hearing. The Commission shall prepare a record of all comments and written responses to questions posed in writing. The record shall include complete copies of scientific or technical comments related to the potential impact of the interbasin transfer. The applicant who petitions the Commission for a certificate under this section shall pay the costs associated with the notice and public hearing on the draft determination.

(k) Final Determination: Factors to be Considered. - In determining whether a certificate may be issued for the transfer, the Commission shall specifically consider each of the following items and state in writing its findings of fact and conclusions of law with regard to each item:

(1) The necessity and reasonableness of the amount of surface water proposed to be transferred and its proposed uses.

(2) The present and reasonably foreseeable future detrimental effects on the source river basin, including present and future effects on public, industrial, economic, recreational, and agricultural water supply needs, wastewater assimilation, water quality, fish and wildlife habitat, electric power generation, navigation, and recreation. Local water supply plans for public water systems with service area located within the source river basin prepared pursuant to G.S. 143-355(l) shall be used to evaluate the projected future water needs in the source river basin that will be met by public water systems. Information on projected future water needs for public water systems with service area located within the source river basin that is more recent than the local water supply plans may be used if the Commission finds the information to be reliable. The determination shall include a specific finding as to measures that are necessary or advisable to mitigate or avoid detrimental impacts on the source river basin.

(3) The cumulative effect on the source major river basin of any water transfer or consumptive water use that, at the time the Commission considers the petition for a certificate is occurring, is authorized under this section, or is projected in any local water supply plan for public water systems with service area located within the source river basin that has been submitted to the Department in accordance with G.S. 143-355(l).

(4) The present and reasonably foreseeable future beneficial and detrimental effects on the receiving river basin, including present and future effects on public, industrial, economic, recreational, and agricultural water supply needs, wastewater assimilation, water quality, fish and wildlife habitat, electric power generation, navigation, and recreation. Local water supply plans prepared pursuant to G.S. 143-355(l) that affect the receiving river basin shall be used to evaluate the projected future water needs in the receiving river basin that will be met by public water systems. Information on projected future water needs that is more recent than the local water supply plans may be used if the Commission finds the information to be reliable. The determination shall include a specific finding as to measures that are necessary or advisable to mitigate or avoid detrimental impacts on the receiving river basin.

(5) The availability of reasonable alternatives to the proposed transfer, including the potential capacity of alternative sources of water, the potential of each alternative to reduce the amount of or avoid the proposed transfer, probable costs, and environmental impacts. In considering alternatives, the Commission is not limited to consideration of alternatives that have been proposed, studied, or considered by the applicant. The determination shall include a specific finding as to why the applicant's need for water cannot be

satisfied by alternatives within the receiving basin, including unused capacity under a transfer for which a certificate is in effect or that is otherwise authorized by law at the time the applicant submits the petition. The determination shall consider the extent to which access to potential sources of surface water or groundwater within the receiving river basin is no longer available due to depletion, contamination, or the declaration of a capacity use area under Part 2 of Article 21 of Chapter 143 of the General Statutes. The determination shall consider the feasibility of the applicant's purchase of water from other water suppliers within the receiving basin and of the transfer of water from another sub-basin within the receiving major river basin. Except in circumstances of technical or economic infeasibility or adverse environmental impact, the Commission's determination as to reasonable alternatives shall give preference to alternatives that would involve a transfer from one sub-basin to another within the major receiving river basin over alternatives that would involve a transfer from one major river basin to another major river basin.

(6) If applicable to the proposed project, the applicant's present and proposed use of impoundment storage capacity to store water during high-flow periods for use during low-flow periods and the applicant's right of withdrawal under G.S. 143-215.44 through G.S. 143-215.50.

(7) If the water to be withdrawn or transferred is stored in a multipurpose reservoir constructed by the United States Army Corps of Engineers, the purposes and water storage allocations established for the reservoir at the time the reservoir was authorized by the Congress of the United States.

(8) Whether the service area of the applicant is located in both the source river basin and the receiving river basin.

(9) Any other facts and circumstances that are reasonably necessary to carry out the purposes of this Part.

(l) Final Determination: Information to be Considered. - In determining whether a certificate may be issued for the transfer, the Commission shall consider all of the following sources of information:

(1) The petition.

(2) The environmental document prepared pursuant to subsection (d) of this section.

(3) All oral and written comment and all accompanying materials or evidence submitted pursuant to subsections (e) and (j) of this section.

(4) Information developed by or available to the Department on the water quality of the source river basin and the receiving river basin, including waters that are identified as impaired pursuant to section 303(d) of the federal Clean Water Act (33 U.S.C. § 1313(d)), that are subject to a total maximum daily load (TMDL) limit under subsections (d) and (e) of section 303 of the federal Clean Water Act, or that would have their assimilative capacity impaired if the certificate is issued.

(5) Any other information that the Commission determines to be relevant and useful.

(m) Final Determination: Burden and Standard of Proof; Specific Findings. - The Commission shall grant a certificate for a water transfer if the Commission finds that the applicant has established by a preponderance of the evidence all of the following:

(1) The benefits of the proposed transfer outweigh the detriments of the proposed transfer. In making this determination, the Commission shall be guided by the approved environmental document and the policy set out in subsection (t) of this section.

(2) The detriments have been or will be mitigated to the maximum degree practicable.

(3) The amount of the transfer does not exceed the amount of the projected shortfall under the applicant's water supply plan after first taking into account all other sources of water that are available to the applicant.

(4) There are no reasonable alternatives to the proposed transfer.

(n) Final Determination: Certificate Conditions and Limitations. - The Commission may grant the certificate in whole or in part, or deny the certificate. The Commission may impose any conditions or limitations on a certificate that the Commission finds necessary to achieve the purposes of this Part including a limit on the period for which the certificate is valid. The conditions and limitations shall include any mitigation measures proposed by the applicant to minimize any detrimental effects within the source and receiving river basins. In addition, the certificate shall require all of the following conditions and limitations:

(1) A water conservation plan that specifies the water conservation measures that will be implemented by the applicant in the receiving river basin to ensure the efficient use of the transferred water. Except in circumstances of technical or economic infeasibility or adverse environmental impact, the water conservation plan shall provide for the mandatory implementation of water conservation measures by the applicant that equal or exceed the most stringent water conservation plan implemented by a public water system that withdraws water from the source river basin.

(2) A drought management plan that specifies how the transfer shall be managed to protect the source river basin during drought conditions or other emergencies that occur within the source river basin. Except in circumstances of technical or economic infeasibility or adverse environmental impact, this drought management plan shall include mandatory reductions in the permitted amount of the transfer based on the severity and duration of a drought occurring within the source river basin and shall provide for the mandatory implementation of a drought management plan by the applicant that equals or exceeds the most stringent water conservation plan implemented by a public water system that withdraws water from the source river basin.

(3) The maximum amount of water that may be transferred, calculated as a daily average of a calendar month, and methods or devices required to be installed and operated that measure the amount of water that is transferred.

(4) A provision that the Commission may amend a certificate to reduce the maximum amount of water authorized to be transferred whenever it appears that an alternative source of water is available to the certificate holder from within the receiving river basin, including, but not limited to, the purchase of water from another water supplier within the receiving basin or to the transfer of water from another sub-basin within the receiving major river basin.

(5) A provision that the Commission shall amend the certificate to reduce the maximum amount of water authorized to be transferred if the Commission finds that the applicant's current projected water needs are significantly less than the applicant's projected water needs at the time the certificate was granted.

(6) A requirement that the certificate holder report the quantity of water transferred during each calendar quarter. The report required by this subdivision shall be submitted to the Commission no later than 30 days after the end of the quarter.

(7) Except as provided in this subdivision, a provision that the applicant will not resell the water that would be transferred pursuant to the certificate to another public water system. This limitation shall not apply in the case of a proposed resale or transfer among public water systems within the receiving river basin as part of an interlocal agreement or other regional water supply arrangement, provided that each participant in the interlocal agreement or regional water supply arrangement is a co-applicant for the certificate and will be subject to all the terms, conditions, and limitations made applicable to any lead or primary applicant.

(o) Administrative and Judicial Review. - Administrative and judicial review of a final decision on a petition for a certificate under this section shall be governed by Chapter 150B of the General Statutes.

(p) Certain Preexisting Transfers. - In cases where an applicant requests approval to increase a transfer that existed on 1 July 1993, the Commission may approve or disapprove only the amount of the increase. If the Commission approves the increase, the certificate shall be issued for the amount of the preexisting transfer plus any increase approved by the Commission. A certificate for a transfer approved by the Commission under G.S. 162A-7 shall remain in effect as approved by the Commission and shall have the same effect as a certificate issued under this Part. A certificate for the increase of a preexisting transfer shall contain all of the conditions and limitations required by subsection (m) of this section.

(q) Emergency Transfers. - In the case of water supply problems caused by drought, a pollution incident, temporary failure of a water plant, or any other temporary condition in which the public health, safety, or welfare requires a transfer of water, the Secretary of Environment and Natural Resources may grant approval for a temporary transfer. Prior to approving a temporary transfer, the Secretary shall consult with those parties listed in subdivision (3) of subsection (c) of this section that are likely to be affected by the proposed transfer. However, the Secretary shall not be required to satisfy the public notice requirements of this section or make written findings of fact and conclusions of law in approving a temporary transfer under this subsection. If the Secretary approves a temporary transfer under this subsection, the Secretary shall specify conditions to protect other water users. A temporary transfer shall not exceed six months in duration, but the approval may be renewed for a period of six months by the Secretary based on demonstrated need as set forth in this subsection.

(r) Relationship to Federal Law. - The substantive restrictions, conditions, and limitations upon surface water transfers authorized in this section may be imposed pursuant to any federal law that permits the State to certify, restrict, or condition any new or continuing transfers or related activities licensed, relicensed, or otherwise authorized by the federal government. This section shall govern the transfer of water from one river basin to another unless preempted by federal law.

(s) Planning Requirements. - When any transfer for which a certificate was issued under this section equals or exceeds eighty percent (80%) of the maximum amount authorized in the certificate, the applicant shall submit to the Department a detailed plan that specifies how the applicant intends to address future foreseeable water needs. If the applicant is required to have a local water supply plan, then this plan shall be an amendment to the local water supply plan required by G.S.143-355(I). When the transfer equals or exceeds ninety percent (90%) of the maximum amount authorized in the certificate, the applicant shall begin implementation of the plan submitted to the Department.

(t) Statement of Policy. - It is the public policy of the State to maintain, protect, and enhance water quality within North Carolina. It is the public policy of this State that the reasonably foreseeable future water needs of a public water system with its service area located primarily in the receiving river basin are subordinate to the reasonably foreseeable future water needs of a public water system with its service area located primarily in the source river basin. Further, it is the public policy of the State that the cumulative impact of transfers from a source river basin shall not result in a violation of the antidegradation policy set out in 40 Code of Federal Regulations § 131.12 (1 July 2006 Edition) and the statewide antidegradation policy adopted pursuant thereto.

(u) Repealed by Session Laws 2013-388, s. 2, effective August 23, 2013.

(v) Modification of Certificate. - A certificate may be modified as provided in this subsection:

(1) The Commission or the Department may make any of the following modifications to a certificate after providing electronic notice to persons who have identified themselves in writing as interested parties:

a. Correction of typographical errors.

b. Clarification of existing conditions or language.

c. Updates, requested by the certificate holder, to a conservation plan, drought management plan, or compliance and monitoring plan.

d. Modifications requested by the certificate holder to reflect altered requirements due to the amendment of this section.

(2) A person who holds a certificate for an interbasin transfer of water may request that the Commission modify the certificate. The request shall be considered and a determination made according to the following procedures:

a. The certificate must have been issued pursuant to G.S. 162A-7, 143-215.22I, or 143-215.22L and the certificate holder must be in substantial compliance with the certificate.

b. The certificate holder shall file a notice of intent to file a request for modification that includes a nontechnical description of the certificate holder's request and identification of the proposed water source.

c. The certificate holder shall prepare an environmental document pursuant to subsection (d) of this section, except that an environmental impact statement shall not be required for the modification of a certificate unless it would otherwise be required by Article 1 of Chapter 113A of the General Statutes.

d. Upon determining that the documentation submitted by the certificate holder is adequate to satisfy the requirements of this subsection, the Department shall publish a notice of the request for modification in the North Carolina Register and shall hold a public hearing at a location convenient to both the source and receiving river basins. The Department shall provide written notice of the request for the modification and the public hearing in the Environmental Bulletin, a newspaper of general circulation in the source river basin, a newspaper of general circulation in the receiving river basin, and as provided in subdivision (3) of subsection (c) of this section. The certificate holder who petitions the Commission for a modification under this subdivision shall pay the costs associated with the notice and public hearing.

e. The Department shall accept comments on the requested modification for a minimum of 30 days following the public hearing.

f. The Commission or the Department may require the certificate holder to provide any additional information or documentation it deems reasonably necessary in order to make a final determination.

g. The Commission shall make a final determination whether to grant the requested modification based on the factors set out in subsection (k) of this section, information provided by the certificate holder, and any other information the Commission deems relevant. The Commission shall state in writing its findings of fact and conclusions of law with regard to each factor.

h. The Commission shall grant the requested modification if it finds that the certificate holder has established by a preponderance of the evidence that the requested modification satisfies the requirements of subsection (m) of this section. The Commission may grant the requested modification in whole or in part, or deny the request, and may impose such limitations and conditions on the modified certificate as it deems necessary and relevant to the modification.

i. The Commission shall not grant a request for modification if the modification would result in the transfer of water to an additional major river basin.

j. The Commission shall not grant a request for modification if the modification would be inconsistent with the December 3, 2010 Settlement Agreement entered into between the State of North Carolina, the State of South Carolina, Duke Energy Carolinas, and the Catawba River Water Supply Project.

(w) Requirements for Coastal Counties. - A petition for a certificate to transfer surface water to supplement ground water supplies in the 15 counties designated as the Central Capacity Use Area under 15A NCAC 2E.0501, or to transfer surface water withdrawn from the mainstem of a river to provide service to one of the coastal area counties designated pursuant to G.S. 113A-103, shall be considered and a determination made according to the following procedures:

(1) The applicant shall file a notice of intent that includes a nontechnical description of the applicant's request and identification of the proposed water source.

(2) The applicant shall prepare an environmental document pursuant to subsection (d) of this section, except that an environmental impact statement shall not be required unless it would otherwise be required by Article 1 of Chapter 113A of the General Statutes.

(3) Upon determining that the documentation submitted by the applicant is adequate to satisfy the requirements of this subsection, the Department shall publish a notice of the petition in the North Carolina Register and shall hold a

public hearing at a location convenient to both the source and receiving river basins. The Department shall provide written notice of the petition and the public hearing in the Environmental Bulletin, a newspaper of general circulation in the source river basin, a newspaper of general circulation in the receiving river basin, and as provided in subdivision (3) of subsection (c) of this section. The applicant who petitions the Commission for a certificate under this subdivision shall pay the costs associated with the notice and public hearing.

(4) The Department shall accept comments on the petition for a minimum of 30 days following the public hearing.

(5) The Commission or the Department may require the applicant to provide any additional information or documentation it deems reasonably necessary in order to make a final determination.

(6) The Commission shall make a final determination whether to grant the certificate based on the factors set out in subsection (k) of this section, information provided by the applicant, and any other information the Commission deems relevant. The Commission shall state in writing its findings of fact and conclusions of law with regard to each factor.

(7) The Commission shall grant the certificate if it finds that the applicant has established by a preponderance of the evidence that the petition satisfies the requirements of subsection (m) of this section. The Commission may grant the certificate in whole or in part, or deny the request, and may impose such limitations and conditions on the certificate as it deems necessary and relevant. (1993, c. 348, s. 1; 1997-443, ss. 11A.119(a), 15.48(c); 1997-524, s. 1; 1998-168, s. 4; 2001-474, s. 28; 2007-484, s. 43.7C; 2007-518, s. 3; 2008-125, s. 1; 2008-198, s. 11.5; 2010-155, ss. 2, 3; 2011-398, s. 50; 2013-388, s. 2.)

Part 3. Dam Safety Law.

§ 143-215.23. Short title.

This Part shall be known and may be cited as the Dam Safety Law of 1967. (1967, c. 1068, s. 1.)

§ 143-215.24. Declaration of purpose.

It is the purpose of this Part to provide for the certification and inspection of dams in the interest of public health, safety, and welfare, in order to reduce the risk of failure of dams; to prevent injuries to persons, damage to downstream property and loss of reservoir storage; and to ensure maintenance of minimum stream flows of adequate quantity and quality below dams. (1967, c. 1068, s. 2; 1977, c. 878, s. 1; 1993, c. 394, s. 1.)

§ 143-215.25. Definitions.

As used in this Part, unless the context otherwise requires:

(1)   "Dam" means a structure and appurtenant works erected to impound or divert water.

(2)   "Minimum stream flow" or "minimum flow" means a stream flow of a quantity and quality sufficient in the judgment of the Department to meet and maintain stream classifications and water quality standards established by the Department under G.S. 143-214.1 and applicable to the waters affected by the project under consideration, and to maintain aquatic habitat in the length of the stream that is affected. (1967, c. 1068, s. 3; 1973, c. 1262, ss. 23, 38; 1977, c. 771, s. 4; c. 878, ss. 2, 4; 1983, c. 306; 1987, c. 827, ss. 154, 175; 1993, c. 394, s. 2.)

§ 143-215.25A. Exempt dams.

(a)   Except as otherwise provided in this Part, this Part does not apply to any dam:

(1)   Constructed by the United States Army Corps of Engineers, the Tennessee Valley Authority, or another agency of the United States government, when the agency designed or approved plans for the dam and supervised its construction.

(2) Constructed with financial assistance from the United States Natural Resources Conservation Service, when that agency designed or approved plans for the dam and supervised its construction.

(3) Licensed by the Federal Energy Regulatory Commission, or for which a license application is pending with the Federal Energy Regulatory Commission.

(4) For use in connection with electric generating facilities regulated by the Nuclear Regulatory Commission.

(5) Under a single private ownership that provides protection only to land or other property under the same ownership and that does not pose a threat to human life or property below the dam.

(6) (See Editor's Note) That is less than 25 feet in height or that has an impoundment capacity of less than 50 acre-feet, unless the Department determines that failure of the dam could result in loss of human life or significant damage to property below the dam.

(7) (See Editor's Note) Constructed for and maintains the purpose of providing water for agricultural use, when a person who is licensed as a professional engineer or is employed by the Natural Resources Conservation Service, county, or local Soil and Water Conservation District, and has federal engineering job approval authority under Chapter 89C of the General Statutes designed or approved plans for the dam, supervised its construction, and registered the dam with the Division of Energy, Mineral, and Land Resources of the Department prior to construction of the dam. This exemption shall not apply to dams that are determined to be high-hazard by the Department.

(b) The exemption from this Part for a dam described in subdivisions (1) and (2) of subsection (a) of this section does not apply after the supervising federal agency relinquishes authority for the operation and maintenance of the dam to a local entity. (1993, c. 394, s. 3; 2009-390, s. 3(a); 2011-394, s. 10(a); 2012-143, s. 1(f); 2013-265, s. 20.)

§ 143-215.26. Construction of dams.

(a) No person shall begin the construction of any dam until at least 10 days after filing with the Department a statement concerning its height, impoundment capacity, purpose, location and other information required by the Department. A person who constructs a dam, including a dam that is otherwise exempt from this Part under subdivisions (4) or (5) of G.S. 143-215.25A(a), shall comply with the malaria control requirements of the Department. If on the basis of this information the Department is of the opinion that the proposed dam is not exempt from the provisions of this Part, it shall so notify the applicant, and construction shall not be commenced until a full application is filed by the applicant and approved as provided by G.S. 143-215.29. The Department may also require of applicants so notified the filing of any additional information it deems necessary, including, but not limited to, streamflow and rainfall data, maps, plans and specifications. Every applicant for approval of a dam subject to the provisions of this Part shall also file with the Department the certificate of an engineer legally qualified in this State. The certificate shall state that the person who files the certificate is responsible for the design of the dam and that the design is safe and adequate.

(b) The Department shall send a copy of each completed application to the State Health Director, the Wildlife Resources Commission, the Department of Transportation, and other State and local agencies it considers appropriate for review and comment. (1967, c. 1068, s. 4; 1973, c. 476, s. 128; c. 507, s. 5; c. 1262, s. 23; 1987, c. 827, s. 176; 1989, c. 727, s. 163; 1993, c. 394, s. 4; 1995, c. 509, s. 80.)

§ 143-215.27. Repair, alteration, or removal of dam.

(a) Before commencing the repair, alteration or removal of a dam, application shall be made for written approval by the Department, except as otherwise provided by this Part. The application shall state the name and address of the applicant, shall adequately detail the changes it proposes to effect and shall be accompanied by maps, plans and specifications setting forth such details and dimensions as the Department requires. The Department may waive any such requirements. The application shall give such other information concerning the dam and reservoir required by the Department, such information concerning the safety of any change as it may require, and shall state the proposed time of commencement and completion of the work. When an application has been completed it may be referred by the Department for agency review and report, as provided by subsection (b) of G.S. 143-215.26 in the case of original construction.

(b) When repairs are necessary to safeguard life and property they may be started immediately but the Department shall be notified forthwith of the proposed repairs and of the work under way, and they shall be made to conform to its orders. (1967, c. 1068, s. 5; 1979, c. 55, s. 1.)

§ 143-215.28. Action by Commission upon applications.

(a) Following receipt of agency comments the Commission shall approve, disapprove, or approve subject to conditions necessary to ensure safety and to satisfy minimum stream flow requirements, all applications made pursuant to this Part.

(b) A defective application shall not be rejected but notice of the defects shall be sent to the applicant by registered mail. If the applicant fails to file a perfected application within 30 days the original shall be canceled unless further time is allowed.

(c) If the Commission disapproves an application, one copy shall be returned with a statement of its objections. If an application is approved, the approval shall be attached thereto, and a copy returned by registered mail. Approval shall be granted under terms, conditions and limitations which the Commission deems necessary to safeguard life and property.

(d) Construction shall be commenced within one year after the date of approval of the application or such approval is void. The Commission upon written application and good cause shown may extend the time for commencing construction. Notice by registered mail shall be given the Commission at least 10 days before construction is commenced. (1967, c. 1068, s. 6; 1973, c. 1262, s. 23; 1987, c. 827, s. 154.)

§ 143-215.28A. Application fees.

(a) In accordance with G.S. 143-215.3(a)(1a), the Commission may establish a fee schedule for processing applications for approvals of construction or removal of dams issued under this Part. In establishing the fee schedule, the Commission shall consider the administrative and personnel costs incurred by the Department for processing the applications and for related compliance activities. The total amount of fees collected in any fiscal year may not exceed one-third of the total personnel and administrative costs incurred by the Department for processing the applications and for related compliance activities in the prior fiscal year. An approval fee may not exceed the larger of two hundred dollars ($200.00) or two percent (2%) of the actual cost of construction or removal of the applicable dam. The provisions of G.S. 143-215.3(a)(1b) do not apply to these fees.

(b) The Dam Safety Account is established as a nonreverting account within the Department. Fees collected under this section shall be credited to the Account and shall be applied to the costs of administering this Part. (1989 (Reg. Sess., 1990), c. 976, s. 1; 1991 (Reg. Sess., 1992), c. 1039, s. 15; 1993, c. 394, s. 5.)

§ 143-215.29. Supervision by qualified engineers; reports and modification during work.

(a) Any project for which the Commission's approval is required under G.S. 143-215.26, 143-215.27, and 143-215.28, and any project undertaken pursuant to an order of the Commission issued pursuant to this section or G.S. 143-215.32 shall be designed and supervised by an engineer legally qualified in the State of North Carolina.

(b) During the construction, enlargement, repair, alteration or removal of a dam, the Commission may require such progress reports from the supervising engineer as it deems necessary.

(c) If during construction, reconstruction, repair, alteration or enlargement of any dam, the Commission finds the work is not being done in accordance with the provisions of the approval and the approved plans and specifications, it shall give written notice by registered mail or personal service to the person who received the approval and to the person in charge of construction at the dam. The notice shall state the particulars in which compliance has not been made, and shall order immediate compliance with the terms of the approval, and the approved plans and specifications. The Commission may order that no further construction work be undertaken until such compliance has been effected and approved by the Commission. A failure to comply with the approval and the approved plans and specifications shall render the approval revocable unless compliance is made after notice as provided in this section. (1967, c. 1068, s. 7; 1973, c. 1262, s. 23; 1977, c. 878, s. 5; 1987, c. 827, s. 154.)

§ 143-215.30. Notice of completion; certification of final approval.

(a) Immediately upon completion, enlargement, repair, alteration or removal of a dam, notice of completion shall be given the Commission. As soon as possible thereafter supplementary drawings or descriptive matter showing or describing the dam as actually constructed shall be filed with the Department in such detail as the Commission may require.

(b) When an existing dam is enlarged, the supplementary drawings and descriptive matter need apply only to the new work.

(c) The completed work shall be inspected by the supervising engineers, and upon finding that the work has been done as required and that the dam is safe and satisfies minimum streamflow requirements, they shall file with the Department a certificate that the work has been completed in accordance with approved design, plans, specifications and other requirements. Unless the Commission has reason to believe that the dam is unsafe or is not in compliance with any applicable rule or law, the Commission shall grant final approval of the work in accordance with the certificate, subject to such terms as it deems necessary for the protection of life and property.

(d) Pending issuance of the Commission's final approval, the dam shall not be used except on written consent of the Commission, subject to conditions it may impose. (1967, c. 1068, s. 8; 1973, c. 1262, s. 23; 1987, c. 827, ss. 154, 177.)

§ 143-215.31. Supervision over maintenance and operation of dams.

(a) The Commission shall have jurisdiction and supervision over the maintenance and operation of dams to safeguard life and property and to satisfy minimum streamflow requirements. The Commission may adopt standards for the maintenance and operation of dams as may be necessary for the purposes of this Part. The Commission may vary the standards applicable to various dams, giving due consideration to the minimum flow requirements of the stream, the type and location of the structure, the hazards to which it may be exposed, and the peril of life and property in the event of failure of a dam to perform its function.

(b) The Department, consistent with rules adopted by the Commission, may impose any condition or requirement in orders and written approvals issued under this Part that is necessary to ensure that stream classifications, water quality standards, and aquatic habitat requirements are met and maintained, including conditions and requirements relating to the release or discharge of designated flows from dams, the location and design of water intakes and outlets, the amount and timing of the withdrawal of water from a reservoir, and the construction of submerged weirs or other devices intended to maintain minimum streamflows.

The Commission shall adopt rules that specify the minimum streamflow in the length of the stream affected.

(c) The minimum streamflow in the length of the stream affected by a dam that is operated by a small power producer, as defined in G.S. 62-3(27a), that diverts water from 4,000 feet or less of the natural streambed and where the water is returned to the same stream shall be:

(1) The minimum average flow for a period of seven consecutive days that would have an average occurrence of once in 10 years in the absence of the dam, or ten percent (10%) of the average annual flow of the stream in the absence of the dam, whichever is less, if prior to 1 January 1995 the small power producer was either licensed by the Federal Energy Regulatory Commission or held a certificate of public convenience and necessity issued by the North Carolina Utilities Commission.

(2) The minimum average flow for a period of seven consecutive days that would have an average occurrence of once in 10 years in the absence of the dam, or ten percent (10%) of the average annual flow of the stream in the absence of the dam, whichever is greater, if subdivision (1) of this subsection does not apply.

(3) To protect the habitat of the Cape Fear Shiner and other aquatic species, 28 cubic feet per second for any dam that diverts water from 2,500 feet or more of the natural streambed of any stream on which six or more dams operated by small power producers were located on 1 January 1995, notwithstanding subdivisions (1) and (2) of this subsection.

(d) Subsection (c) of this section establishes the policy of this State with respect to minimum streamflows in the length of the stream affected by a dam that is operated by a small power producer, as defined in G.S. 62-3(27a), that diverts water from 4,000 feet or less of the natural streambed and where the water is returned to the same stream, whether the dam is subject to or exempt from this Part. In its comments and recommendations to the Federal Energy Regulatory Commission regarding the minimum streamflow in the length of the stream affected by a dam that is operated by a small power producer, as defined in G.S. 62-3(27a), that diverts water from 4,000 feet or less of the natural streambed and where the water is returned to the same stream, the Commission and the Department shall not advocate or recommend a minimum streamflow that exceeds the minimum streamflow that would be required under subsection (c) of this section.

(e) The minimum streamflow in the length of the stream affected by a dam to which subsections (c) and (d) of this section do not apply shall be established as provided in subsection (b) of this section. Subsections (c) and (d) of this section do not apply if the length of the stream affected:

(1) Receives a discharge of waste from a treatment works for which a permit is required under Part 1 of this Article; or

(2) Includes any part of a river or stream segment that:

a. Is designated as a component of the State Natural and Scenic Rivers System by G.S. 113A-35.1 or G.S. 113A-35.2.

b. Is designated as a component of the national Wild and Scenic Rivers System by 16 U.S.C. § 1273 and 1274. (1967, c. 1068, s. 9; 1973, c. 1262, s. 23; 1987, c. 827, s. 154; 1993, c. 394, s. 6; c. 553, s. 80; 1995, c. 184, s. 1; c. 439, s. 1.)

§ 143-215.32. Inspection of dams.

(a) The Department may at any time inspect any dam, including a dam that is otherwise exempt from this Part, upon receipt of a written request of any affected person or agency, or upon a motion of the Environmental Management Commission. Within the limits of available funds the Department shall endeavor to provide for inspection of all dams at intervals of approximately five years.

(b) If the Department upon inspection finds that any dam is not sufficiently strong, is not maintained in good repair or operating condition, is dangerous to life or property, or does not satisfy minimum streamflow requirements, the Department shall present its findings to the Commission and the Commission may issue an order directing the owner or owners of the dam to make at his or her expense maintenance, alterations, repairs, reconstruction, change in construction or location, or removal as may be deemed necessary by the Commission within a time limited by the order, not less than 90 days from the date of issuance of each order, except in the case of extreme danger to the safety of life or property, as provided by subsection (c) of this section.

(c) If at any time the condition of any dam becomes so dangerous to the safety of life or property, in the opinion of the Environmental Management Commission, as not to permit sufficient time for issuance of an order in the manner provided by subsection (b) of this section, the Environmental Management Commission may immediately take such measures as may be essential to provide emergency protection to life and property, including the lowering of the level of a reservoir by releasing water impounded or the destruction in whole or in part of the dam or reservoir. The Environmental Management Commission may recover the costs of such measures from the owner or owners by appropriate legal action.

(d) An order issued under this Part shall be served on the owner of the dam as provided in G.S. 1A-1, Rule 4. (1967, c. 1068, s. 10; 1973, c. 1262, s. 23; 1977, c. 878, s. 3; 1987, c. 827, s. 154; 1993, c. 394, s. 7.)

§ 143-215.33. Administrative hearing.

A person to whom a decision or a dam safety order is issued under this Part may contest the decision or order by filing a contested case petition in accordance with G.S. 150B-23. A person to whom a decision is issued must file a contested case petition within 30 days after the decision is mailed to that person. A person to whom a dam safety order is issued must file a contested case petition within 10 days after the order is served. (1967, c. 1068, s. 11; 1973, c. 1262, s. 23; 1975, c. 842, s. 4; 1977, c. 878, s. 6; 1979, c. 55, s. 2; 1987, c. 827, s. 178, 1993, c. 394, s. 8.)

§ 143-215.34. Investigations by Department; employment of consultants.

The Department shall make such investigations and assemble such data as it deems necessary for a proper review and study of the design and construction of dams, reservoirs and appurtenances, and for such purposes may enter upon private property. The Department may employ or make such agreements with geologists, engineers, or other expert consultants and such assistants as it deems necessary to carry out the provisions of this Part. (1967, c. 1068, s. 12; 1973, c. 1262, s. 23; 1987, c. 827, s. 179.)

§ 143-215.35. Liability for damages.

No action shall be brought against the State of North Carolina, the Department, or the Commission or any agent of the Commission or any employee of the State or the Department for damages sustained through the partial or total failure of any dam or its maintenance by reason of any supervision or other action taken pursuant to or under this Part. Nothing in this Part shall relieve an owner or operator of a dam from the legal duties, obligations and liabilities arising from such ownership or operation. (1967, c. 1068, s. 13; 1973, c. 1262, s. 23; 1987, 827, s. 154.)

§ 143-215.36. Enforcement procedures.

(a)   Criminal Penalties. - Any person who shall be adjudged to have violated this Article shall be guilty of a Class 3 misdemeanor and shall only be liable to a penalty of not less than one hundred dollars ($100.00) nor more than one thousand dollars ($1,000) for each violation. In addition, if any person is adjudged to have committed such violation willfully, the court may determine that each day during which such violation continued constitutes a separate violation subject to the foregoing penalty.

(b)   Civil Penalties. -

(1)   The Secretary may assess a civil penalty of not less than one hundred dollars ($100.00) nor more than five hundred dollars ($500.00) against any person who violates any provisions of this Part, a rule implementing this Part, or an order issued under this Part.

(2) If any action or failure to act for which a penalty may be assessed under this Part is willful, the Secretary may assess a penalty not to exceed five hundred dollars ($500.00) per day for each day of violation.

(3) In determining the amount of the penalty, the Secretary shall consider the factors set out in G.S. 143B-282.1(b). The procedures set out in G.S. 143B-282.1 shall apply to civil penalty assessments that are presented to the Commission for final agency decision.

(4) The Secretary shall notify any person assessed a civil penalty of the assessment and the specific reasons therefor by registered or certified mail, or by any means authorized by G.S. 1A-1, Rule 4. Contested case petitions shall be filed in accordance with G.S. 150B-23 within 30 days of receipt of the notice of assessment.

(5) Requests for remission of civil penalties shall be filed with the Secretary. Remission requests shall not be considered unless made within 30 days of receipt of the notice of assessment. Remission requests must be accompanied by a waiver of the right to a contested case hearing pursuant to Chapter 150B and a stipulation of the facts on which the assessment was based. Consistent with the limitations in G.S. 143B-282.1(c) and G.S. 143-282.1(d), remission requests may be resolved by the Secretary and the violator. If the Secretary and the violator are unable to resolve the request, the Secretary shall deliver remission requests and his recommended action to the Committee on Civil Penalty Remissions of the Environmental Management Commission appointed pursuant to G.S. 143B-282.1(c).

(6) If any civil penalty has not been paid within 30 days after notice of assessment has been served on the violator, the Secretary shall request the Attorney General to institute a civil action in the Superior Court of any county in which the violator resides or has his or its principal place of business to recover the amount of the assessment, unless the violator contests the assessment as provided in subdivision (4) of this subsection. If any civil penalty has not been paid within 30 days after the final agency decision or court order has been served on the violator, the Secretary shall request the Attorney General to institute a civil action in the Superior Court of any county in which the violator resides or has his or its principal place of business to recover the amount of the assessment. A civil action shall be filed within three years of the date the final agency decision was served on the violator.

(7) The Secretary may delegate his powers and duties under this section to the Director of the Division of Energy, Mineral, and Land Resources of the Department.

(8) The clear proceeds of civil penalties assessed pursuant to this subsection shall be remitted to the Civil Penalty and Forfeiture Fund in accordance with G.S. 115C-457.2.

(c) Injunctive Relief. - Upon violation of any of the provisions of this Part, a rule implementing this Part, or an order issued under this Part, the Secretary may, either before or after the institution of proceedings for the collection of the penalty imposed by this Part for such violations, request the Attorney General to institute a civil action in the superior court of the county or counties where the violation occurred in the name of the State upon the relation of the Department for injunctive relief to restrain the violation or require corrective action, and for such other or further relief in the premises as said court shall deem proper. Neither the institution of the action nor any of the proceedings thereon shall relieve any party to such proceedings from the penalty prescribed by this Part for any violation of the same. (1967, c. 1068, s. 14; 1973, c. 1262, s. 23; 1975, c. 842, s. 3; 1977, c. 771, s. 4; 1987, c. 827, ss. 154, 180; 1989 (Reg. Sess., 1990), c. 1036, s. 5; 1991, c. 342, ss. 10, 11; 1993, c. 394, s. 9; c. 539, s. 1021; 1994, Ex. Sess., c. 24, s. 14(c); 1998-215, s. 65; 2012-143, s. 1(f).)

§ 143-215.37. Rights of investigation, entry, access, and inspection.

The Commission shall have the right to direct the conduct of such investigations as it may reasonably deem necessary to carry out its duties prescribed in this Part, and the Department shall have the right to conduct such investigations, and for this purpose the employees of the Department and agents of the Commission have the right to enter at reasonable times on any property, public or private, for the purpose of investigating the condition, construction, or operation of any dam or associated equipment facility or property, and to require written statements or the filing of reports under oath, with respect to pertinent questions relating to the construction or operation of any dam: Provided, that no person shall be required to disclose any secret formula, processes or methods used in any manufacturing operation or any confidential information concerning business activities carried on by him or under his supervision. No person shall refuse entry or access to any authorized representative of the Commission or Department who requests entry for purposes of inspection, and who presents appropriate credentials, nor shall any person obstruct, hamper or interfere with any such representative while in the process of carrying out his official duties. (1967, c. 1068, s. 15; 1973, c. 1262, s. 23.)

Part 4. Federal Water Resources Development Projects.

§ 143-215.38. Short title.

This Part shall be known as and may be cited as the Federal Water Resources Development Law of 1969. (1969, cc. 724, 968.)

§ 143-215.39. Public policy.

It is hereby declared the public policy of the State of North Carolina to encourage development of such river and harbor, flood control and other similar civil works projects as will accrue to the general or special benefit of any county or municipality of North Carolina or to any region of the State. To this end, it is also hereby declared that within the meaning of the North Carolina Constitution expenditures for such projects and obligations incurred for such projects are for public purposes, that county and municipal and other local government expenditures and obligations incurred therefor are necessary expenses, and that county expenditures therefor are for special purposes for which the special approval of the General Assembly is hereby given. (1969, cc. 724, 968.)

§ 143-215.40. Resolutions and ordinances assuring local cooperation.

(a)   The boards of commissioners of the several counties, in behalf of their respective counties, the governing bodies of the several municipalities, in behalf of their respective municipalities, the governing bodies of any other local government units, in behalf of their units, and the North Carolina Environmental Management Commission, in behalf of the State of North Carolina, subject to the approval of the Governor, are hereby authorized to adopt such resolutions or ordinances as may be required giving assurances to any appropriate agency of the United States government for the fulfillment of the required items of local cooperation as expressed in acts of Congress or congressional documents, as conditions precedent to the accomplishment of river and harbor, flood control or other such civil works projects, when it shall appear, and is determined by such board or governing body that any such project will accrue to the general or special benefit of such county or municipality or to a region of the State. In each case where the subject of such local cooperation requirements comes before a board of county commissioners or the governing body of any municipality or other local unit a copy of its final action, whether it be favorable or unfavorable, shall be sent to the Secretary of Environment and Natural Resources for the information of the Governor.

(b) Within the meaning of this Part, a "local government unit" means any local subdivision or unit of government or local public corporate entity (other than a county or municipality), including any manner of special district or public authority. (1969, cc. 724, 968; 1973, c. 1262, s. 23; 1977, c. 771, s. 4; 1983, c. 717, s. 69; 1985 (Reg. Sess., 1986), c. 955, ss. 91, 92; 1989, c. 727, s. 218(108); 1997-443, s. 11A.119(a); 2006-203, s. 89.)

§ 143-215.41. Items of cooperation to which localities and the State may bind themselves.

Such resolutions and ordinances may irrevocably bind such county, municipality, other local unit, or the State of North Carolina, acting through the Commission, to the following when included as requirements of local cooperation for a federal water resources development project:

(1) To provide, without cost to the United States, all lands, easements, and rights-of-way required for construction and subsequent maintenance of the project and for aids to navigation, if required, upon the request of the Chief of Engineers, or other official to be required in the general public interest for initial and subsequent disposal of spoil, and also necessary retaining dikes, bulkheads, and embankments therefor, or the costs of such retaining works;

(2) To hold and save the United States free from damages due to the construction works and subsequent maintenance of the project;

(3) To provide firm assurances that riverside terminal and transfer facilities will be constructed at the upper limit of the modified project to permit transfer of commodities from or to plants and barges;

(4) To provide and maintain, without cost to the United States, depths in berthing areas and local access channels serving the terminals commensurate with depths provided in related project areas;

(5) To accomplish, without cost to the United States, such alterations, if any, as required in sewer, water supply, drainage, electrical power lines, and other utility facilities, as well as their maintenance;

(6) To provide, without cost to the United States, all lands, easements, rights-of-way, utility relocations and alterations, and, with the concurrence and under the direction of the Board of Transportation, highway or highway bridge construction and alterations necessary for project construction;

(7) To adjust all claims concerning water rights;

(8) To maintain and operate the project after completion, without cost to the United States, in accordance with regulations prescribed by the Secretary of the Army or other responsible federal official, board, or agency;

(9) To provide a cash contribution for project costs assigned to project features other than flood control;

(10) To prevent future encroachment which might interfere with proper functioning of the project for flood control;

(11) To provide or satisfy any other items or conditions of local cooperation as stipulated in the congressional or other federal document covering the particular project involved.

This section shall not be interpreted as limiting but as descriptive of the items of local cooperation, the accomplishment of which counties, municipalities and the State are herein authorized to irrevocably bind themselves; it being intended to authorize counties, municipalities and the Commission in behalf of the State to comply fully and completely with all of the items of local cooperation as contemplated by Congress and as stipulated in the congressional acts or documents concerned, or project reports by the Army Chief of Engineers, the Administrator of the Soil Conservation Service, the Board of Directors of the Tennessee Valley Authority, or other responsible federal official, board or agency. (1969, cc. 724, 968; 1973, c. 507, s. 5; c. 1262, s. 23; c. 1446, s. 14; 1987, c. 827, s. 154.)

§ 143-215.42. Acquisition of lands.

(a) For the purpose of complying with the terms of local cooperation as specified in this Part, and as stipulated in the congressional document covering the particular project involved, any county, municipality, other local government unit or the State of North Carolina, acting on behalf of the Commission, may acquire the necessary lands, or interest in lands, by lease, purchase, gift or condemnation. A municipality, county or other local government unit may acquire such lands by any of the aforesaid means outside as well as inside its territorial boundaries, if the local governing body finds that substantial benefits will accrue to property inside such territorial boundaries as a result of such acquisition.

(b) The power of condemnation herein granted to counties, municipalities and other local government units may be exercised only after:

(1) The municipality, county or other local unit makes application to the Commission, identifying the land sought to be condemned and stating the purposes for which said land is needed; and

(2) The Commission finds that the land is sought to be acquired for a proper purpose within the intent of this Part. The findings of the Commission will be conclusive in the absence of fraud, notwithstanding any other provision of law.

(c) The Department shall certify copies of the Commission's findings to the applicant municipality, county, or other local unit, and to the clerk of superior court of the county or counties wherein any of the land sought to be condemned lies for recordation in the special proceedings thereof.

(d) For purposes of this section:

(1) The term "interest in land" means any land, right-of-way, rights of access, privilege, easement, or other interest in or relating to land. Said "interest in land" does not include an interest in land which is held or used in whole or in part for a public water supply, unless such "interest in land" is not necessary or essential for such uses or purposes.

(2) A "description" of land shall be sufficient if the boundaries of the land are described in such a way as to convey an intelligent understanding of the location of the land. In the discretion of the applicant, boundaries may be described by any of the following methods or by any combination thereof: by

reference to a map; by metes and bounds; by general description referring to natural boundaries, or to boundaries of existing political subdivisions or municipalities, or to boundaries of particular tracts or parcels of land.

(e) The procedure in all condemnation proceedings pursuant to this section shall conform as nearly as possible to the procedure provided in Article 3 of Chapter 40A of the General Statutes.

(f) Interests in land acquired pursuant to this section may be used in such manner and for such purpose as the condemning authority deems best. If the local government unit so determines, such lands may be sold, leased, or rented, subject to the prior approval of the Commission. The State may sell, lease or rent any lands acquired by it, and if the Commission is participating with any local government unit or units in a water resources project under this Article, may convey such lands or interests to the unit or units as a part of its participation therein.

(g) This section is intended to confer supplementary and additional authority, and not to confer exclusive authority nor to impose cumulative requirements. If a municipality, county or other local government unit is authorized to acquire lands or interests in lands by some other law (such as by General Statutes Chapter 139, 153A, 160A, or 162A) as well as by this section, compliance with the requirements of this section or the requirements of such other law will be sufficient.

(h) This section shall not authorize acquisition by condemnation of interests in land within the boundaries of any project to be constructed by the Tennessee Valley Authority, its agents or subdivision or any project licensed by the Federal Power Commission or interests in land owned or held for use by a public utility, as defined in G.S. 62-3. No commission created pursuant to G.S. 158-8 shall condemn or acquire any property to be used by the Tennessee Valley Authority, its agents or subdivision. (1969, cc. 724, 968; 1973, c. 621, ss. 2-4; c. 1262, s. 23; 1977, c. 771, s. 4; 1987, c. 827, ss. 154, 181; 2013-360, s. 15.28(d); 2013-363, s. 5.7(b).)

§ 143-215.43. Additional powers.

For the purpose of complying with requirements of local cooperation as described in this Part, county and municipal governing bodies shall also have the power to accept funds, and to use general tax funds for necessary project purposes, including project maintenance. (1969, cc. 724, 968.)

Part 5. Right of Withdrawal of Impounded Water.

§ 143-215.44. Right of withdrawal.

(a) A person who lawfully impounds water for the purpose of withdrawal shall have a right of withdrawal of excess volume of water attributable to the impoundment. Within the meaning of this subsection, the word "purpose" shall include one of several purposes in a multiple purpose impoundment.

(b) A "right of withdrawal," within the meaning of this Part, is an interest which establishes a right to withdraw an excess volume of water superior to other interests in the water.

(c) "Excess volume of water," within the meaning of this Part, is that volume which may be withdrawn from an impoundment or from a watercourse below the impoundment without foreseeably reducing the rate of flow of a watercourse below that which would obtain in that watercourse if the impoundment did not exist.

(d) "Impound," within the meaning of this Part, shall include but is not limited to financial contributions or the assurance of financial contributions in the construction or operation of an impoundment.

(e) Repealed by Session Laws 1987, c. 827, s. 182. (1971, c. 111, s. 1; 1987, c. 827, s. 182.)

§ 143-215.45. Transfer of right of withdrawal.

A person with a right of withdrawal may assign or transfer it in whole or in part to another, subject to those rights of reassignment or transfer by the State specified in G.S. 143-354(a)(11). A person who has a right of withdrawal of excess volume of water by virtue of an assignment or transfer has an interest in water superior to other interests only to the extent that his withdrawal is in accordance with the terms of the assignment or transfer. (1971, c. 111, s. 1; 1991, c. 342, s. 12.)

§ 143-215.46. Exercise of right of withdrawal.

A person may exercise right of withdrawal by withdrawing directly from the impoundment, from a watercourse below the impoundment, or from both; provided, however, that the exercise of the right of withdrawal shall not require any person other than the holder of said right to incur additional capital expenditures in order to enable the holder of said right to withdraw any excess volume of water from a watercourse below the impoundment. (1971, c. 111, s. 1.)

§ 143-215.47. Effect of right of withdrawal on discharges of water.

Neither a right of withdrawal nor any assignment or transfer of said right may be asserted in defense against a claim that the method of releasing or discharging water is improper, that the quality of water has been impaired by the withdrawal or release of the water or by its return to the stream following its use, that water has been diverted without authority from the basin from which it was withdrawn, or that water resulting from augmentation of the natural streamflow to control water quality has been withdrawn. (1971, c. 111, s. 1.)

§ 143-215.48. Determining streamflows.

(a) In litigation in which the rate of flow of water that would exist in the absence of an impoundment is in issue, that rate shall be deemed to be the minimum average flow for a period of seven consecutive days that have an average recurrence of once in 10 years unless a party to the litigation introduces a calculation that more closely approximates the actual rate. A determination made by the Commission (i) of either that minimum average flow, or (ii) that adopts a calculation that more closely approximates the actual rate of flow, and introduced by one of the parties to the litigation, shall be prima facie correct.

(b) The Commission is authorized to make the determinations specified in subsection (a) of this section and to require the submission of such reports and such inspections as are necessary to permit those determinations. (1971, c. 111, s. 1; 1973, c. 1262, s. 23; 1987, c. 827, s. 154.)

§ 143-215.49. Right of withdrawal for use in community water supply.

A person operating a municipal, county, community or other local water distribution or supply system and having a right of withdrawal may assert that right when its withdrawal is for use in any such water system as well as in other circumstances. (1971, c. 111, s. 1.)

§ 143-215.50. Interpretation with other statutes.

Whether rights of withdrawal shall have effect in a capacity use area declared by the Commission under the Water Use Act of 1967 shall be in the discretion of the Commission. This Part shall be subject to the provisions of the Water and Air Resources Act, and the Dam Safety Law of 1967. (1971, c. 111, s. 1; 1973, c. 1262, s. 23; 1987, c. 827, s. 154.)

Part 6. Floodway Regulation.

§ 143-215.51. Purposes.

The purposes of this Part are to:

(1) Minimize the extent of floods by preventing obstructions that inhibit water flow and increase flood height and damage.

(2) Prevent and minimize loss of life, injuries, property damage, and other losses in flood hazard areas.

(3) Promote the public health, safety, and welfare of citizens of North Carolina in flood hazard areas. (1971, c. 1167, s. 3; 1973, c. 621, s. 5; 2000-150, s. 1.)

§ 143-215.52. Definitions.

(a) As used in this Part:

(1) "Artificial obstruction" means any obstruction to the flow of water in a stream that is not a natural obstruction, including any that, while not a significant obstruction in itself, is capable of accumulating debris and thereby reducing the flood-carrying capacity of the stream.

(1a) "Base flood" or "100-year flood" means a flood that has a one percent (1%) chance of being equaled or exceeded in any given year. The term "base flood" is used in the National Flood Insurance Program to indicate the minimum level of flooding to be addressed by a community in its floodplain management regulations.

(1b) "Base floodplain" or "100-year floodplain" means that area subject to a one percent (1%) or greater chance of flooding in any given year, as shown on the current floodplain maps prepared pursuant to the National Flood Insurance Program or approved by the Department.

(1c) "Department" means the Department of Public Safety.

(1d) "Flood hazard area" means the area designated by a local government, pursuant to this Part, as an area where development must be regulated to prevent damage from flooding. The flood hazard area must include and may exceed the base floodplain.

(2) Repealed by Session Laws 2000, c. 150, s. 1, effective August 2, 2000.

(3) "Local government" means any county or city, as defined in G.S. 160A-1.

(3a) "Lowest floor", when used in reference to a structure, means the lowest enclosed area, including a basement, of the structure. An unfinished or flood resistant enclosed area, other than a basement, that is usable solely for parking vehicles, building access, or storage is not a lowest floor.

(4) "Natural obstruction" includes any rock, tree, gravel, or other natural matter that is an obstruction and has been located within the 100-year floodplain by a nonhuman cause.

(4b) "Secretary" means the Secretary of Public Safety.

(5) "Stream" means a watercourse that collects surface runoff from an area of one square mile or greater.

(6) "Structure" means a walled or roofed building, including a mobile home and a gas or liquid storage tank.

(b) As used in this Part, the terms "artificial obstruction" and "structure" do not include any of the following:

(1) An electric generation, distribution, or transmission facility.

(2) A gas pipeline or gas transmission or distribution facility, including a compressor station or related facility.

(3) A water treatment or distribution facility, including a pump station.

(4) A wastewater collection or treatment facility, including a lift station.

(5) Processing equipment used in connection with a mining operation.
(1971, c. 1167, s. 3; 2000-150, s. 1; 2011-145, s. 19.1(g).)

§ 143-215.53: Repealed by Session Laws 2000-150, s. 1.

§ 143-215.54. Regulation of flood hazard areas; prohibited uses.

(a) A local government may adopt ordinances to regulate uses in flood hazard areas and grant permits for the use of flood hazard areas that are consistent with the requirements of this Part.

(b) The following uses may be made of flood hazard areas without a permit issued under this Part, provided that these uses comply with local land-use ordinances and any other applicable laws or regulations:

(1) General farming, pasture, outdoor plant nurseries, horticulture, forestry, mining, wildlife sanctuary, game farm, and other similar agricultural, wildlife and related uses;

(2) Ground level loading areas, parking areas, rotary aircraft ports and other similar ground level area uses;

(3) Lawns, gardens, play areas and other similar uses;

(4) Golf courses, tennis courts, driving ranges, archery ranges, picnic grounds, parks, hiking or horseback riding trails, open space and other similar private and public recreational uses.

(5) Land application of waste at agronomic rates consistent with a permit issued under Part 1 or Part 1A of Article 21 of Chapter 143 of the General Statutes or an approved animal waste management plan.

(6) Land application of septage consistent with a permit issued under G.S. 130A-291.1.

(c) New solid waste disposal facilities, hazardous waste management facilities, salvage yards, and chemical storage facilities are prohibited in the 100-year floodplain except as authorized under G.S. 143-215.54A(b). (1971, c. 1167, s. 3; 1973, c. 621, s. 8; 1979, c. 413, ss. 1, 2; 2000-150, s. 1.)

§ 143-215.54A. Minimum standards for ordinances; variances for prohibited uses.

(a) A flood hazard prevention ordinance adopted by a county or city pursuant to this Part shall, at a minimum:

(1) Meet the requirements for participation in the National Flood Insurance Program and of this section.

(2) Prohibit new solid waste disposal facilities, hazardous waste management facilities, salvage yards, and chemical storage facilities in the 100-year floodplain except as authorized under subsection (b) of this section.

(3) Provide that a structure or tank for chemical or fuel storage incidental to a use that is allowed under this section or to the operation of a water treatment plant or wastewater treatment facility may be located in a 100-year floodplain only if the structure or tank is either elevated above base flood elevation or designed to be watertight with walls substantially impermeable to the passage of water and with structural components capable of resisting hydrostatic and hydrodynamic loads and the effects of buoyancy.

(b) A flood hazard prevention ordinance may include a procedure for granting variances for uses prohibited under G.S. 143-215.54(c). A county or city shall notify the Secretary of its intention to grant a variance at least 30 days prior to granting the variance. A county or city may grant a variance upon finding that all of the following apply:

(1) The use serves a critical need in the community.

(2) No feasible location exists for the location of the use outside the 100-year floodplain.

(3) The lowest floor of any structure is elevated above the base flood elevation or is designed to be watertight with walls substantially impermeable to the passage of water and with structural components capable of resisting hydrostatic and hydrodynamic loads and the effects of buoyancy.

(4) The use complies with all other applicable laws and regulations. (2000-150, s. 1.)

§ 143-215.55. Acquisition of existing structures.

A local government may acquire, by purchase, exchange, or condemnation an existing structure located in a flood hazard area in the area regulated by the local government if the local government determines that the acquisition is necessary to prevent damage from flooding. The procedure in all condemnation proceedings pursuant to this section shall conform as nearly as possible to the procedure provided in Article 3 of Chapter 40A of the General Statutes. (1971, c. 1167, s. 3; 1987, c. 827, s. 183; 2000-150, s. 1.)

§ 143-215.56. Delineation of flood hazard areas and 100-year floodplains; powers of Department; powers of local governments and of the Department.

(a) For the purpose of delineating a flood hazard area and evaluating the possibility of flood damages, a local government may:

(1) Request technical assistance from the competent State and federal agencies, including the Army Corps of Engineers, the Natural Resources Conservation Service, the Tennessee Valley Authority, the Federal Emergency Management Agency, the North Carolina Department of Public Safety, the North Carolina Geodetic Survey, the North Carolina Geological Survey, and the U.S. Geological Survey, or successor agencies.

(2) Utilize the reports and data supplied by federal and State agencies as the basis for the exercise by local ordinance or resolution of the powers and responsibilities conferred on responsible local governments by this Part.

(b) The Department shall provide advice and assistance to any local government having responsibilities under this Part. In exercising this function the Department may furnish manuals, suggested standards, plans, and other technical data; conduct training programs; give advice and assistance with respect to delineation of flood hazard areas and the development of appropriate ordinances; and provide any other advice and assistance that the Department deems appropriate. The Department shall send a copy of every rule adopted to implement this Part to the governing body of each local government in the State.

(c) A local government may delineate any flood hazard area subject to its regulation by showing it on a map or drawing, by a written description, or any combination thereof, to be designated appropriately and filed permanently with the clerk of superior court and with the register of deeds in the county where the land lies. A local government may also delineate a flood hazard area by reference to a map prepared pursuant to the National Flood Insurance Program. Alterations in the lines delineated shall be indicated by appropriate entries upon or addition to the appropriate map, drawing, or description. Entries or additions shall be made by or under the direction of the clerk of superior court. Photographic, typed or other copies of the map, drawing, or description, certified by the clerk of superior court, shall be admitted in evidence in all courts and shall have the same force and effect as would the original map or description. A local government may provide for the redrawing of any map. A redrawn map shall supersede for all purposes the earlier map or maps that it is designated to replace upon the filing and approval thereof as designated and provided above.

(d) The Department may prepare a floodplain map that identifies the 100-year floodplain and base flood elevations for an area for the purposes of this Part if all of the following conditions apply:

(1) The 100-year floodplain and base flood elevations for the area are not identified on a floodplain map prepared pursuant to the National Flood Insurance Program within the previous five years.

(2) The Department determines that the 100-year floodplain and the base flood elevations for the area need to be identified and the use of the area regulated in accordance with the requirements of this Part in order to prevent damage from flooding.

(3) The Department prepares the floodplain map in accordance with the federal standards required for maps to be accepted for use in administering the National Flood Insurance Program.

(e) Prior to preparing a floodplain map pursuant to subsection (d) of this section, the Department shall advise each local government whose jurisdiction includes a portion of the area to be mapped.

(f) Upon completing a floodplain map pursuant to subsection (d) of this section, the Department shall both:

(1) Provide copies of the floodplain map to every local government whose jurisdiction includes a portion of the 100-year floodplain identified on the floodplain map.

(2) Submit the floodplain map to the Federal Emergency Management Agency for approval for use in administering the National Flood Insurance Program.

(g) Upon approval of a floodplain map prepared pursuant to subsection (d) of this section by the Federal Emergency Management Agency for use in administering the National Flood Insurance Program, it shall be the responsibility of each local government whose jurisdiction includes a portion of the 100-year floodplain identified in the floodplain map to incorporate the revised map into its floodplain ordinance. (1971, c. 1167, s. 3; 1973, c. 621, ss. 6, 7; c. 1262, s. 23; 1977, c. 374, s. 2; c. 771, s. 4; 1987, c. 827, ss. 154, 184; 2000-150, s. 1; 2002-165, s. 1.6; 2011-145, s. 19.1(g).)

§ 143-215.56A. Floodplain Mapping Fund.

The Floodplain Mapping Fund is established as a special revenue fund. The Fund consists of the fees credited to it under G.S. 161-11.5. Revenue in the fund may be used only to offset the Department's cost in preparing floodplain maps and performing its other duties under this Part. (2008-107, s. 29.7(c); 2013-225, s. 7(d).)

§ 143-215.57. Procedures in issuing permits.

(a) A local government may establish application forms and require maps, plans, and other information necessary for the issuance of permits in a manner consonant with the objectives of this Part. For this purpose a local government may take into account anticipated development in the foreseeable future that may be adversely affected by the obstruction, as well as existing development. They shall consider the effects of a proposed artificial obstruction in a stream in creating danger to life and property by:

(1) Water that may be backed up or diverted by the obstruction.

(2) The danger that the obstruction will be swept downstream to the injury of others.

(3) The injury or damage at the site of the obstruction itself.

(b) In prescribing standards and requirements for the issuance of permits under this Part and in issuing permits, local governments shall proceed as in the case of an ordinance for the better government of the county or city as the case may be. A city may exercise the powers granted in this Part not only within its corporate boundaries but also within the area of its extraterritorial zoning jurisdiction. A county may exercise the powers granted in this Part at any place within the county that is outside the zoning jurisdiction of a city in the county. If a city does not exercise the powers granted in this Part in the city's extraterritorial zoning jurisdiction, the county may exercise the powers granted in this Part in the city's extraterritorial zoning jurisdiction. The county may regulate territory within the zoning jurisdiction of any city whose governing body, by resolution, agrees to the regulation. The governing body of a city may, upon one year's written notice, withdraw its approval of the county regulations, and those regulations shall have no further effect within the city's jurisdiction.

(c) The local governing body is hereby empowered to adopt regulations it may deem necessary concerning the form, time, and manner of submission of applications for permits under this Part. These regulations may provide for the issuance of permits under this Part by the local governing body or by an agency designated by the local governing body, as prescribed by the governing body. Every final decision granting or denying a permit under this Part shall be subject to review by the superior court of the county, with the right of jury trial at the election of the party seeking review. The time and manner of election of a jury trial shall be governed by G.S. 1A-1, Rule 38(b) of the Rules of Civil Procedure. Pending the final disposition of an appeal, no action shall be taken that would be unlawful in the absence of a permit issued under this Part. (1971, c. 1167, s. 3; 2000-150, s. 1.)

§ 143-215.58. Violations and penalties.

(a) Any willful violation of this Part or of any ordinance adopted (or of the provisions of any permit issued) under the authority of this Part shall constitute a Class 1 misdemeanor.

(a1) A local government may use all of the remedies available for the enforcement of ordinances under Chapters 153A and 160A of the General Statutes to enforce an ordinance adopted pursuant to this Part.

(b) Failure to remove any artificial obstruction or enlargement or replacement thereof, that violates this Part or any ordinance adopted (or the provision of any permit issued) under the authority of this Part, shall constitute a separate violation of this Part for each day that the failure continues after written notice from the county board of commissioners or governing body of a city.

(c) In addition to or in lieu of other remedies, the county board of commissioners or governing body of a city may institute any appropriate action or proceeding to restrain or prevent any violation of this Part or of any ordinance adopted (or of the provisions of any permit issued) under the authority of this Part, or to require any person, firm or corporation that has committed a violation to remove a violating obstruction or restore the conditions existing before the placement of the obstruction. (1971, c. 1167, s. 3; 1993, c. 539, s. 1022; 1994, Ex. Sess., c. 24, s. 14(c); 2000-150, s. 1.)

§ 143-215.59. Other approvals required.

(a) The granting of a permit under the provisions of this Part shall in no way affect any other type of approval required by any other statute or ordinance of the State or any political subdivision of the State, or of the United States, but shall be construed as an added requirement.

(b) No permit for the construction of any structure to be located within a flood hazard area shall be granted by a political subdivision unless the applicant has first obtained the permit required by any local ordinance adopted pursuant to this Part. (1971, c. 1167, s. 3; 2000-150, s. 1.)

§ 143-215.60. Liability for damages.

No action for damages sustained because of injury or property damage caused by a structure or obstruction for which a permit has been granted under this Part shall be brought against the State or any political subdivision of the State, or their employees or agents. (1971, c. 1167, s. 3; 2000-150, s. 1.)

§ 143-215.61. Floodplain management.

The provisions of this Part shall not preclude the imposition by responsible local governments of land use controls and other regulations in the interest of floodplain management for the 100-year floodplain. (1971, c. 1167, s. 3; 2000-150, s. 1.)

Part 6A. Hurricane Flood Protection and Beach Erosion Control Project Revolving Fund.

§ 143-215.62. Revolving fund established; conditions and procedures.

(a) There is established under the control and direction of the Department a Hurricane Flood Protection and Beach Erosion Control Project Revolving Fund, to consist of any moneys that may be appropriated for use through the fund by the General Assembly or that may be made available to it from any other source for the purpose of financing the local portion of the nonfederal share of the cost of hurricane flood protection and beach erosion control projects. The Department shall, when funds are available, and in accordance with priorities established by the Commission, make advances from the fund to any county or municipality for:

(1) Advance planning and engineering work necessary or desirable in order to promote the development, construction, or preservation of hurricane flood protection and beach erosion works or projects;

(2) Construction of hurricane flood protection and beach erosion control works or projects, or other related costs which are a responsibility of local government, including costs associated with construction, such as the acquisition of land or rights-of-way or the relocation of public roads and utilities;

(3) Maintenance and nourishment of the constructed works or project.

Such advances shall be subject to repayment by the recipient to the Department from the proceeds of bonds or other obligations for the beach erosion control and hurricane flood protection works or projects, or from other funds available to the recipient, including grants.

(b) Prior to making any advance to a county or municipal government the Commission shall advise the county or municipal government:

(1) Its opinion as to whether or not the projected works or project would further beach erosion control or provide protection to life or property from floodwaters resulting from hurricanes;

(2) Its opinion as to whether or not there is a reasonable prospect of federal aid in the financing of the projected works or project and whether or not the advance will exceed the local portion of the nonfederal share of the cost of the works or project to be financed by the county or municipality making the application;

(3) Its opinion as to whether or not the anticipated financial outlays in connection with the projected works or project for the county or municipality making the application would constitute an unreasonable burden on the citizens of the county or municipality.

The Commission shall authorize no advance to a county or municipal government without first receiving satisfactory assurances from such government that the projected works or project shall be undertaken and the funds advanced repaid as provided herein.

(c)   Repayment of any advance may be in equal installments or in a lump sum, but the term for such repayment shall not exceed a term of 10 years. All moneys received from repayments on advances shall be paid into the revolving fund and shall be used for the purposes set forth in this section.

(d)   Repealed by Session Laws 1987, c. 827, s. 185. (1971, c. 1159, s. 1; 1973, c. 1262, s. 23; 1977, c. 771, s. 4; 1987, c. 827, ss. 154, 185 .)

Part 7. Water and Air Quality Reporting.

§ 143-215.63. Short title.

This Part shall be known and may be cited as the Water and Air Quality Reporting Act of 1971. (1971, c. 1167, s. 9.)

§ 143-215.64. Purpose.

The purpose of this Article is to require all persons who are subject to the provisions of G.S. 143-215.1, 143-215.108, or 143-215.109 to file reports with the Commission covering the discharge of waste and air contaminants to the waters and outdoor atmosphere of the State and to establish and maintain approved systems for monitoring the quantity and quality of such discharges and their effects upon the water and air resources of the State. (1971, c. 1167, s. 9; 1973, c. 1262, s. 23; 1987, c. 827, s. 154; 1989, c. 135, s. 3.)

§ 143-215.65. Reports required.

All persons subject to the provisions of G.S. 143-215.1, 143-215.108, or 143-215.109 who discharge wastes to the waters or emit air contaminants to the outdoor atmosphere of this State shall file at such frequencies as the

Commission may specify and at least quarterly reports with the Commission setting forth the volume and characteristics of wastes discharged or air contaminants emitted daily or such other period of time as may be specified by the Commission in its rules. Such reports may be required less frequently than quarterly for any permit for a minor activity as defined in G.S. 143-215.1(b)(4)d. and e. Such reports shall be filed on forms provided by the Department and approved by the Commission and shall include such pertinent data with reference to the total and average volume of wastes or air contaminants discharged, the strength and amount of each waste substance or air contaminant discharged, the type and degree of treatment such wastes or air contaminants received prior to discharge and such other information as may be specified by the Commission in its rules. The information shall be used by the Commission only for the purpose of air and water pollution control. The Department shall provide proper and adequate facilities and procedures and the Commission shall adopt rules to safeguard the confidentiality of proprietary manufacturing processes except that confidentiality shall not extend to wastes discharged or air contaminants emitted. (1971, c. 1167, s. 9; 1973, c. 1262, s. 23; 1975, c. 655, s. 4; 1987, c. 827, ss. 154, 186; 1989, c. 135, s. 4, c. 453, s. 3.)

§ 143-215.66. Monitoring required.

In order to provide for adequately monitoring the discharge of wastes to the waters and the emission of contaminants to the outdoor atmosphere and their effects upon the quality of the environment, all persons subject to the provisions of G.S. 143-215.1, 143-215.108, or 143-215.109 who cause such discharges or emissions shall establish and maintain adequate water and air quality monitoring systems and report the data obtained therefrom to the Commission. Each monitoring system shall include the collection of water or air quality data as appropriate from such locations, in such detail, and with such frequency as required by rule of the Commission for evaluating the efficiency of treatment facilities or air-cleaning devices and the effects of the discharges or emissions upon the waters and air resources of the State. (1971, c. 1167, s. 9; 1973, c. 1262, s. 23; 1987, c. 827, ss. 154, 187; 1989, c. 135, s. 5.)

§ 143-215.67. Acceptance of wastes to disposal systems and air-cleaning devices.

(a) No person subject to the provisions of G.S. 143-215.1, 143-215.108, or 143-215.109 shall willfully cause or allow the discharge of any wastes or air contaminants to a waste-disposal system or air-cleaning device in excess of the capacity of the disposal system or cleaning device or any wastes or air contaminants which the disposal system or cleaning device cannot adequately treat. This subsection does not prohibit the discharge of waste to a treatment works operated by a public utility or unit of local government in excess of the capacity of the treatment works by any person who holds a valid building permit issued prior to the date on which the public utility or unit of local government receives the notice required by subsection (c) of this section if the Commission finds that the discharge of waste will not result in any significant degradation in the quality of the waters ultimately receiving the discharge as provided in subsection (b) of this section.

(b) The Commission may authorize a unit of government subject to the provisions of subsection (a) of this section to accept additional wastes to its waste-disposal system upon a finding by the Commission (i) that the unit of government has secured a grant or has otherwise secured financing for planning, design, or construction of a new or improved waste disposal system which will adequately treat the additional waste, and (ii) the additional waste will not result in any significant degradation in the quality of the waters ultimately receiving the discharge. The Commission may impose such conditions on permits issued under G.S. 143-215.1 as it deems necessary to implement the provisions of this subsection, including conditions on the size, character, and number of additional dischargers. Nothing in this subsection shall be deemed to authorize a unit of government to violate water quality standards, effluent limitations or the terms of any order or permit issued under Part 1 of this Article nor does anything herein preclude the Commission from enforcing by appropriate means the provisions of Part 1 of this Article.

(c) The Commission may impose a moratorium on the addition of waste to a treatment works if the Commission determines that the treatment works is not capable of adequately treating additional waste. The Commission shall give notice of its intention to impose a moratorium at least 45 days prior to the effective date of the moratorium to any person who holds a permit for a treatment works subject to the moratorium. Except to the extent that the provisions of subsection (b) of this section apply, the Commission shall not issue a permit for a sewer line that will connect to a treatment works that the Commission has determined to be incapable of treating additional waste from the date on which the Commission determines that the treatment works is incapable of adequately treating additional waste until the moratorium on the addition of waste to the treatment works is lifted.

(d) A public utility or unit of local government that operates a treatment works shall give notice of a moratorium on the discharge of additional waste to the treatment works within 15 days of the date on which the public utility or unit of local government receives notice of the moratorium from the Commission. The public utility or unit of local government shall give public notice of a moratorium by publication of the notice one time in a newspaper having general circulation in the county in which the treatment works is located. The Commission shall prescribe the form and content of the notice. (1971, c. 1167, s. 9; 1979, c. 566; 1987, c. 827, s. 154; 1989, c. 135, s. 6; 1995, c. 202, s. 1.)

§ 143-215.68. Repealed by Session Laws 1987, c. 827, s. 188.

§ 143-215.69. Enforcement procedures.

(a) (1) Criminal Penalties. - Except as provided in subdivision (2) of this subsection, any person who violates any provisions of this Part or any rules adopted by the Commission for its implementation shall be guilty of a Class 3 misdemeanor and shall be only liable to a penalty of not less than one hundred dollars ($100.00), nor more than one thousand dollars ($1,000) for each violation and each day such person shall fail to comply after having been officially notified by the Commission shall constitute a separate offense subject to the foregoing penalty.

(2) Any person who violates any provision of this Part or any rule adopted by the Commission to implement this Part that imposes a requirement that is also a requirement under Title V or any rule adopted by the Commission to implement Title V shall be subject to punishment as provided by G.S. 143-215.114B.

(b) Civil Penalties. - The Commission may assess a civil penalty against a person who violates this Part or a rule of the Commission implementing this Part. For persons subject to the provisions of G.S. 143-215.1, the amount of the penalty shall not exceed the maximum imposed in G.S. 143-215.6A and shall be assessed in accordance with the procedure set out in G.S. 143-215.6A for assessing a civil penalty. For persons subject to the provisions of Title V, G.S. 143-215.108, or G.S. 143-215.109, the amount of penalty shall not exceed the maximum imposed in G.S. 143-215.114A and shall be assessed in accordance with the procedure set out in G.S. 143-215.114A for assessing a civil penalty. The clear proceeds of civil penalties assessed under this subsection shall be remitted to the Civil Penalty and Forfeiture Fund in accordance with G.S. 115C-457.2.

(c)   Injunctive Relief. - Upon violation of any of the provisions of this Part, a rule implementing this Part, or an order issued under this Part, the Secretary may, either before or after the institution of proceedings for the collection of the penalty imposed by this Part for such violations, request the Attorney General to institute a civil action in the superior court of the county or counties where the violation occurred in the name of the State upon the relation of the Department for injunctive relief to restrain the violation or require corrective action, and for such other or further relief in the premises as said court shall deem proper. Neither the institution of the action nor any of the proceedings thereon shall relieve any party to such proceedings from the penalty prescribed by this Part for any violation of same.

(d)   Repealed by Session Laws 1987, c. 827, s. 189. (1971, c. 1167, s. 9; 1973, c. 1262, s. 23; 1975, c. 842, s. 5; 1977, c. 771, s. 4; 1987, c. 827, ss. 154, 189; 1989 (Reg. Sess., 1990), c. 1045, s. 10; 1993, c. 400, s. 6; c. 539, s. 1023; 1994, Ex. Sess., c. 24, s. 14(c); 1998-215, s. 66.)

Part 8. Grants for Water Resources Development Projects.

§ 143-215.70. Secretary of Environment and Natural Resources authorized to accept applications.

The Secretary is authorized to accept applications for grants for nonfederal costs relating to water resources development projects from units of local government sponsoring such projects, except that this shall not include small watershed projects reviewed by the State Soil and Water Conservation Commission pursuant to G.S. 139-55. (1979, c. 1046, s. 1; 1987, c. 827, s. 154; 1989, c. 727, s. 218(109); 1997-443, s. 11A.119(a).)

§ 143-215.71. Purposes for which grants may be requested.

Applications for grants may be made for the nonfederal share of water resources development projects for the following purposes in amounts not to exceed the percentage of the nonfederal costs indicated:

(1) General navigation projects that are sponsored by local governments - eighty percent (80%);

(2) Recreational navigation projects - twenty-five percent (25%);

(3) Construction costs for water management (flood control and drainage) purposes, including utility and road relocations not funded by the State Department of Transportation - sixty-six and two-thirds percent (66 2/3%), but only of that portion of the project specifically allocated for such flood control or drainage purposes;

(4) Stream restoration - sixty-six and two-thirds percent (66 2/3%);

(5) Protection of privately owned beaches where public access is allowed and provided for - seventy-five percent (75%);

(6) Land acquisition and facility development for water-based recreation sites operated by local governments - fifty percent (50%);

(7) Aquatic weed control projects sponsored by local governments - fifty percent (50%). (1979, c. 1046, s. 1; 1983, c. 450; 1987, c. 781, s. 1.)

§ 143-215.72. Review of applications.

(a) The Secretary shall receive and review applications for the grants specified in this Part and approve, approve in part, or disapprove such applications.

(b) In reviewing each application, the Secretary shall consider:

(1) The economic, social, and environmental benefits to be provided by the projects;

(2) Regional benefits of projects to an area greater than the area under the jurisdiction of the local sponsoring entity;

(3) The financial resources of the local sponsoring entity;

(4) The environmental impact of the project;

(5) Any direct benefit to State-owned lands and properties. (1979, c. 1046, s. 1.)

§ 143-215.73. Recommendation and disbursal of grants.

After review of grant applications, project funds shall be disbursed and monitored by the Department. (1979, c. 1046, s. 1; 1983, c. 717, s. 70; 1985 (Reg. Sess., 1986), c. 955, s. 93; 1987, c. 827, s. 154; 2006-203, s. 90.)

Part 8A. Water Resources Development Projects.

§ 143-215.73A. Water Resources Development Plan.

(a) Plan prepared. - Before 1 July in each calendar year, the Department of Environment and Natural Resources shall prepare a statewide plan for water resources development projects for a period of six years into the future. The plan shall be known as the Water Resources Development Plan. If the plan differs from the Water Resources Development Plan adopted for the preceding calendar year, the Department shall indicate the changes and the reasons for such changes. The Department shall submit the plan to the Director of the Budget for review.

(b) Projects listed. - The plan shall list the following water resources development projects based on their status as of 1 May of the year in which the plan is prepared:

(1) Projects approved by the Congress of the United States.

(2) Projects for which the Congress of the United States has appropriated funds.

(3) Projects for which grant applications have been submitted under Part 8 of Article 21 of Chapter 143 of the General Statutes.

(4) Projects for which grant applications have been submitted under Article 4 of Chapter 139 of the General Statutes.

(5) Projects planned as federal reservoir projects but for which no federal funds are scheduled and for which local governments are seeking State financial assistance.

(c) Project priorities and funding recommendations. - The Department shall assign a priority to each project within each of the five categories listed under subsection (b) of this section either by giving the project a number, with "1" assigned to the highest priority, or by recommending no funding. The Department shall state its reasons for recommending the funding, deferral, or elimination of a project. The Department shall determine the priority of a project based on the following criteria: local interest in the project, the cost of the project to the State, the benefit of the project to the State, and the environmental impact of the project.

(c1) The Department shall provide information annually to appropriate county or municipal officials about the availability, requirements, and process to secure federal and State funding under the Water Resource Development Program.

(d) Project information. - For each project listed under subsection (b) of this section, the Water Resources Development Plan shall:

(1) Provide a brief description.

(2) If federal, list the estimated cost of each of the following phases that have not been completed as of 1 July, (i) feasibility study, (ii) construction, (iii) operation and maintenance, and the amount of State funds required to match the federal funds needed.

(3) If State or local, list the estimated cost to complete the project and amount of State funds required under G.S. 143-215.71 or G.S. 139-54.

(4) Indicate the total cost to date and the State share of that cost.

(5) Indicate the status.

(6) Indicate the estimated completion date.

(e) Distribution of the plan. - The Director of the Budget shall provide copies of the plan to the General Assembly along with the recommended biennial budget and the recommended revised budget for the second year of the biennium.

(f) Budget recommendations. - The Director of the Budget shall determine which projects, if any, will be included in the recommended biennial budget and in the recommended revised budget for the second year of the biennium. The budget document transmitted to the General Assembly shall identify the projects or types of projects recommended for funding. (1991, c. 181, s. 1; 1997-443, s. 11A.119(a); 2006-203, s. 91; 2011-145, s. 30.3(e).)

§ 143-215.73B: Reserved for future codification purposes.

§ 143-215.73C: Reserved for future codification purposes.

§ 143-215.73D: Reserved for future codification purposes.

§ 143-215.73E: Reserved for future codification purposes.

Part 8B. Shallow Draft Navigation Channel and Lake Dredging Fund.

§ 143-215.73F. Shallow Draft Navigation Channel and Lake Dredging Fund.

The Shallow Draft Navigation Channel and Lake Dredging Fund is established as a special revenue fund. The Fund consists of fees credited to it under G.S. 75A-3, 75A-38, and 105-449.126. Revenue in the Fund may only be used to provide the State's share of the costs associated with any dredging project designed to keep shallow draft navigation channels located in State waters or waters of the state located within lakes navigable and safe. Any project funded by revenue from the Fund must be cost-shared with non-State dollars on a one-to-one basis. For purposes of this section, "shallow draft navigation channel" means (i) a waterway connection with a maximum depth of 16 feet between the Atlantic Ocean and a bay or the Atlantic Intracoastal Waterway, (ii) a river entrance to the Atlantic Ocean through which tidal and other currents flow, or (iii) other interior coastal waterways. "Shallow draft navigation channel" includes the Atlantic Intracoastal Waterway and its side channels, Beaufort Harbor, Bogue Inlet, Carolina Beach Inlet, the channel from Back Sound to Lookout Back, channels connected to federal navigation channels, Lockwoods Folly

River, Manteo/Shallowbag Bay, including Oregon Inlet, Masonboro Inlet, New River, New Topsail Inlet, Rodanthe, Rollinson, Shallotte River, Silver Lake Harbor, and the waterway connecting Pamlico Sound and Beaufort Harbor. (2013-360, s. 14.22(h).)

Part 9. Nonpoint Source Pollution Control Program.

§§ 143-215.74 through 143-215.74B: Recodified as Article 72 of Chapter 106, G.S. 106-850 through G.S. 106-852, by Session Laws 2011-145, s. 13.22A(t), effective July 1, 2011.

Part 9A. Application of Animal Waste.

§§ 143-215.74C through 143-215.74E: Repealed by Session Laws 1995 (Regular Session, 1996), c. 626, s. 13.

Part 10. Stream Watch Program.

§ 143-215.74F. Program authorized.

The Department of Environment, Health, and Natural Resources may establish a Stream Watch Program to recognize and assist civic, environmental, educational, and other volunteer groups interested in good water resources management and protection. The goals of the Stream Watch Program are to encourage volunteer groups to adopt streams and other water bodies and to work toward their good management and protection; to increase public awareness of and involvement in water resources management; and to promote cooperative activities among volunteer groups, local government, industry, the Department of Environment, Health, and Natural Resources, and other agencies and entities for improved protection and management of water resources. (1989, c. 412, c. 727, s. 218; 1997-443, s. 11A.119(a).)

§ 143-215.74G. Applications.

The Department may accept and approve applications to affiliate with the Stream Watch Program from volunteer groups willing to adopt a specific body of water and to conduct at least one project each year to promote the protection of the adopted body of water or to increase public understanding of water resources. (1989, c. 412.)

§ 143.215.74H. Assistance.

The Department may provide technical, organizational, and financial assistance to stream watch groups from such resources as may be available to the Department. (1989, c. 412.)

§ 143-215.74I. Projects.

The Department may encourage and assist stream watch groups to carry out projects for stream cleanup and restoration, stream surveillance and water quality monitoring, public education, the establishment of trails and greenways, recreational use of water bodies, and other activities in furtherance of the goals of the Stream Watch Program. (1989, c. 412.)

§ 143-215.74J. Reserved for future codification purposes.

§ 143-215.74K. Reserved for future codification purposes.

§ 143-215.74L. Reserved for future codification purposes.

Part 11. Community Conservation Assistance Program.

§ 143-215.74M: Recodified as Article 73 of Chapter 106, G.S. 106-860, by Session Laws 2011-145, s. 13.22A(x), effective July 1, 2011.

Article 21A.

Oil Pollution and Hazardous Substances Control.

Part 1. General Provisions.

§ 143-215.75. Title.

This Article shall be known and may be cited as the "Oil Pollution and Hazardous Substances Control Act of 1978." (1973, c. 534, s. 1; 1979, c. 535, s. 1.)

§ 143-215.76. Purpose.

It is the purpose of this Article to promote the health, safety, and welfare of the citizens of this State by protecting the land and the waters over which this State has jurisdiction from pollution by oil, oil products, oil by-products, and other hazardous substances. It is not the intention of this Article to exercise jurisdiction over any matter as to which the United States government has exclusive jurisdiction, nor in any wise contrary to any governing provision of federal law, and no provision of this Article shall be so construed. The General Assembly further declares that it is the intent of this Article to support and complement applicable provisions of the Federal Water Pollution Control Act, as amended, 33 U.S.C. section 1251 et seq., as amended, and the National Contingency Plan for removal of oil adopted pursuant thereto. (1973, c. 534, s. 1; 1979, c. 535, s. 2.)

§ 143-215.77. Definitions.

As used in this Article, unless the context otherwise requires:

(1)   "Barrel" shall mean 42 U.S. gallons at 60 degrees Fahrenheit.

(2)   "Commission" means the North Carolina Environmental Management Commission.

(3) "Secretary" shall mean the North Carolina Secretary of Environment and Natural Resources.

(4) "Discharge" shall mean, but shall not be limited to, any emission, spillage, leakage, pumping, pouring, emptying, or dumping of oil or other hazardous substances into waters of the State or into waters outside the territorial limits of the State which affect lands, waters or uses related thereto within the territorial limits of the State, or upon land in such proximity to waters that oil or other hazardous substances is reasonably likely to reach the waters, but shall not include amounts less than quantities which may be harmful to the public health or welfare as determined pursuant to G.S. 143-215.77A; provided, however, that this Article shall not be construed to prohibit the oiling of driveways, roads or streets for reduction of dust or routine maintenance; provided further, that the use of oil or other hazardous substances, oil-based products, or chemicals on the land or waters by any State, county, or municipal government agency in any program of mosquito or other pest control, or their use by any person in accepted agricultural, horticultural, or forestry practices, or in connection with aquatic weed control or structural pest and rodent control, in a manner approved by the State, county, or local agency charged with authority over such uses, shall not constitute a discharge; provided, further, that the use of a pesticide regulated by the North Carolina Pesticide Board in a manner consistent with the labelling required by the North Carolina Pesticide Law shall not constitute a "discharge" for purposes of this Article. The word "discharge" shall also include any discharge upon land, whether or not in proximity to waters, which is intentional, knowing or willful.

(5) "Having control over oil or other hazardous substances" shall mean, but shall not be limited to, any person, using, transferring, storing, or transporting oil or other hazardous substances immediately prior to a discharge of such oil or other hazardous substances onto the land or into the waters of the State, and specifically shall include carriers and bailees of such oil or other hazardous substances. This definition shall not include any person supplying or delivering oil into a petroleum underground storage tank that is not owned or operated by the person, unless:

a. The person knows or has reason to know that a discharge is occurring from the petroleum underground storage tank at the time of supply or delivery;

b. The person's negligence is a proximate cause of the discharge; or

c. The person supplies or delivers oil at a facility that requires an operating permit under G.S. 143-215.94U and a currently valid operating permit certificate is not held or displayed at the time of the supply or delivery.

(5a) "Hazardous substance" shall mean any substance, other than oil, which when discharged in any quantity may present an imminent and substantial danger to the public health or welfare, as designated pursuant to G.S. 143-215.77A.

(6) Repealed by Session Laws 1979, c. 981, s. 5.

(7) "Department" shall mean the Department of Environment and Natural Resources.

(8) "Oil" shall mean oil of any kind and in any form, including, but specifically not limited to, petroleum, crude oil, diesel oil, fuel oil, gasoline, lubrication oil, oil refuse, oil mixed with other waste, oil sludge, petroleum related products or by-products, and all other liquid hydrocarbons, regardless of specific gravity, whether singly or in combination with other substances.

(9) "Bailee" shall mean any person who accepts oil or other hazardous substances to hold in trust for another for a special purpose and for a limited period of time.

(10) "Carrier" shall mean any person who engages in the transportation of oil or other hazardous substances for compensation.

(11) "Oil terminal facility" shall mean any facility of any kind and related appurtenances located in, on or under the surface of any land, or water, including submerged lands, which is used or capable of being used for the purpose of transferring, transporting, storing, processing, or refining oil; but shall not include any facility having a storage capacity of less than 500 barrels, nor any retail gasoline dispensing operation serving the motoring public. A vessel shall be considered an oil terminal facility only in the event that it is utilized to transfer oil from another vessel to an oil terminal facility; or to transfer oil between one oil terminal facility and another oil terminal facility; or is used to store oil.

(12) "Operator" shall mean any person owning or operating an oil terminal facility or pipeline, whether by lease, contract, or any other form of agreement.

(13) "Person" shall mean any and all natural persons, firms, partnerships, associations, public or private institutions, municipalities or political subdivisions, governmental agencies, or private or public corporations organized or existing under the laws of this State or any other state or country.

(14) "Pipeline" shall mean any conduit, pipe or system of pipes, and any appurtenances related thereto and used in conjunction therewith, used, or capable of being used, for transporting or transferring oil to, from, or between oil terminal facilities.

(15) "Restoration" or "restore" shall mean any activity or project undertaken in the public interest or to protect public interest or to protect public property or to promote the public health, safety or welfare for the purpose of restoring any lands or waters affected by an oil or other hazardous substances discharge as nearly as is possible or desirable to the condition which existed prior to the discharge.

(16) "Transfer" shall mean the transportation, on-loading or off-loading of oil or other hazardous substances between or among two or more oil terminal facilities; between or among oil terminal facilities and vessels; and between or among two or more vessels.

(17) "Vessel" shall include every description of watercraft or other contrivance used, or capable of being used, as a means of transportation on water, whether self-propelled or otherwise, and shall include, but shall not be limited to, barges and tugs; provided that the term "vessel" as used herein shall not apply to any pleasure, sport or commercial fishing vessel which has a fuel capacity of less than 500 gallons and is not used to transport petroleum, petroleum products, or general cargo.

(18) "Waters" shall mean any stream, river, creek, brook, run, canal, swamp, lake, sound, tidal estuary, bay, reservoir, waterway, wetlands, or any other body or accumulation of water, surface or underground, public or private, natural or artificial, which is contained within, flows through, or borders upon this State, or any portion thereof, including those portions of the Atlantic Ocean over which this State has jurisdiction. (1973, c. 534, s. 1; c. 1262, s. 23; 1977, c. 771, s. 4; 1979, c. 535, ss. 3-10; c. 981, ss. 3-5; 1979, 2nd Sess., c. 1209, ss. 1, 2; 1987, c. 827, s. 155; 1989, c. 656, s. 1; c. 727, s. 218(111); 1995, c. 377, s. 12; 1997-443, s. 11A.119(a).)

§ 143-215.77A. Designation of hazardous substances and determination of quantities which may be harmful.

(a) Those substances designated as hazardous as of June 1, 1980, by the Administrator of the United States Environmental Protection Agency under 33 U.S.C. 1321(b)(2)(A) are designated as hazardous substances for purposes of this Article.

(b) Such quantities of hazardous substances as may be harmful as determined as of June 1, 1980, by the Administrator of the United States Environmental Protection Agency under 33 U.S.C. 1321(b)(4) are quantities which may be harmful for purposes of this Article.

(c) Changes by Administrator of the United States Environmental Protection Agency in the designation of hazardous substances and the determination of quantities which may be harmful shall be deemed to be made to the designation of hazardous substances and the determination of quantities for purposes of this Article, unless the Commission objects within 120 days of publication of the action in the Federal Register. The Commission may object to a change by the Administrator on the basis that the change is not consistent with the standards for determining hazardous substances or harmful quantities. Upon objection by the Commission to a change, the Commission shall initiate rule-making proceedings on the change. The change will not be made pending the hearing and a final determination by the Commission. After the hearing, the Commission may reject the change upon a finding that the change is not consistent with the standards for determining hazardous substances or harmful quantities. (1979, 2nd Sess., c. 1209, s. 3; 1987, c. 827, s. 190.)

§ 143-215.78. Oil pollution control program.

The Department shall establish an oil pollution control program for the administration of this Article. The Department may employ and prescribe the duties of employees assigned to this activity. (1973, c. 534, s. 1; c. 1262, s. 23; 1979, c. 535, s. 11.)

§ 143-215.79. Inspections and investigations; entry upon property.

The Commission, through its authorized representatives, is empowered to conduct such inspections and investigations as shall be reasonably necessary to determine compliance with the provisions of this Article; to determine the person or persons responsible for violation of this Article; to determine the nature and location of any oil or other hazardous substances discharged to the land or waters of this State; and to enforce the provisions of this Article. The authorized representatives of the Commission are empowered upon presentation of their credentials to enter upon any private or public property, including boarding any vessel, for the purpose of inspection or investigation or in order to conduct any project or activity to contain, collect, disperse or remove oil or other hazardous substances discharges or to perform any restoration necessitated by an oil or other hazardous substances discharge. Neither the State nor its agencies, employees or agents shall be liable in trespass or damages arising out of the conduct of any inspection, investigation, or oil or other hazardous substances removal or restoration project or activity other than liability for damage to property or injury to persons arising out of the negligent or willful conduct of an employee or agent of the State during the course of an inspection, investigation, project or activity. (1973, c. 534, s. 1; c. 1262, s. 23; 1979, c. 535, s. 12; 1987, c. 827, s. 154.)

§ 143-215.80. Confidential information.

Any information relating to a secret process, device or method of manufacturing or production discovered or obtained in the course of an inspection, investigation, project or activity conducted pursuant to this Article shall not be revealed except as may be required by law or lawful order or process. (1973, c. 534, s. 1.)

§ 143-215.81. Authority supplemental.

The authority and powers granted under this Article shall be in addition to, and not in derogation of, any authority or powers vested in the Commission under any other provision of law, except to the extent that such other powers or authority may conflict directly with the powers and authority granted under this Article. (1973, c. 534, s. 1; c. 1262, s. 23; 1987, c. 827, ss. 154, 191.)

§ 143-215.82. Local ordinances.

Nothing in the Article shall be construed to deny any county, municipality, sanitary district, metropolitan sewerage district or other authorized local governmental entity, by ordinance, regulation or law, from exercising police powers with reference to the prevention and control of oil or other hazardous substances discharges to sewers or disposal systems. (1973, c. 534, s. 1; 1979, c. 535, s. 13.)

Part 2. Oil Discharge Controls.

§ 143-215.83. Discharges.

(a) Unlawful Discharges. - It shall be unlawful, except as otherwise provided in this Part, for any person to discharge, or cause to be discharged, oil or other hazardous substances into or upon any waters, tidal flats, beaches, or lands within this State, or into any sewer, surface water drain or other waters that drain into the waters of this State, regardless of the fault of the person having control over the oil or other hazardous substances, or regardless of whether the discharge was the result of intentional or negligent conduct, accident or other cause.

(b) Excepted Discharges. - This section shall not apply to discharges of oil or other hazardous substances in the following circumstances:

(1) When the discharge was authorized by an existing rule of the Commission.

(2) When any person subject to liability under this Article proves that a discharge was caused by any of the following:

a. An act of God.

b. An act of war or sabotage.

c. Negligence on the part of the United States government or the State of North Carolina or its political subdivisions.

d. An act or omission of a third party, whether any such act or omission was or was not negligent.

e. Any act or omission by or at the direction of a law-enforcement officer or fireman.

(c) Permits. - Any person who desires or proposes to discharge oil or other hazardous substances onto the land or into the waters of this State shall first make application for and secure the permit required by G.S. 143-215.1. Application shall be made pursuant to the rules adopted by the Commission. Any permit granted pursuant to this subsection may contain such terms and conditions as the Commission shall deem necessary and appropriate to conserve and protect the land or waters of this State and the public interest therein. (1973, c. 534, s. 1; c. 1262, s. 23; 1979, c. 535, s. 14; 1987, c. 827, ss. 154, 192.)

§ 143-215.84. Removal of prohibited discharges.

(a) Person Discharging. - Except as provided in subsection (a2) of this section, any person having control over oil or other hazardous substances discharged in violation of this Article shall immediately undertake to collect and remove the discharge and to restore the area affected by the discharge as nearly as may be to the condition existing prior to the discharge. If it is not feasible to collect and remove the discharge, the person responsible shall take all practicable actions to contain, treat and disperse the discharge; but no chemicals or other dispersants or treatment materials which will be detrimental to the environment or natural resources shall be used for such purposes unless they shall have been previously approved by the Commission. The owner of an underground storage tank who is the owner of the tank only because he is the owner of the land on which the underground storage tank is located, who did not know or have reason to know that the underground storage tank was located on his property, and who did not become the owner of the land as the result of a transfer or transfers to avoid liability for the underground storage tank shall not be deemed to be responsible for a release or discharge from the underground storage tank.

(a1) The Commission shall not require collection or removal of a discharge or restoration of an affected area under subsection (a) of this section if the person having control over oil or other hazardous substances discharged in violation of this Article complies with rules governing the collection and removal of a discharge and the restoration of an affected area adopted by the Commission pursuant to G.S. 143-214.1 or G.S. 143-215.94V. This subsection shall not be construed to affect the rights of any person under this Article or any other provision of law.

(a2) Discharges of Mineral Oil From Electrical Equipment. - As used in this subsection, "mineral oil" means a light nontoxic liquid petroleum distillate used as a coolant and insulator in electrical equipment owned by a public utility. Any person having control over mineral oil discharged from electrical equipment owned by a public utility, as defined in G.S. 62-100, including, but not limited to, transformers, regulators, bushings, and capacitors, shall restore the area affected by the discharge as nearly as may be to the condition existing prior to the discharge. A person shall notify the applicable regional office of the Department by telephone, hand delivery, electronic mail, or fax when the restoration has been properly completed for a discharge that (i) exceeds 25 gallons, (ii) is directly to surface waters or causes a sheen on surface waters of the State, or (iii) is at a distance of 100 feet or less from any surface water and contains 50 parts per million or more of polychlorinated biphenyls. Where soil removal is necessary as part of a cleanup, all visible traces of the mineral oil shall be removed. For discharges of mineral oil which contain 50 parts per million or more of polychlorinated biphenyls, cleanup shall be performed in compliance with applicable provisions of the Toxic Substances Control Act, 15 U.S.C. § 2601, et seq., as amended. If it is not feasible to collect and remove the discharge of mineral oil from electrical equipment within 24 hours of confirmation of the release, the person responsible shall take all practicable actions to contain, treat, and disperse the discharge, except that no chemical or other dispersants or treatment materials which will be detrimental to the environment or natural resources shall be used for such purposes unless they shall have been previously approved by the Commission.

(b) Removal by Department. - Notwithstanding the requirements of subsections (a) and (a2) of this section, the Department is authorized and empowered to utilize any staff, equipment and materials under its control or supplied by other cooperating State or local agencies and to contract with any agent or contractor that it deems appropriate to take such actions as are necessary to collect, investigate, perform surveillance over, remove, contain, treat or disperse oil or other hazardous substances discharged onto the land or into the waters of the State and to perform any necessary restoration. The Secretary shall keep a record of all expenses incurred in carrying out any project or activity authorized under this section, including actual expenses incurred for services performed by the State's personnel and for use of the State's equipment and material. The authority granted by this subsection shall be limited to projects and activities that are designed to protect the public interest or public property, and shall be compatible with the National Contingency Plan established pursuant to the Federal Water Pollution Control Act, as amended, 33 U.S.C. section 1251 et seq.

(c), (d) Repealed by Session Laws 1989, c. 656, s. 2.

(e) Notification of Completed Removal of Prohibited Discharges. - The definitions set out in G.S. 130A-310.31(b) apply to this subsection. Any person may submit a written request to the Department for a determination that a discharge of oil or a hazardous substance in violation of this Article has been remediated to unrestricted use standards. A request for a determination that a discharge has been remediated to unrestricted use standards shall be accompanied by the fee required by G.S. 130A-310.39(a)(2). If the Department determines that the discharge has been remediated to unrestricted use standards, the Department shall issue a written notification that no further remediation of the discharge will be required. The notification shall state that no further remediation of the discharge will be required unless the Department later determines, based on new information or information not previously provided to the Department, that the discharge has not been remediated to unrestricted use standards or that the Department was provided with false or incomplete information. Under any of those circumstances, the Department may withdraw the notification and require responsible parties to remediate the discharge to unrestricted use standards.

(f) In order to reduce or eliminate the danger to public health or the environment posed by a discharge or release of oil or a hazardous substance, an owner, operator, or other responsible party may impose restrictions on the current or future use of the real property comprising any part of the site if the restrictions meet the requirements of this subsection. The restrictions must be agreed to by the owner of the real property, included in a remedial action plan for the site that has been approved by the Secretary, and implemented as a part of the remedial action program for the site. The Secretary may approve restrictions included in a remedial action plan in accordance with standards determined: (i) pursuant to rules for remediation of soil or groundwater contamination adopted by the Commission; (ii) with respect to the cleanup of a discharge or release from a petroleum underground storage tank, pursuant to rules adopted by the Commission pursuant to G.S. 143-215.94V; or (iii) as provided in G.S. 130A-310.3(d). Restrictions may apply to activities on, over, or under the land, including, but not limited to, use of groundwater, building, filling, grading, excavating, and mining. Any approved restriction shall be enforced by any owner, operator, or other party responsible for the oil or hazardous substance discharge site. Any land-use restriction may also be enforced by the Department through the remedies provided in this Article, Part 2 of Article 1 of Chapter 130A of the General Statutes, or by means of a civil action. The Department may enforce any land-use restriction without first having exhausted any available administrative remedies. A land-use restriction may also be enforced by any unit of local government having jurisdiction over any part of the site. A land-use restriction shall not be declared unenforceable due to lack of privity of estate or contract, due to lack of benefit to particular land, or due to lack of any property interest in particular land. Any person who owns or leases a property subject to a land-use restriction under this Part shall abide by the land-use restriction. (1973, c. 534, s. 1; c. 1262, s. 23; 1975, c. 885; 1977, c. 771, s. 4; 1979, c. 535, s. 15; 1987, c. 827, ss. 154, 193; 1989, c. 656, s. 2; 1991, c. 538, s. 14; 1995, c. 377, s. 13; 1997-357, s. 7; 1997-394, s. 4; 1997-456, s. 50; 2001-384, s. 11; 2011-38, s. 2.)

§ 143-215.85. Required notice.

(a) Except as provided in G.S. 143-215.94E(a1) and subsections (b) and (c) of this section, every person owning or having control over oil or other substances discharged in any circumstances other than pursuant to a rule adopted by the Commission, a regulation of the U.S. Environmental Protection Agency, or a permit required by G.S. 143-215.1 or the Federal Water Pollution Control Act, upon notice that such discharge has occurred, shall immediately notify the Department, or any of its agents or employees, of the nature, location and time of the discharge and of the measures which are being taken or are proposed to be taken to contain and remove the discharge. The agent or employee of the Department receiving the notification shall immediately notify the Secretary or such member or members of the permanent staff of the Department as the Secretary may designate. If the discharged substance of which the Department is notified is a pesticide regulated by the North Carolina Pesticide Board, the Department shall immediately inform the Chairman of the Pesticide Board. Removal operations under this Article of substances identified as pesticides defined in G.S. 143-460 shall be coordinated in accordance with the Pesticide Emergency Plan adopted by the North Carolina Pesticide Board; provided that, in instances where entry of such hazardous substances into waters of the State is imminent, the Department may take such actions as are necessary to physically contain or divert such substance so as to prevent entry into the surface waters.

(b) As used in this subsection, "petroleum" has the same meaning as in G.S. 143-215.94A. A person who owns or has control over petroleum that is discharged into the environment shall immediately take measures to collect and remove the discharge, report the discharge to the Department within 24 hours of the discharge, and begin to restore the area affected by the discharge in accordance with the requirements of this Article if the volume of the petroleum that is discharged is 25 gallons or more or if the petroleum causes a sheen on nearby surface water or if the petroleum is discharged at a distance of 100 feet or less from any surface water body. If the volume of petroleum that is discharged is less than 25 gallons, the petroleum does not cause a sheen on nearby surface water, and the petroleum is discharged at a distance of more than 100 feet from all surface water bodies, the person who owns or has control over the petroleum shall immediately take measures to collect and remove the discharge. If a discharge of less than 25 gallons of petroleum cannot be cleaned up within 24 hours of the discharge or if the discharge causes a sheen on nearby surface water, the person who owns or has control over the petroleum shall immediately notify the Department.

(c) As used in this subsection, "mineral oil" means a light nontoxic liquid petroleum distillate used as a coolant and insulator in electrical equipment owned by a public utility. Any person who owns or has control over mineral oil discharged from electrical equipment owned by a public utility, as defined in G.S. 62-100, including, but not limited to, transformers, regulators, bushings, and capacitors, shall report the discharge to the applicable regional office of the Department within 24 hours of confirmation of a discharge when the discharge (i) exceeds 25 gallons, (ii) is directly to surface waters or causes a sheen on surface waters of the State, or (iii) is at a distance of 100 feet or less from any surface water and contains 50 parts per million or more of polychlorinated biphenyls. The notification shall include the time of discovery, address or location of the release, immediate actions taken, estimated amount of the release, and, if known, the concentration of polychlorinated biphenyls present in the discharge. This information may be submitted by telephone, hand delivery, electronic mail, or fax. (1973, c. 534, s. 1; c. 1262, s. 23; 1977, c. 771, s. 4; c. 858, s. 1; 1979, c. 535, ss. 16, 17; 1987, c. 827, ss. 154, 194; 2000-54, s. 1; 2011-38, s. 1.)

§ 143-215.85A. Recordation of oil or hazardous substance discharge sites.

(a) The owner of the real property on which a site is located that is subject to current or future use restrictions approved as provided in G.S. 143-215.84(f) shall submit to the Department a survey plat as required by this section within 180 days after the owner is notified to do so. The survey plat shall identify areas designated by the Department, shall be prepared and certified by a professional land surveyor, and shall be entitled "NOTICE OF OIL OR HAZARDOUS SUBSTANCE DISCHARGE SITE". Where an oil or hazardous substance discharge site is located on more than one parcel or tract of land, a composite map or plat showing all parcels or tracts may be recorded. The Notice shall include a legal description of the site that would be sufficient as a description in an instrument of conveyance, shall meet the requirements of G.S. 47-30 for maps and plats, and shall identify:

(1) The location and dimensions of the disposal areas and areas of potential environmental concern with respect to permanently surveyed benchmarks.

(2) The type, location, and quantity of oil or hazardous substances known to the owner of the site to exist on the site.

(3) Any restrictions approved by the Department on the current or future use of the site.

(b) After the Department approves and certifies the Notice, the owner of the site shall file the certified copy of the Notice in the register of deeds office in the county or counties in which the land is located within 15 days of the date on which the owner receives approval of the Notice from the Department.

(c) Repealed by Session Laws 2012-18, s. 1.20, effective July 1, 2012.

(d) In the event that the owner of the site fails to submit and file the Notice required by this section within the time specified, the Secretary may prepare and file the Notice. The costs thereof may be recovered by the Secretary from any responsible party. In the event that an owner of a site who is not a responsible party submits and files the Notice required by this section, he may recover the reasonable costs thereof from any responsible party.

(e) When an oil or hazardous substance discharge site that is subject to current or future land-use restrictions under this section is sold, leased, conveyed, or transferred, the deed or other instrument of transfer shall contain in the description section, in no smaller type than that used in the body of the deed or instrument, a statement that the property has been used as an oil or hazardous substance discharge site and a reference by book and page to the recordation of the Notice.

(f) A Notice of Oil or Hazardous Substance Discharge Site filed pursuant to this section may, at the request of the owner of the land, be cancelled by the Secretary after the hazards have been eliminated. If requested in writing by the owner of the land and if the Secretary concurs with the request, the Secretary shall send to the register of deeds of each county where the Notice is recorded a statement that the hazards have been eliminated and request that the Notice be cancelled of record. The Secretary's statement shall contain the names of the owners of the land as shown in the Notice and reference the plat book and page where the Notice is recorded. (1997-394, s. 5; 1997-443, s. 11A.119(b); 1997-456, s. 55.6(a), (b); 2012-18, s. 1.20.)

§ 143-215.86. Other State agencies and State-designated local agencies.

(a) Planning. - The State Emergency Response Commission shall be responsible for developing a program, including training, for the waters of the State, including offshore marine waters, to enable the State to respond to an emergency oil or other hazardous substances spillage. In carrying out its duties under this section, designated representatives of the State Emergency Response Commission, the Board of Transportation, the Wildlife Resources Commission, the Environmental Management Commission, the Division of Marine Fisheries, the Outer Continental Shelf Lands Office of the Department of Administration, and any other agency or agencies of the State which the State Emergency Response Commission shall deem necessary and appropriate, shall confer and establish plans and procedures for the assignment and utilization of personnel, equipment and material to be used in carrying out the purposes of this Part. Every State agency involved is authorized to adopt such rules as shall be necessary to effectuate the purposes of this section.

(b) Cooperative Effort. - The Board of Transportation, the North Carolina Wildlife Resources Commission, the Division of Marine Fisheries, and any other agency of this State and any local agency designated by the State shall cooperate with and lend assistance to the Commission by assigning to the Commission upon its request personnel, equipment, and material to be utilized in any project or activity related to the containment, collection, dispersal, or removal of oil or other hazardous substances discharged upon the land or discharged into waters affecting this State.

(c) Trucks. - The Secretary of Transportation may, after consultation with the Secretary of Environment and Natural Resources, purchase and equip a sufficient number of trucks designed to carry out the provisions of subsection (b) of this section. These trucks shall be maintained by the Department of Transportation and shall be strategically located at various locations throughout the State so as to furnish a ready response when word of an oil or other hazardous substances discharge has been received. The Secretary of Environment and Natural Resources or his designee will, after consultation, decide where the trucks are to be located.

(d) Rules. - The Secretary of Transportation and the Secretary of Environment and Natural Resources or their designees shall adopt rules for the placement of these trucks and shall determine the manner and way in which they are to be used. The Secretary of Environment and Natural Resources shall reimburse the Department of Transportation for expenses incurred by the Department of Transportation during cleanups as provided in G.S. 143-215.88.

(e) Accounts. - Every State agency or other State-designated local agency participating in the containment, collection, dispersal, or removal of an oil or other hazardous substances discharge or in restoration necessitated by such discharge, shall keep a record of all expenses incurred in carrying out any such project or activity including the actual services performed by the agency's personnel and the use of the agency's personnel and the use of the agency's equipment and material. A copy of all records shall be delivered to the Commission upon completion of the project or activity. (1973, c. 507, s. 5; c. 534, s. 1; c. 1262, s. 23; 1979, c. 535, ss. 18, 19; 1987, c. 827, ss. 154, 195; 1989, c. 656, s. 3; c. 727, ss. 164, 165; 1997-443, s. 11A.119(a).)

Vision Books Order Form

Fax Orders: 1-980-299-5965

Phone Orders: 1-704-898-0770

E-mail Orders: www.visionbooks.org

Mail Orders: Vision Books, LLC
P.O. Box 42406
Charlotte, NC 28215

Shipp To:
Name_____
Address_____
City_____State_____Zip_____
Phone_____Fax_____
Email_____@_____

Bill To: We can bill a third party on your behalf.
Name_____
Address_____
City_____State_____Zip_____
Phone____(_____)_____Fax_____
Email_____@_____

Pamphlet Number ($15.00 Each)	Qty	Total Cost
_____	_____	_____
_____	_____	_____
_____	_____	_____
_____	_____	_____
_____	_____	_____
_____	_____	_____
_____	_____	_____
Full Volume Set 1-92	**92 Pamphlets**	**1,380.00**

Free Shipping & Handling on Full Volume Orders
Add $1.00 Shipping & Handling Per Pamphlet $_____

Total Cost $_____

Thank you for your support. Management!

DID YOU ENJOY THIS BOOK?

Vision Books, LLC would like to hear from you! If you or someone you know has been fasely imprisoned, we would like to hear your story. If the 'North Carolina Criminal Law and Procedure' has had an effect in your life or if you have suggestions, we would like to hear from you. Send your letters to:

Vision Books, LLC
Attn: Staff Writers
P.O. Box 42406
Charlotte, NC 28215
Email: staff@visionbooks.org

Order Additional Copies:

Fax Orders:	1-980-299-5965
Phone Orders:	1-704-898-0770
E-mail Orders:	www.visionbooks.org
Mail Orders:	Vision Books, LLC P.O. Box 42406 Charlotte, NC 28215

www.ingramcontent.com/pod-product-compliance
Lightning Source LLC
Chambersburg PA
CBHW051629170526
45167CB00001B/122